Test Your Skills in C# Programming

Review and Analyze Important Features of C#

Vaskaran Sarcar

Apress®

Test Your Skills in C# Programming: Review and Analyze Important Features of C#

Vaskaran Sarcar
Garia, Kolkata, West Bengal, India

ISBN-13 (pbk): 978-1-4842-8654-8 ISBN-13 (electronic): 978-1-4842-8655-5
https://doi.org/10.1007/978-1-4842-8655-5

Managing Director, Apress Media LLC: Welmoed Spahr
Acquisitions Editor: Smriti Srivastava
Development Editor: Laura Berendson
Coordinating Editor: Shrikant Vishwakarma
Copy Editor: Kim Wimpsett

Cover designed by eStudioCalamar

Cover image designed by Freepik (www.freepik.com)

Distributed to the book trade worldwide by Springer Science+Business Media New York, 1 New York Plaza, Suite 4600, New York, NY 10004-1562, USA. Phone 1-800-SPRINGER, fax (201) 348-4505, e-mail orders-ny@springer-sbm.com, or visit www.springeronline.com. Apress Media, LLC is a California LLC and the sole member (owner) is Springer Science + Business Media Finance Inc (SSBM Finance Inc). SSBM Finance Inc is a **Delaware** corporation.

For information on translations, please e-mail booktranslations@springernature.com; for reprint, paperback, or audio rights, please e-mail bookpermissions@springernature.com.

Apress titles may be purchased in bulk for academic, corporate, or promotional use. eBook versions and licenses are also available for most titles. For more information, reference our Print and eBook Bulk Sales web page at www.apress.com/bulk-sales.

Any source code or other supplementary material referenced by the author in this book is available to readers on GitHub (https://github.com/apress/test-your-skills-cs-programming). For more detailed information, please visit www.apress.com/source-code.

Printed on acid-free paper

I dedicate this book to the programming lovers of C#.

Table of Contents

About the Author

Vaskaran Sarcar obtained his master's of engineering in software engineering from Jadavpur University, Kolkata (India), and his MCA from Vidyasagar University, Midnapore (India). He was a National Gate Scholar (2007-2009) and has more than 12 years of experience in education and the IT industry. Vaskaran devoted his early years (2005–2007) to the teaching profession at various engineering colleges, and later he joined HP India PPS R&D Hub Bangalore. He worked there until August 2019. At the time of his retirement from HP, he was a senior software engineer and team lead. To follow his dream of writing books, Vaskaran is now a full-time author. These are the other Apress books he has written:

- *Java Design Patterns, Third Edition* (Apress, 2022)
- *Simple and Efficient Programming in C#* (Apress, 2021)
- *Design Patterns in C#, Second Edition* (Apress, 2020)
- *Getting Started with Advanced C#* (Apress, 2020)
- *Interactive Object-Oriented Programming in Java, Second Edition* (Apress, 2019)
- *Java Design Patterns, Second Edition* (Apress, 2019)
- *Design Patterns in C#* (Apress, 2018)
- *Interactive C#* (Apress, 2017)
- *Interactive Object-Oriented Programming in Java* (Apress, 2016)
- *Java Design Patterns* (Apress, 2016)

The following are his non-Apress books:

- *Python Bookcamp* (Amazon, 2021)
- *Operating System: Computer Science Interview Series* (Createspace, 2014)

About the Technical Reviewer

Carsten Thomsen is a back-end developer primarily but works with smaller front-end bits as well. He has authored and reviewed a number of books and created numerous Microsoft Learning courses, all to do with software development. He works as a freelancer/contractor in various countries in Europe; Azure, Visual Studio, Azure DevOps, and GitHub are some of the tools he works with regularly. He is an exceptional troubleshooter, and he also enjoys working with architecture, research, analysis, development, testing, and bug fixing. Carsten is a great communicator with mentoring and team-lead skills, and he also enjoys researching and presenting new material.

Acknowledgments

First, I thank the Almighty. I sincerely believe that His blessings were the reason I could complete this book. I also extend my deepest gratitude and thanks to the following people:

Ratanlal Sarkar and Manikuntala Sarkar: My dear parents, thank you for your blessings.

Indrani, my wife; **Ambika**, my daughter; **Aryaman**, my son: Sweethearts, I love you all.

Sambaran, my brother: Thank you for your constant encouragement.

Carsten, the technical editor: I know that whenever I was in need, your support was there. Thank you one more time.

Celestin, Smriti, Laura, Shrikant, Nirmal: Thanks for giving me another opportunity to work with you and Apress.

Kim Wimpsett, Linthaa, Sivachandran, Pradap: Thank you for your exceptional support to improve my work. I thank you all for your extraordinary supports.

Introduction

Welcome to your journey through *Test Your Skills in C# Programming: Review and Analyze Important Features of C#*. C# is a powerful, popular programming language that helps you make a wide range of applications. This is one of the primary reasons that it is continuously growing and is always in demand as a skill. It is not a surprise that new developers want to get better at programming with C#.

Many developers try to learn C# in the shortest possible time frame and like to claim that they know C# well. Trying to learn something as quickly as possible is a great idea, but do you know the problem with that approach? We are living in a world that offers you lots of content, advertisements, and quick fixes to distract you. Many products claim that you can master C# in a day, a week, or a month. But is this true? Obviously not.

Sir Isaac Newton, one of the greatest mathematicians and physicists of all time, said the following:

> *I do not know what I may appear to the world, but to myself I seem to have been only like a boy playing on the seashore, and diverting myself in now and then finding a smoother pebble or a prettier shell than ordinary, whilst the great ocean of truth lay all undiscovered before me.*

You can find similar quotes from other great personalities too. For now, let me give you one more example: Malcom Gladwell in his book *Outliers* (Little, Brown, and Company) talked about the 10,000-hour rule. This rule says that the key to achieving world-class expertise in any skill, is, to a large extent, a matter of practicing the correct way, for a total of around 10,000 hours. So, even though we may claim that we know something very well, we actually know very little. Learning is a continuous process, and there is no end to it. This is why you can surely assume that if anyone makes a 1,000-page book, that also may not be sufficient to cover all the topics and features in C#.

But there is something called *effective learning*. It teaches you how to learn fast to serve your need. Have you heard of the Pareto principle, or 80-20 rule? This rule simply states that 80 percent of outcomes come from 20 percent of all causes. This is useful in programming too. When you learn the fundamental and most important features of a programming language, you will be confident in using it. Though you may not know every aspect of a programming language, you will know the common constructs and widely used features. This book is for those who acknowledge this fact. It will help you to review your understanding of the core constructs and features of C# using 15 chapters that have 430+ questions (170+ theoretical, and 260+ programming) and answers with lots of explanations. I tried to keep a balance between the most recent features and commonly used features in C#.

How Is the Book Organized?

The book has three major parts.

- Part I contains the first three chapters, in which you will see a detailed discussion on .NET fundamentals, useful data types in C#, and different kinds of programming statements. These are the fundamental building blocks for the rest of the book.
- C# is a powerful object-oriented language. So, understanding the concepts of classes, objects, inheritance, encapsulation, polymorphism, and abstraction is essential for you. In Part II, you'll see a detailed discussion on each of these topics in Chapters 4 through 9; this is the heart of this book. Once you understand them, you will be a better programmer.
- There is no end to learning. So, Part III includes some interesting topics such as delegates, events, lambda expressions, generics, and multithreading. These are advanced concepts, and particularly, the last two of them are really big chapters. A quick overview of these topics will help you make better applications. They will also make your foundation strong for more advanced C# topics. The last chapter of the book discusses a few important topics including the preview features of C# 11.
- The best way to learn is by doing and analyzing case studies. So, throughout this book, you will see interesting program segments, and I'll ask you to predict the output. To help you understand the code better, at the beginning of each chapter you will see theoretical questions and answers too.

- Each theorical question is marked with <chapter_no>.T<Question_no>, and each programming question is marked with <chapter_no>.P<Question_no>. For example, 5.T3 means theoretical question number 3 from Chapter 5, and 10.P2 means programming question number 2 from Chapter 10.
- You can download all the source code in the book from the publisher's website (`www.apress.com`). I plan to maintain the "Errata" list, and if required, I can also make some updates/announcements there. So, I suggest that you visit Apress.com periodically to receive any important corrections or updates.

Prerequisite Knowledge

The target readers for this book are those who have completed a basic tutorial, a book, or a course on C# but want to prepare themselves for an examination or a job interview. I assume that you are familiar with the basic language constructs in C# and have an idea about the pure object-oriented concepts such as polymorphism, inheritance, abstraction, encapsulation, and, most importantly, how to compile or run a C# application in Visual Studio. This book does not invest time in easily available topics, such as how to install Visual Studio on your system or how to write a "Hello World" program in C#, and so forth. The code examples and questions and answers (Q&As) are straightforward. I believe that by analyzing these Q&As, you can evaluate your understanding of C#. These discussions will make your future learning easier and enjoyable, but most importantly, they will make you confident about using C#.

Who Is This Book For?

In short, you will get the most from this book if you can answer "yes" to the following questions:

- Are you familiar with basic constructs in C# and object-oriented concepts such as polymorphism, inheritance, abstraction, and encapsulation?
- Do you know how to set up your coding environment?

- Have you completed at least one basic course on C# and now you are interested in reviewing your understanding?
- Are you interested in knowing how the core constructs of C# can help you make useful applications?

You probably shouldn't pick up this book if you can answer "yes" to any of the following questions:

- Are you looking for a C# tutorial or reference book?
- Are you looking for advanced concepts in C# excluding the topics mentioned previously?
- Are you interested in exploring a book where the focus is not on the Q&As?
- Have you ever said, "I do not like Windows, Visual Studio, and/or .NET. I want to learn and use C# without them."

Useful Software

These are the important software and tools that I used for this book:

- I started this book with the latest edition of C# (C# 10.0) using Microsoft's Visual Studio Community 2022 in a Windows 10 environment. During the process of writing, the C# 11 preview was released. So, I kept updating the code to test C# 11 with .NET 7. When I finished my initial draft, I had the updated edition of Visual Studio (version 17.2.3). It was the latest edition at that time. Applying some specific settings (discussed in Chapter 15), you can test some of those preview features with this edition of Visual Studio too.
- In C# programming, there are different channels. They target different users. At a particular time, you may work on any of the following channels: Preview channel, Current channel, Long-term support channel (LTSC). The current channel was not sufficient to test all of the preview features. So, to test some specific preview features, I used the preview channel as well. For example, in 15.p3, to test the auto-default struct, I used Visual Studio version 17.3.0 (Preview 1.1).

- In this context, it is useful to know that nowadays the C# language version is automatically selected based on your project's target framework so that you can always get the highest compatible version by default. In the latest versions, Visual Studio doesn't support the UI to change the value, but you can change it by editing the `.csproj` file.
- As per the new rules, C# 11 is supported only on .NET 7 and newer versions. C# 10 is supported only on .NET 6 and newer versions. C# 9 is supported only on .NET 5 and newer versions. C# 8.0 is supported only on .NET Core 3.x and newer versions. If you are interested in the C# language versioning, you can visit `https://docs.microsoft.com/en-us/dotnet/csharp/language-reference/configure-language-version`.
- The good news for you is that the community edition is free of cost. If you do not use the Windows operating system, you can also use Visual Studio Code, which is a source code editor developed by Microsoft to support the Windows, Linux, and Mac operating systems. This multiplatform IDE is free. At the time of this writing, Visual Studio 2022 for Mac is also available, but I did not test my code on it.

Guidelines for Using This Book

Here are some suggestions so you can use the book more effectively:

- This book suits you best if you've gone through some introductory courses on C# already and are familiar with common programming concepts. If not, please do this before you start reading this book.
- I suggest you go through the chapters sequentially. The reason is that some useful and related topics may be already discussed in a previous chapter, and I have not repeated those discussions in the later chapters.

- You can predict that version updates will come continuously, but I strongly believe that these version details should not matter much for your learning. This is because I have used the fundamental constructs of C# in this book. Also, if a particular piece of code can run in a newer version of C#, but not in an old version of C#, I have mentioned it in the explanation. For example, see 15.P3, where I have written: "This code produced a compile-time error in 3.P20 (Chapter 3). But the Visual Studio preview version 17.3.0 (Preview 1.1) allows you to compile this code." Here I also inform you that auto-default struct is a new feature that was added in Visual Studio 2022 version 17.3. It ensures that all fields (or autoproperties) of a struct type are initialized to their default values if a constructor does not initialize them.
- In short, the code in this book should give you the expected output in upcoming versions of C#/Visual Studio. Though I believe that the results should not vary in other environments, you know the nature of software—it is naughty. So, I recommend that if you want to see the same output, it will be better if you can mimic the same environment.
- You can download and install the Visual Studio IDE from `https://visualstudio.microsoft.com/downloads/` (see Figure I-1).

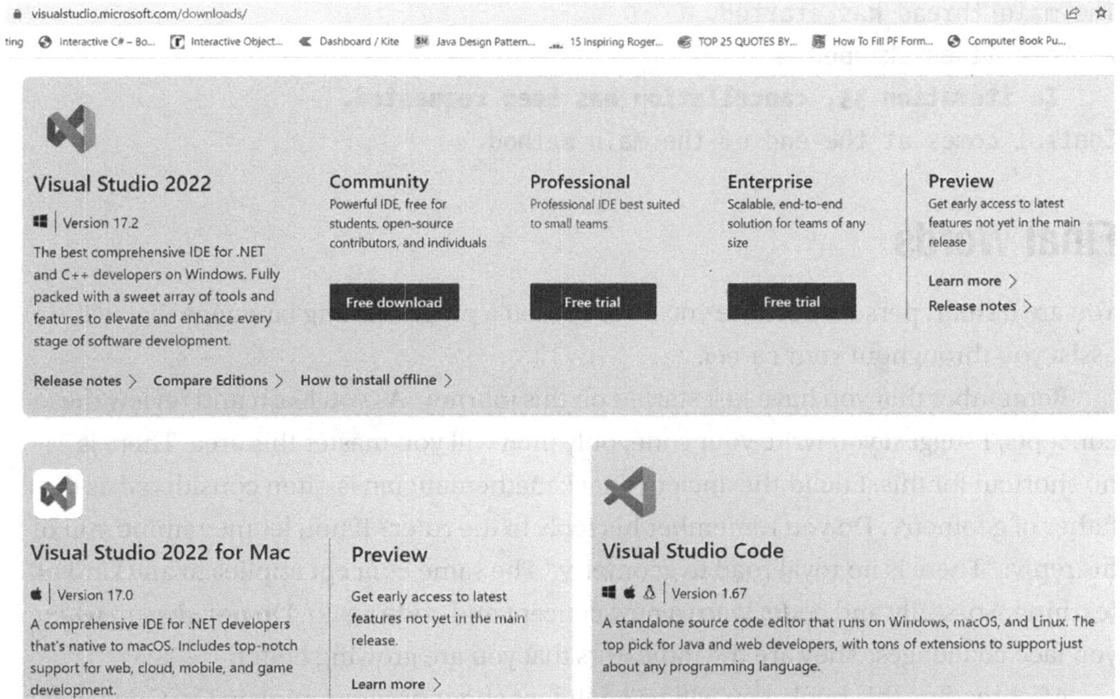

Figure I-1. *Download link for Visual Studio 2022, Visual Studio for Mac, and Visual Studio Code*

Note At the time of this writing, this link works fine, and the information is correct. But the link and policies may change in the future. The same comment applies to all the links in this book.

Conventions Used in This Book

In many places, I have provided you with links to Microsoft's documentation. Why? They are the authenticated source of information to describe a feature.

Finally, all the output and code in the book uses the same font and structure. To draw your attention to a particular piece of code, in some places, I have made code bold. For example, consider the following output fragment (taken from Chapter 14 where I discuss managed thread cancellation) and the line that contains the bold letters:

```
The main thread has started.
// Some lines skipped
    In iteration 33, cancellation has been requested.
Control comes at the end of the Main method.
```

Final Words

You are a smart person, because you have chosen a programming language that will assist you throughout your career.

Remember that you have just started on this journey. As you learn and review these concepts, I suggest you write your code; only then will you master this area. There is no shortcut for this. Euclid,the ancient Greek mathematician is often considered as the father of geometry. Do you remember his reply to the ruler? If not, let me remind you of his reply: "There is no royal road to geometry." The same concept applies to any kind of learning. So, study and code; learn a new concept and code again. Do not give up when you face challenges. They are the indicators that you are growing better.

After reading this book, you will be confident about programming in C#. Good luck.

PART I

Foundations

Part I consists of three chapters.

- Chapter 1 focuses on the most important concepts in .NET and the fundamentals of C#. It discusses the basic programming constructs in C#, useful operators, explicit casting, selection statements with case guards, iteration statements, jump statements, and so on.
- Chapter 2 covers various aspects of using strings and arrays in C#.
- Chapter 3 covers various aspects of using structures and enumerations in C#.

Since its inception in 2002, C# has continued to evolve and introduce new features to meet developers' expectations. This book is not meant to cover every aspect of C#; instead, it reviews the recently-added and most commonly used features in C#, so that you can be confident about C# and prepare quickly before an examination or a job interview. Most importantly, this book can help you understand the C# language better.

CHAPTER 1

Fundamentals of .NET and C#

Welcome to the first chapter of the book! Before you jump into it, let me quickly remind you that in each of the chapters I'll focus on some specific topics that are important for you to learn in order to master programming in C#. In addition, you probably know that C# heavily depends on .NET. So, before we review your C# programming skills, I will review some .NET basics. This chapter covers the following topics:

- The important concepts in .NET
- The basic programming constructs in C#
- Use of some useful data types including the var type
- Use of some useful operators and explicit casting
- Use of the selection statements and case guards
- Use of the iteration statements
- Use of the jump statements
- Use of the ternary operator

Let us start now.

Theoretical Concepts

This section includes questions and answers on C# programming basics and defines common terms in Microsoft .NET.

Common .NET Terminology

1.T1 What do you mean by .NET?

Answer:

V. Sarcar, *Test Your Skills in C# Programming*, https://doi.org/10.1007/978-1-4842-8655-5_1

.NET is a common term to mean .NET Standard and all the .NET implementations and workloads. It is recommended that you use it for all upcoming development, meaning .NET 5 (and .NET Core) and later versions. It is a cross-platform, high-performance, open source implementation of .NET.

It is important to note that a plus sign after a version number means "and newer versions." For example, .NET 5+ should be interpreted as .NET 5 and the subsequent versions.

Author's Note: Initially, this book was based on .NET 6. But when I was completing the initial drafts, the C# 11 preview was released. So, later I tested many of these programs with C# 11 and .NET 7. In Chapter 15 of this book, you'll see some of the preview features as well.

1.T2 In the previous answer you mentioned the word *cross-platform*. What does that word mean?

Answer:

We use the term *cross-platform* to mean that a developer can make an application that can be used on different operating systems, such as Windows or Linux. As a result, the developer can avoid writing new code for each specific platform.

This facility saves time and effort. In programming terminology, we say that the developer can reuse code across applications and platforms.

1.T3 What is the CLR and the Core CLR?

Answer:

CLR means the Common Language Runtime. The Core CLR is used as the CLR for .NET Core, .NET 5, and newer versions. So, an exact meaning depends on the context, depending on whether you are referring to the .NET Framework or .NET 5+. If you mean the .NET Framework, the CLR implementation targets Windows only; otherwise, it targets cross-platform support.

A CLR is a virtual machine that generates and compiles code on the fly using a just-in-time (JIT) compiler. It also handles memory allocations. Simply, you can say that it is an intermediary that exists on top of operating systems and handles the execution of .NET applications. The programs must go through the CLR so that there is no direct communication with the OS.

1.T4 What do you mean by a JIT compiler?

Answer:

A CLR uses a just-in-time (JIT) compiler to compile the intermediate language (IL) code to native executable code, for example, in `.exe` or `.dll` (which must be machine and OS-specific). Afterward, the CLR reuses the same compiled copy so that repeated compilation time can be avoided.

When we call a function, the conversion of IL to native code takes place just in time, and the part that is not used in any particular run is never converted. The Microsoft documentation (`https://docs.microsoft.com/en-us/dotnet/standard/glossary#implementation-of-net`) says the following:

> *Since JIT compilation occurs during the execution of the application, compile time is part of the run time. Thus, JIT compilers have to balance time spent optimizing code against the savings that the resulting code can produce. But a JIT knows the actual hardware and can free developers from having to ship different implementations.*

1.T5 What do you mean by IL?

Answer:

IL is the Intermediate Language. Sometimes, we also refer to it as MSIL (Microsoft's IL) or CIL (Common IL). A higher-level .NET language like C# first compiles down to the IL code, which is the operating system and hardware independent. This code is similar for each .NET language so we can make cross-language relationships with it.

The Common Language Runtime (CLR) converts this IL code to machine-specific code using a JIT compiler. Figure 1-1 describes the overall process.

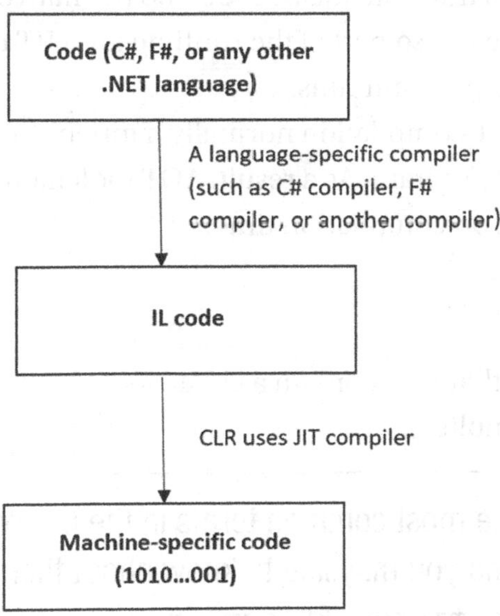

***Figure 1-1.** The process through which the C# code converts to a machine-specific code*

1.T6 How is .NET Core different from the .NET Framework?

Answer:

The .NET Framework runs only on Windows. It includes the CLR, base class library (BCL), and the application framework libraries such as Windows Forms and WPF. On the other hand, .NET Core has cross-platform support, and it is the earlier version of .NET, which we already discussed in 1.T1. To make things clear, here are some important points from the official site:

- The version numbers 4.x was skipped to avoid confusion with .NET Framework 4.x.
- They dropped "Core" from the name to emphasize that this is the main implementation of .NET going forward.
- .NET 5 supports more types of apps and more platforms. It is the next major release of .NET Core following 3.1

1.T7 What is .NET Native?

Answer:

It is a compiler toolchain that can produce native code ahead of time (AOT).

1.T8 How does an AOT compiler differ from a JIT compiler?

Answer:

Both of these compilers translate the IL code into the native code. But you already know that the compile time is also part of the runtime for a JIT compiler because this compilation occurs when a program runs.

On the contrary, an AOT compilation normally happens on a different machine before the execution of the program. As a result, AOT toolchains can put the full focus on code optimization, but not on compilation time.

1.T9 What is an assembly?

Answer:

It is a `.dll` or `.exe` file that may contain a collection of APIs, which can be used by an application (or other assemblies).

Note I have covered the most common terms in the previous Q&As. But there are many other terms, and you may like to know about them. So, I recommend you visit `https://docs.microsoft.com/en-us/dotnet/standard/glossary#implementation-of-net`. Here you'll also see that .NET is always fully capitalized, never written as ".Net."

Preliminary Concepts in C#

1.T10 Can you distinguish a project from a solution?

Answer:

A project contains executables and libraries (in general) to make an application or module. Its extension is `.csproj` in C# (e.g., Console Application, Class Library, Windows Form Application, etc.).

A solution is a placeholder that contains different logically related projects. Its extension is `.sln`. (e.g., a solution can contain a console application project and Windows form project application together).

1.T11 What is the significance of `using System`?

Answer:

It allows you to access all classes defined in the `System` namespace (but not the classes in its child namespaces).

1.T12 How do you choose among a float, a double, and a decimal data type?

Answer:

If you want more precision in an application such as an application that deals with financial computations or interest rates, use a `decimal` data type. But when optimizing performance or minimizing the storage is more important than precisions, you can use a `double` (or `float`) data type.

The online documentation at `https://docs.microsoft.com/en-us/dotnet/csharp/language-reference/builtin-types/floating-point-numeric-types` tells the following:

> *However, any difference in performance would go unnoticed by all but the most calculation-intensive applications. Another possible reason to avoid decimal is to minimize storage requirements. For example, ML.NET uses float because the difference between 4 bytes and 16 bytes adds up for very large data sets.*

Author's Note: The C# types float, double, and decimal represent the .NET types `System.Single`, `System.Double`, and `System.Decimal`, respectively. All these floating-point numeric types are used to represent real numbers, and their default value is 0.

1.T13 "If you want more precision in an application such as the applications that deal with financial computations or interest rates, use a decimal data type." Can you explain this statement with a program?

Answer:

The float and double data types work best for numbers with base 2. But the decimal data type is used for the numbers with base 10. So, as said before, you should pick decimals when your calculations (such as financial computations) are very sensitive to rounding errors. To understand this, consider the following code:

```
var b = 6;
decimal flag1 =(decimal) 10.0 / b;
double flag2 = 10.0/ b;
float flag3 = (float)10.0 / b;

Console.WriteLine(flag1);
Console.WriteLine(flag2);
Console.WriteLine(flag3);
```

Now compile and run this code. You'll see the following output:

```
1.6666666666666666666666666667
1.6666666666666667
1.6666666
```

1.T14 Is the conditional operator left-associative or right-associative?
Answer:

It is right-associative. So, an expression of type `e1 ? e2 : e3 ? e4 : e5` is evaluated as `e1 ? e2 : (e3 ? e4 : e5)`.

1.T15 Name the different types of iteration statements in C#. Why do we need these statements?
Answer:

The `while`, `do`, `for`, and `foreach` are examples of iteration statements in C#.

These are useful to create loops. Alternatively, they help you to execute a code block repeatedly.

1.T16 How can you distinguish between a while loop and a do-while loop?
Answer:

In the case of the `do-while` loop, the condition is checked at the end of the loop. So, even if the condition is false, a `do-while` loop executes at least once. On the contrary, if the condition is false, the `while` loop does not execute at all. So, you can say that a `do-while` loop executes one or more times, whereas a `while` loop executes zero or more times.

Consider the following program and notice the output to understand the difference between them:

```
Console.WriteLine("***Illustration: do-while loop***");
int j = 1;
do
{
    Console.WriteLine($"Inside loop: j is now {j}");
    j++;
} while (j < 1);
Console.WriteLine($"Outside loop: j's final value is {j}");

Console.WriteLine("\n***Illustration: while loop***");
j = 1;
while (j < 1)
{
    Console.WriteLine($"Inside loop: j is now {j}");
    j++;
};
Console.WriteLine($"Outside loop: j's final value is {j}");
```

When you run this code, you'll get the following output:

```
***Illustration: do-while loop***
Inside loop: j is now 1
Outside loop: j's final value is 2

***Illustration: while loop***
Outside loop: j's final value is 1
```

POINT TO REMEMBER

Sometimes a `do-while` loop is referred to as a do loop. But I want you to note that if you use `do{..}` without a `while{..}`, the C# compiler raises the following error: `CS1003 Syntax error, 'while' expected.`

1.T17 What is a foreach loop?

Answer:

We use a foreach statement to iterate over each element in an enumerable object. It simply means that we are considering a type that implements either the System.Collections.IEnumerable or System.Collections.Generic.IEnumerable<T> interface. For example, the string data type is enumerable. So, we can enumerate the characters in a string. Here is a sample code:

```
string text = "hello";
Console.WriteLine($"The string \"hello\" contains the
                    following characters:");
foreach (char c in text)
{
    Console.WriteLine(c);
}
```

This code can produce the following output:

```
The string "hello" contains the following characters:
h
e
l
l
o
```

Author's Note: The string data type is discussed in detail in Chapter 2. Probably you have noticed how I printed the double quotes in the console using an escape sequence (a backslash followed by a double-quote).

1.T18 How do you choose between a for loop or a foreach loop?

Answer:

I have seen some discussions where developers claim that for is slightly faster. However, to make the distinction simpler, these are my opinions:

- If you are dealing with collections and do not want to bother with the indexes, use a foreach loop. It is easier to write, and you do not need to put any bounds on that operations.
- If you want to use, print, or access every second or third item (or any such similar operation), the for loop is convenient.

- The `for` loop can work with other data, and it is not restricted to collections.

To understand these suggestions, let us examine the following code segment:

```
List<int> list = new () { 1, 2, 3,4,5 };
Console.WriteLine("Executing the 'foreach' loop:");
foreach (int index in list)
{
    Console.WriteLine("\t" + index);
}
Console.WriteLine("Executing the 'for' loop :");
for (int index = 0; index < list.Count; index++)
{
   Console.WriteLine("\t" + list[index]);
}
```

This code produces the following output:

```
Executing the 'foreach' loop:
        1
        2
        3
        4
        5
Executing the 'for' loop :
        1
        2
        3
        4
        5
```

You can see that I have created similar operations using a `for` loop and a `foreach` loop. Now notice that if you want to print the values, like 1,3,5 (or any particular order you like), writing code using the `for` loop is easier, and I need to change only the increment part of the `for` loop, as follows (i.e., instead of `i++`, I'll use `i+=2`):

```
for (int i = 0; i < list.Count; i+=2)
```

Note Collections are advanced concepts. If you do not have any idea about them, it is better to skip this question for now. You can learn about collections later and come back here.

1.T19 Name the different types of jump statements in C#. Why do we need these statements?

Answer:

The `break`, `continue`, `return`, `goto`, and `throw` are the jump statements in C#. These statements are used to transfer control unconditionally.

Programming Skills

Using the following questions you can test your programming skills in C#. Note that if I do not mention the namespace, you assume that all parts of the program belong to the same namespace.

Basic Programming Concepts

1.P1 Can you compile the following code?

```
Console.WriteLine("Hello");
class A
{
    // Some code
}
class A
{
    // Some code
}
```

Answer:

No. You'll receive the following compile-time error:

```
CS0101   The namespace '<global namespace>' already contains a
definition for 'A'
```

Explanation:

In a namespace, you cannot declare multiple classes with the same name. If you want to use the same name for your classes, you can place them in separate namespaces. Here is a sample:

```
Console.WriteLine("Hello");
class A
{
    // Some code
}

namespace AnotherNamespace
{
    class A
    {
        // Some code
    }
}
```

1.P2 Predict the output of the following code segment:

```
int flag1 = 1, flag2 = 1;
Console.WriteLine($"Currently, the flag1 is: {flag1++}");
Console.WriteLine($"Currently, the flag2 is: {++flag2}");
```

Answer:

This code can compile and run successfully. You'll get the following output:

```
Currently, the flag1 is: 1
Currently, the flag2 is: 2
```

Explanation:

You have seen the usage of the unary operators: prefix increment and postfix increment. The result of ++`flag` is the value of the `flag` after the operation (i.e., increment it before, so you call it a pre-increment), and the result of `flag`++ is the value of the `flag` before the operation (i.e., increment it later, so you call it a post-increment).

1.P3 Predict the output of the following code segment:

```
Console.WriteLine($"The max value of an int
                            is:{int.MaxValue}");
```

```
Console.WriteLine($"The min value of an int
                                    is:{int.MinValue}");
int flag = int.MaxValue;
Console.WriteLine($"Currently, the flag is: {flag}");
flag++;
Console.WriteLine($"Post increment,the flag is: {flag}");
```

Answer:

You'll get the following output:

```
The max value of an int is:2147483647
The min value of an int is:-2147483648
Currently, the flag is: 2147483647
Post increment,the flag is: -2147483648
```

Explanation:

MaxValue and MinValue in this example help you to verify the largest and smallest possible value of an int. So, the first two lines of this output are straightforward. But it becomes interesting when you notice the last line of the output.

Why did this happen? The answer is that, silently, the result of an arithmetic operation on integral types can overflow, and you may be unaware of it because you do not see any exception message. Here I demonstrate such a case: I incremented an integer value by 1 when it was already containing the maximum possible value. The result of this addition operation causes you to get the minimum possible int value.

So, if you want to be careful, what should you do? You can use the checked keyword like the following:

```
// The previous code skipped
int flag = int.MaxValue;
Console.WriteLine($"Currently, the flag is: {flag}");
checked
{
    flag++;
    Console.WriteLine($"Post increment,the flag is: {flag}");
}
```

As a result, when you execute the previous code segment, you can see the exception, as shown here:

```
Currently, the flag is: 2147483647
Unhandled exception. System.OverflowException: Arithmetic operation
resulted in an overflow.
```

Author's Note: The unchecked operator can be used for the opposite purpose.

1.P4 In the previous code (1.P3), I saw that by default there is no exception message. So, I do not understand the need for an unchecked operator. Can you please explain?

Answer:

The official documentation at `https://docs.microsoft.com/en-us/dotnet/csharp/language-reference/keywords/checked` confirms that the overflow checking can be enabled by compiler options, environment configuration, or the `checked` keyword. So, when you use the compiler option in **Visual Studio's Advanced Build Settings** as shown in Figure 1-2, you enable overflow checking by default for all the possible expressions in a similar context.

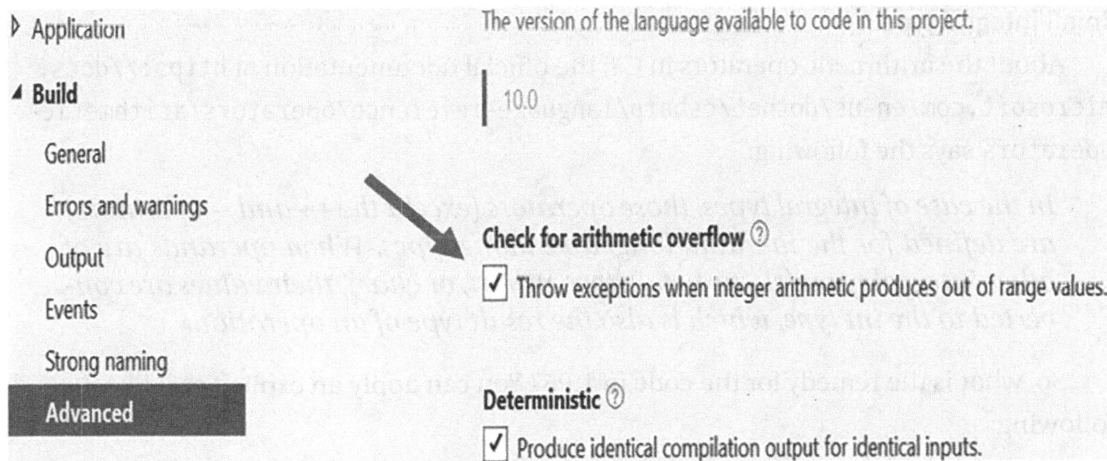

***Figure 1-2.** Enabling overflow checking for the arithmetic expressions in a program*

Now let us assume that you need to disable overflow checking for a small number of expressions. So, instead of disabling the overflow checks for all expressions, you can use the `unchecked` operator for these few expressions.

1.P5 Can you compile the following code?

```
byte flag1 = 1;
byte flag2 = 2;
byte flag3 = flag1 + flag2;
Console.WriteLine($"The flag3 is: {flag3}");
```

Answer:

No. You'll receive the following compile-time error:

```
CS0266   Cannot implicitly convert type 'int' to 'byte'. An explicit
conversion exists (are you missing a cast?)
```

Explanation:

See the official note at `https://docs.microsoft.com/en-us/dotnet/csharp/language-reference/builtin-types/integral-numeric-types`. You can see that byte is an "Unsigned 8-bit integer," whereas int is a "Signed 32-bit integer." Small-sized integers (8-bit and 16-bit integral types) do not have their arithmetic operators. If required, C# implicitly can convert them to larger types as required to support an operation. But you'll see the compile-time error if you try to assign the result back to the small integral type.

About the arithmetic operators in C#, the official documentation at `https://docs.microsoft.com/en-us/dotnet/csharp/language-reference/operators/arithmetic-operators` says the following:

> *In the case of integral types, those operators (except the ++ and -- operators) are defined for the int, uint, long, and ulong types. When operands are of other integral types (sbyte, byte, short, ushort, or char), their values are converted to the int type, which is also the result type of an operation.*

So, what is the remedy for the code in 1.P5? You can apply an explicit cast like the following:

```
byte flag3 = (byte)(flag1 + flag2); // OK
```

Author's Note: The official documentation also states that when operands are of different integral or floating-point types, their values are converted to the closest containing type, if such a type exists. This information is helpful for you to understand certain code segments.

1.P6 Can you compile the following code segment?

```
Console.WriteLine($"5.25/0.0 = {5.25 / 0.0}");
Console.WriteLine($"1.27/-0 = {1.27 / -0.0}");
Console.WriteLine($"0/-2.5 = {0 / -2.5}");
Console.WriteLine($"0.0/0.0 = {0.0 / 0.0}");
Console.WriteLine($"0/5 = {0/5}");
Console.WriteLine($"-0.0 = {-0.0}");
Console.WriteLine($"-0.0f = {-0.0f}");
Console.WriteLine($"double.PositiveInfinity =
              {double.PositiveInfinity}");
Console.WriteLine($"-5*PositiveInfinity =
              {-5 * double.PositiveInfinity}");
Console.WriteLine($"float.PositiveInfinity =
              {float.PositiveInfinity}");
```

Answer:

Yes, this code can compile and run successfully. You'll get the following output:

```
5.25/0.0 = ∞
1.27/-0 = -∞
0/-2.5 = -0
0.0/0.0 = NaN
0/5 = 0
-0.0 = -0
-0.0f = -0
double.PositiveInfinity = ∞
-5*PositiveInfinity = -∞
float.PositiveInfinity = ∞
```

Explanation:

I have shown this example to remind you that you can see negative infinity or negative zero in your program output. In C# programming, the float and double types can have some special values: NaN (Not a Number), +∞, -∞, and -0. There are certain operations that can produce these special values. You have seen some of these operations. For example, you can see that dividing a nonzero number by zero produces an infinite value. In this case, the resultant sign is positive if both the numerator and the denominator have the same sign only. You can also see that both the constants, -0.0 and -0.0f, show the special value -0.

Now, Figure 1-3 shows a partial snapshot of the `Double` class from the Visual Studio IDE so that you can see some of its constants for these special values.

```
public readonly partial struct Double : System.IComparable, System.IComparable<double>, System.IConverti
{
    private readonly double _dummyPrimitive;
    public const double E = 2.718281828459045;
    public const double Epsilon = 5E-324;
    public const double MaxValue = 1.7976931348623157E+308;
    public const double MinValue = -1.7976931348623157E+308;
    public const double NaN = 0.0 / 0.0;
    public const double NegativeInfinity = -1.0 / 0.0;
    public const double NegativeZero = -0;
    public const double Pi = 3.141592653589793;
    public const double PositiveInfinity = 1.0 / 0.0;
    public const double Tau = 6.283185307179586;
    static double System.Numerics.IAdditiveIdentity<System.Double,System.Double>.AdditiveIdentity { get
    static double System.Numerics.IFloatingPointIeee754<System.Double>.E { get { throw null; } }
    static double System.Numerics.IFloatingPointIeee754<System.Double>.Epsilon { get { throw null; } }
    static double System.Numerics.IFloatingPointIeee754<System.Double>.NaN { get { throw null; } }
    static double System.Numerics.IFloatingPointIeee754<System.Double>.NegativeInfinity { get { throw nu
    static double System.Numerics.IFloatingPointIeee754<System.Double>.NegativeZero { get { throw null;
```

***Figure 1-3.** Special values inside the built-in Double class in C#*

You can see that the `Double` class has the specific constants such as `NaN`, `PositiveInfinity`, `NegativeInfinity`, and so on. It is useful for you to note that the float and double types follow the specification of the IEEE 754 format types. From the lower part of Figure 1-3, by seeing the naming conventions, you can get this hint.

1.P7 Can you compile the following code?

```
Console.WriteLine($"5/0 = {5 / 0}");
```

Answer:

No. You'll receive the following compile-time error:

```
CS0020   Division by constant zero
```

1.P8 Can you compile the following code?

```
int b = 0;
Console.WriteLine($"5/0 = {5 / b}");
```

Answer:

This code can compile, but you'll get the following runtime error:

```
Unhandled exception. System.DivideByZeroException: Attempted to divide
by zero.
```

Author's Note: If you declare b as a constant, then you can catch this error at compile time (similar to 1.P7). Chapter 8 is dedicated to exception handling.

Selection Statements

1.P9 Predict the output of the following code segment:

```
Console.WriteLine("---Use of an if-else chain.---");
int input = 7;
if (input % 2 == 0)
{
    Console.WriteLine($"{input} is an even number.");
}
else
{
    Console.WriteLine($"{input} is an odd number.");
}
```

Answer:

You have seen a simple use of an `if-else` chain. In this case, you'll get the following output:

```
---Use of an if-else chain.---
7 is an odd number.
```

1.P10 Can you compile the following code?

```
CheckNumber(25.5);
CheckNumber(125.5);
CheckNumber(10.000);

void CheckNumber(double number)
{
    switch (number)
    {
        case double.NaN:
```

```
            Console.WriteLine($"{number} is not a number.");
            break;
        case < 10.0:
            Console.WriteLine($"{number} is less than 10.0");
            break;
        default:
            Console.WriteLine($"{number} is equal to 10.0");
            break;
        case >= 10.0:
            Console.WriteLine($"{number} is greater than or
                                  equal to 10.0");
            break;
    }
}
```

Answer:

Yes, this code can compile and run successfully. But you'll see the following warning:

```
CS0162   Unreachable code detected
```

Once you run this code, you'll get the following output:

```
25.5 is greater than or equal to 10.0
125.5 is greater than or equal to 10.0
10 is greater than or equal to 10.0
```

Explanation:

This program demonstrates the following important points:

- You should not assume that the default case should be placed at the end of a switch block. However, it is a standard practice because this case is evaluated at the end (if required). The official documentation (`https://docs.microsoft.com/en-us/dotnet/csharp/language-reference/statements/selection-statements`) also says this:

  The default case can appear in any place within a switch statement. Regardless of its position, the default case is always evaluated last and only if all other case patterns aren't matched.

- Why do you see the warning? For the number 10.000, both the default case and `case >= 10.0` satisfy the matching criteria. But as per the language documentation, the default case is evaluated only if other case patterns are not matched. So, you see the output statement corresponding to the case pattern `case >= 10.0`.

So, if you remove the equal sign (=) from this case and use `case > 10.0` instead of `case >= 10.0`, you won't see this warning, and the last line of the output will be changed. It is because this time the supplied number meets the criteria of the default case only. Here is the corresponding output:

```
25.5 is greater than or equal to 10.0
125.5 is greater than or equal to 10.0
10 is equal to 10.0
```

1.P11 Can you compile the following program?

```
CheckNumbers(5,23);
CheckNumbers(12,5+7);
CheckNumbers(-7,239);

void CheckNumbers(int num1,int num2)
{
    switch (num1,num2)
    {

        case ( > 0, > 0) when num1 != num2:
            Console.WriteLine($"{num1} and {num2} are unequal
                                    positive numbers.");
            break;
        case ( > 0, > 0):
            Console.WriteLine($"{num1} and {num2} are the same
                                  positive numbers.");
            break;
        default:
            Console.WriteLine($"At least one of {num1} or
                                   {num2} is 0 or negative.");
            break;
    }
}
```

Answer:

Yes, this program can compile and run successfully. You'll get the following output:

```
5 and 23 are unequal positive numbers.
12 and 12 are the same positive numbers.
At least one of -7 or 239 is 0 or negative.
```

Explanation:

Here you see an example of a case guard (which is a Boolean expression) inside a `switch` block. It is useful when a case pattern is not expressive enough to specify the condition. Basically, this is an additional condition that must be satisfied together with a matched pattern. You specify a case guard after the `when` keyword, as shown in this program.

1.P12 Can you compile the following code?

```
EvaluateNumber(5);
EvaluateNumber(125);
EvaluateNumber(-2);

void EvaluateNumber(int num)
{
    switch (num)
    {
        case >100:
            Console.WriteLine($"{num} is greater than 100.");
            break;
        case > 5:
            Console.WriteLine($"{num} is greater than 5.");
            // break;
        default:
            Console.WriteLine($"{num} is less than 5.");
            break;
    }
}
```

Answer:

No. You'll receive the following compile-time error:

```
CS0163  Control cannot fall through from one case label ('case > 5:')
to another
```

Explanation:

At the time of this writing, the C# compiler will not allow the control to fall through from one `switch` section to the next within a `switch` statement. Typically you use the `break` statement at the end of each switch section. Sometimes you also see the use of the `return`, `goto`, and `throw` statements to pass control out of a `switch` statement.

1.P13 Can you compile the following code?

```
ShowNumber(5);
ShowNumber(125);
ShowNumber(-2);

void ShowNumber(int num)
{
    switch (num)
    {

        case < 5:
        case < 50:
        case < 100:
            Console.WriteLine($"{num} is less than 100.");
            break;
        default:
            Console.WriteLine($"{num} is greater than or equal
                                 to 100.");

            break;
    }
}
```

Answer:

Yes, this code can compile and run successfully. You'll get the following output:

```
5 is less than 100.
125 is greater than or equal to 100.
-2 is less than 100.
```

Explanation:

You should not confuse it with the previous program. The C# compiler allows you to specify multiple case patterns for one section of a `switch` statement. So, this program can compile and run. But if you use something like the following (the changes are in bold):

```
// The previous code skipped
void ShowNumber(int num)
{
    switch (num)
    {

        case < 5:
        case < 50: Console.WriteLine("Some statements.");
        case < 100:
            Console.WriteLine($"{num} is less than 100.");
            break;
        default:
            Console.WriteLine($"{num} is greater than or equal
                                        to 100.");
            break;
    }
}
```

you'll see the compile-time error:

```
CS0163  Control cannot fall through from one case label ('case < 50:')
to another
```

Ternary Operator

1.P14 Predict the output of the following code segment:

```
int flag = 7;
string output= flag<3?"less than 3":"greater than 3";
Console.WriteLine($"{flag} is {output}");
```

Answer:

You have seen a simple use of a conditional operator (`?:`). It is also known as the ternary operator because it takes three operands. It evaluates a Boolean expression and returns the result of one of the two expressions, depending on whether this expression evaluates to true or false. When you use it, you use the following form:

```
expression? true_case: false_case,
```

Here if the condition of the `expression` is true, `true_case` is evaluated; otherwise, the `false_case` is evaluated.

Since the Boolean expression becomes `false` in this program, you'll get the following output:

```
7 is greater than 3
```

Author's Note: Conditional expressions have become more useful over a period of time. For example, in C# 7.2 onward, conditional `ref` expressions are more flexible: you can assign a `ref local` or `ref readonly` local variable conditionally with such an expression. In C# 9.0 onward, conditional expressions are also target-typed. This is the beginning of the book, and we have not covered the advanced concepts yet. So, I prefer to skip those discussions here. If interested, you can take a quick look at these new capabilities of the conditional expression at `https://docs.microsoft.com/en-us/dotnet/csharp/language-reference/operators/conditional-operator`.

Iteration Statements

1.P15 Here is a code segment that uses a `while` loop:

```
int i = 0;
while (i < 3)
{
    Console.WriteLine($"The current value: {i}");
    i++;
}
```

Can you write an equivalent for loop?

Answer:

Here is a sample:

```
for (int j = 0; j < 3; j++)
{
    Console.WriteLine($"The current value: {j}");
}
```

In each case, you'll see the following output:

```
The current value: 0
The current value: 1
The current value: 2
```

1.P16 Can you compile the following code?

```
for (int k1 = 0; ; k1++)
{
    Console.WriteLine($"The current value: {k1}");
}
```

Answer:

Yes, but you'll fall into an infinite loop:

1.P17 Can you compile the following code?

```
for (int k2 = 0; k2 < 3; )
{
    Console.WriteLine($"The current value: {k2}");
}
```

Answer:

Yes, but you'll fall into an infinite loop again.

1.P18 Predict the output of the following code segment:

```
for (int k = 0; k < 8; k+=3)
{
    Console.WriteLine($"The current value: {k}");
}
```

Answer:

This code can compile and run successfully. You'll get the following output:

```
The current value: 0
The current value: 3
The current value: 6
```

Explanation:

Each time the loop is executed, the value of k is incremented by 3. The upper limit was set to 8. So, you see these values: `0, 0+3=3, 3+3=6`.

1.P19 Can you compile the following code?

```
int i = 5;
while (i)
{
    Console.WriteLine($"i is now {i}");
    i++;
}
```

Answer:

No. In C# programming, this type of coding is not allowed. You'll receive the following compile-time error:

```
CS0029   Cannot implicitly convert type 'int' to 'bool'
```

1.P20 Can you compile the following code?

```
int i = 5;
while ()
{
    Console.WriteLine($"i is now {i}");
    i++;
}
```

Answer:

No. You'll receive the following compile-time error:

```
CS1525   Invalid expression term ')'
```

1.P21 Can you compile the following code?

```
int j = 0, m = 0;
while (true)
{
    Console.WriteLine($"j is now {j}");
    m++;
}
```

Answer:

Yes, but you'll fall into an infinite loop again.

Explanation:

The Boolean expression for the `while` statement is always `true`, so the loop cannot terminate.

1.P22 Can you compile the following code?

```
int flag = 1;
while (flag != 3)
{
    Console.WriteLine($"flag is now {flag}");
    flag++;
    if (flag == 2)
        goto level_1;
}
flag = 50;
Console.WriteLine($"flag is now {flag}");

level_1:
flag = 100;
Console.WriteLine($"flag is now {flag}");
```

Answer:

This code can compile and run successfully. You'll get the following output:

```
flag is now 1
flag is now 100
```

Explanation:

When the variable `flag` becomes 2, it jumps to `level_1`. There it sets a new value (100) for the `flag` variable and finally prints this information. So, you have seen an example of a `goto` statement here.

1.P23 Here is a code segment that uses a `while` loop:

```
int i = 0;
while (i < 3)
{
```

```
    Console.WriteLine($"The current value: {i}");
    i++;
}
```

Can you write an equivalent program using a goto statement?

Answer:

Here is a sample:

```
int k = 0;
level_2:
Console.WriteLine($"The current value: {k}");
k++;
if (k < 3) goto level_2;
```

In each case, you'll see the following output:

```
The current value: 0
The current value: 1
The current value: 2
```

Jump Statements

1.P24 Can you compile the following code?

```
DummyMethod(true);
void DummyMethod(bool b)
{
    b = false;
    goto level_3;
}
level_3:
Console.WriteLine("Reached to the level_3");
```

Answer:

No. You'll receive the following compile-time error:

```
CS0159    No such label 'level_3' within the scope of the goto statement
```

Explanation:

You'll see the compile-time error when the level referenced by the goto statement are not placed within the scope of the goto statement.

POINTS TO NOTE

To get out of a nested loop or inside a `switch` statement to transfer control, you can use `goto` statements. But in general, I try to avoid these statements in my program. Microsoft also recommends the same for both C++ and C# programmers. For C++ programmers, Microsoft says the following (see `https://docs.microsoft.com/en-us/cpp/cpp/goto-statement-cpp?view=msvc-170`):

> *It is a good programming style to use the break, continue, and return statements instead of the goto statement whenever possible. However, because the break statement exits from only one level of a loop, you might have to use a goto statement to exit a deeply nested loop.*

For C# programmers, Microsoft says the following (see `https://docs.microsoft.com/en-us/dotnet/csharp/language-reference/statements/jump-statements#the-goto-statement`):

> *When you work with nested loops, consider refactoring separate loops into separate methods. That may lead to a simpler, more readable code without the goto statement. When you work with nested loops, consider refactoring separate loops into separate methods. That may lead to a simpler, more readable code without the goto statement.*

1.P25 How can you distinguish between a **break** statement and a **continue** statement?

Answer:

A `break` statement terminates the closest enclosing iteration statement (or `switch` statement), whereas a `continue` statement starts a new iteration of the closest enclosing iteration statement. To understand this better, let us run a program. At first, we will use the `break` statement. In the next run, we'll replace the `break` statement with the `continue` statement. Here is the code segment:

```
Console.WriteLine("***Illustration: break vs continue ***");
int i = 1;
while (i != 5)
{
    Console.WriteLine($"Now, i= {i}");
```

```
        i++;
        if (i == 4)
        {
            Console.WriteLine(" Entered inside if loop");
            break;
            //continue;
        }
    }
```

When you run this code, you'll see the following output:

```
***Illustration: break vs continue ***
Now, i= 1
Now, i= 2
Now, i= 3
 Entered inside if loop
```

Now replace the break statement with the continue statement and run the program again. This time you'll see the following output (notice the change in bold):

```
***Illustration: break vs continue ***
Now, i= 1
Now, i= 2
Now, i= 3
 Entered inside if loop
Now, i= 4
```

Author's Note: The use of the throw statement is discussed in Chapter 8. The use of return statements will be shown in various code segments in this book. So, I have skipped the separate discussion on them in this section.

Use of the var Keyword

1.P26 Can you compile the following code?

```
var i = 25;
var j1 = 25.5f;
var j2 = 25.5;
```

```
var j3 = 25.5M;
var k = 'c';
var l = "hello";

Console.WriteLine($"The type of i is {i.GetType()}");
Console.WriteLine($"The type of j1 is {j1.GetType()}");
Console.WriteLine($"The type of j2 is {j2.GetType()}");
Console.WriteLine($"The type of j3 is {j3.GetType()}");
Console.WriteLine($"The type of k is {k.GetType()}");
Console.WriteLine($"The type of l is {l.GetType()}");
```

Answer:

Yes, this code can compile and run successfully. You'll get the following output:

```
The type of i is System.Int32
The type of j1 is System.Single
The type of j2 is System.Double
The type of j3 is System.Decimal
The type of k is System.Char
The type of l is System.String
```

Explanation:

You have seen the usage of the var type. You can use it to declare an implicit type variable that specifies the type of a variable based on the initial value. This program also shows that a var type declaration can be used to figure out an implicitly typed local variable. Remember the following points:

- We use a literal without a suffix or with the `d` or `D` suffix for the double type variable.
- We use a literal with the `f` or `F` suffix for the float type variable.
- We use a literal with the `m` or `M` suffix for the decimal type variable.
- The `float` is an alias for the .NET type `System.Single`.

CHAPTER 2

Strings and Arrays

In C# programming, you have various data types. For example, to store integers with various ranges, you can use the integral types (int, short, long, byte, sbyte, uint, ushort, ulong, and char). Similarly, you have floating-point types (float, double, and decimal) to store floating-point numbers. These types support different levels of precision and range. You also have bool type to store true or false values, as well as the string data type to store text. There are also custom data types, which you'll learn about in Part II of this book.

The goal of this chapter is not to check whether you remember all of these types and the ranges they support. I know that they cannot be memorized in one reading, and the information about their supporting ranges is easily available from a reference book or online material. In the first chapter, I covered some useful data types. In this chapter, I'll cover two more important data types: strings and arrays. You can guess the reason: they also belong to the most common building blocks in C# programming. Once you finish this chapter, you will be able to answer the following questions:

- How can you use the string data type in your program?
- How can you use the common built-in methods from the `String` class?
- How is a `String` variable different from a `StringBuilder`?
- How can you convert a string to an int?
- How can you use a nullable reference type in a program?
- How do you create arrays in C#?
- What are the different types of C# arrays, and how can you use them?
- How can you use the common built-in methods from the `System.Array` class?
- How can you iterate over a string or an array?

Let us review and test your understanding of these topics now.

V. Sarcar, *Test Your Skills in C# Programming*, https://doi.org/10.1007/978-1-4842-8655-5_2

Theoretical Concepts

This section includes the theoretical questions and answers about strings and arrays in C#.

Strings in C#

2.T1 What is a string data type in C#?

Answer:

You use the string type to store the text of an arbitrary length. In C#, you can use the `string` keyword to represent strings. To create a string data type or assign a value to it, you use double quotes as follows (this code initializes the string variable with a regular string literal):

```
string title = "Welcome to C# Programming.";
```

You need to remember that these are an *immutable* sequence of Unicode characters.

Author's Note: A string object is a sequential collection of `System.Char` objects. A `System.Char` object corresponds to a UTF-16 code unit. So, you can say that a string represents text that is a sequence of UTF-16 code units. In C#, the `string` keyword is an alias for `System.String`. Similarly, you can use the `int` and `char` keywords for the .NET types `System.Int32` and `System.Char`, respectively.

2.T2 We can print a string variable in the console using different methods. Can you demonstrate some of them?

Answer:

Here is some sample code with supporting comments for your reference:

```
string name= "John";
double balance = 250.56;
// Using formatting
Console.WriteLine("Hi {0}, you have ${1} left.",
                  name,balance);

// Using String.Format
string str = String.Format("Hi {0}, you have ${1} left.",
                          name, balance);
Console.WriteLine(str);
```

```
// Using string concatenation
Console.WriteLine("Hi " + name + ", you have $" + balance + "
                  left.");

// Using string interpolation (C# 6 onwards)
Console.WriteLine($"Hi {name}, you have ${balance} left.");
```

When you run this code, you'll see that each line produces the same output as follows:

```
Hi John, you have $250.56 left.
Hi John, you have $250.56 left.
Hi John, you have $250.56 left.
Hi John, you have $250.56 left.
```

2.T3 Is string a value type or a reference type?

Answer:

The string data type in C# is a reference type.

Author's Note: The object, string, and dynamic types are examples of reference types. The int, float, double, decimal, etc., are examples of value types. Chapter 3 discusses the value types in C# in detail. In Chapter 9, you'll learn more about value types and reference types in C#.

2.T4 What is the difference between `String` and `StringBuilder`?

Answer:

Strings are immutable (not editable). This means that if you do some operations on a given string instance and if those operations cause some changes to the original string, then a new string instance with the updated value will be created (in a different location in memory).

On the other hand, the `StringBuilder` *does not create a new instance for such an operation, which is why it is mutable.* It updates the change in the existing instance.

Author's Note: You should also remember that the `String` class resides in the `System` namespace, but `StringBuilder` resides in the `System.Text` namespace. 2.P10 demonstrates a program to show the difference between a `String` and a `StringBuilder`.

2.T5 How do you differentiate between the `String.Join()` and `String.Concat()` methods?

Answer:

Using `String.Join()` is better when you believe that the strings should be separated by a delimiter. Consider the following program and see the output to understand it better:

```
string[] animalStore = { "Tigers","Lions","Elephants" };

string animals = string.Concat(animalStore);
Console.WriteLine($"The circus has {animals}");

animals = string.Join(",", animalStore);
Console.WriteLine($"The circus has {animals}");
```

When you run this code, you'll see the following output:

```
The circus has TigersLionsElephants
The circus has Tigers,Lions,Elephants
```

You can see the invocation of the `String.Join` method makes a more readable output in this case.

Author's Note: The Q&A in 2.T6 belongs to the advanced topics of C#. You may need to understand the concept of objects, references, and string interning. The need for string interning can be understood through the Flyweight design pattern. But I have made it easier for you to understand this concept with a small code segment. Still, if it is tough for you, you can skip it for now!

2.T6 Suppose you see the following code segment:

```
string str1 = "Hello reader!";
string str2 = "Hello reader!";
```

Will this code create two string objects?

Answer:

No, both the references, `str1` and `str2`, will point to a single object. To confirm this answer, you can use the `ReferenceEquals` method, which helps you to determine whether the specified `System.Object` instances are the same instance. So, consider the following code:

```
string str1 = "Hello reader!";
string str2 = "Hello reader!";
Console.WriteLine(object.ReferenceEquals(str1,str2)); // True
```

When you run this code, you'll see the following output:

```
True
```

What is the reason behind this? The Microsoft documentation at `https://docs.microsoft.com/en-us/dotnet/api/system.string.intern?view=net-6.0` says the following:

> *The common language runtime conserves string storage by maintaining a table, called the intern pool, that contains a single reference to each unique literal string declared or created programmatically in your program. Consequently, an instance of a literal string with a particular value only exists once in the system.*

But it is interesting to note that if you have the following code segment (see the changes in bold):

```
string str1 = "Hello reader!";
string str2 = "Hello reader!";
string str3 = "reader!";
string str4 = "Hello " + str3;
Console.WriteLine(object.ReferenceEquals(str1,str2)); // True
Console.WriteLine(object.ReferenceEquals(str1, str4));// False
```

then when you run this code, you'll see the following output (notice the last line in bold):

```
True
False
```

Confused about the last line of output? Let me explain: though `str3` is a constant, `str4` is not. This is because the combination of a constant and a variable cannot be a constant. So, the compiler does not know the value of this expression in advance. Therefore, in this case, `str1` and `str2` do not point to the same object; instead, they point to different objects.

The Use of Arrays in C#

2.T7 What do you mean by arrays in C#?

Answer:

Arrays contain homogeneous data. Their length is fixed (`System.Collection` can provide dynamically sized arrays, however), and the elements in them are stored in a contiguous location. Arrays can be single-dimensional, multidimensional (often referred to as rectangular), or jagged.

Author's Note: An array can contain elements of any type, including an array type.

2.T8 How do you create an array in C#?

Answer:

An array is denoted with square brackets after the element type. The following line of code can be used to declare a single-dimensional array of three ints:

```
int[] numbers = new int[3];
```

Here is some sample code to insert the elements in this array:

```
numbers[0] = 5;
numbers[1] = 12;
numbers[2] = 7;
```

You can display these elements using a `for` loop (though it is optional) as follows:

```
for (int i = 0; i < 3; i++)
{
    Console.WriteLine(numbers[i]);
}
```

This is a simple demonstration, and we know that there are only three elements in this array. But it is always better to use the `Length` property of the array to traverse the array. Here is an example:

```
for (int i = 0; i < numbers.Length; i++)
{
    Console.WriteLine(numbers[i]);
}
```

You could have used either of these alternatives to create the array.

```
// Alternative approach-2.
int[] numbers = new int[] { 5, 12,7 };

// Alternative approach-3.
int[] numbers = { 5, 12, 7 };

// Alternative approach-4.
// For an explicit instantiation, var is also allowed
var numbers = new int[] { 5, 12, 7 };
```

Here you used integer arrays. If needed, you can create other types of arrays too.

2.T9 What is a multidimensional array in C#?

Answer:

Multidimensional arrays come in two flavors: rectangular and jagged.

- In a rectangular array, each row has an equal number of columns.
- A jagged array is an array of arrays, possibly of different sizes. In other words, in a jagged array, each row can have a different number of columns. A jagged array is also known as a ragged array.

POINTS TO REMEMBER

Remember that to declare a rectangular array, you use commas to separate each dimension such as `int[,] elements = new int[row, column];`.

For a jagged array, you use successive square brackets to represent each dimension such as `int[][] matrix = new int[outmost_dimension][];`.

2.T10 How can you create a rectangular array in C#?

Answer:

You can create a rectangular array with explicit values like the following:

```
int[,] rectArray = {
  {10, 20,30},
  {40, 50,60},
  };
```

Alternatively, you can see the following style:

```
int row = 2, column = 3;
int[,] elements = new int[row, column];
elements[0, 0] = 10;
elements[0, 1] = 20;
elements[0, 2] = 30;
elements[1, 0] = 40;
elements[1, 1] = 50;
elements[1, 2] = 60;
```

Since it is a rectangular array with the dimensions 2x3, you can use the following code to print the array elements:

```
Console.WriteLine("The rectangular array is as follows:");
for (int i = 0; i< 2; i++)
{
    for (int j = 0; j < 3; j++)
    {
        Console.Write(rectArray[i, j] + "\t");
    }
    Console.WriteLine();
}
Here is a sample output for your reference:
The rectangular array is as follows:
10      20      30
40      50      60
```

Author's Note: All arrays implement `IEnumerable`. So, you can also use a `foreach` statement to iterate through an array. But the Microsoft documentation (`https://docs.microsoft.com/en-us/dotnet/csharp/programming-guide/arrays/using-foreach-with-arrays`) tells us that in the case of multidimensional arrays, using a nested `for` loop can be more beneficial to control the processing order of the array elements.

2.T11 How can you create a jagged array in C#?

Answer:

Let us assume that you want to create a jagged array in which the first row contains three elements, and the second row contains four elements, as represented in Figure 2-1.

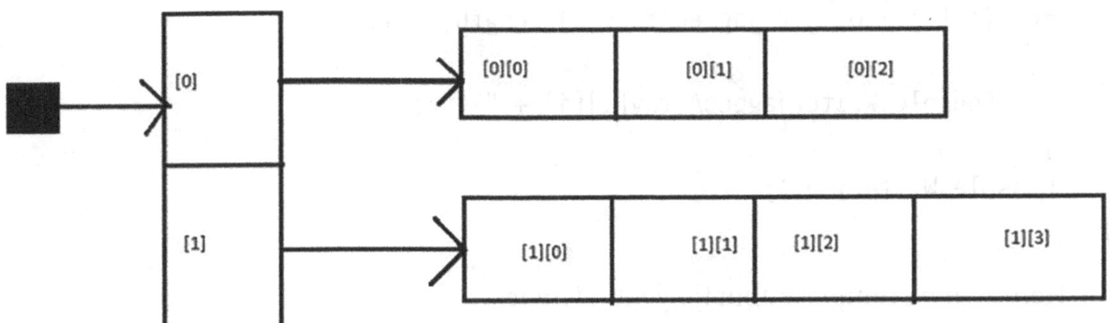

Figure 2-1. *A jagged array representation in which the first row contains three elements and the second row contains four elements*

Here is some sample code to initialize such a jagged array with explicit values:

```
int[][] jaggedArray = new int[][]
{
  new int[] {0,1},
  new int[] {2,3,4},
};
```

There are different styles of coding. Here is one such style:

```
int[][] jaggedArray = new int[2][];// Contains two 1D array
jaggedArray[0] = new int[2];// First row has 2 elements
jaggedArray[1] = new int[3];// Second row has 3 elements

// Initializing the first row
jaggedArray[0][1] = 0;
jaggedArray[0][1] = 1;

// Initializing the second row
jaggedArray[1][0] = 2;
jaggedArray[1][1] = 3;
jaggedArray[1][2] = 4;
```

You can use the following code to print the array elements:

```
Console.WriteLine("The jagged array is as follows:");
for (int i = 0; i < jaggedArray.Length; i++)
{
```

```
    for (int j = 0; j < jaggedArray[i].Length; j++)
    {
        Console.Write(jaggedArray[i][j] + "\t");
    }
    Console.WriteLine();
}
```

Here is some sample output for your reference:

```
The jagged array is as follows:
0       1
2       3       4
```

Note Eric Lippert has written a nice article (`https://ericlippert.com/2009/08/17/arrays-of-arrays/`) where the conclusion was: "Multidimensional ragged arrays are almost certainly a bad code smell. But life is much better if you can instead use generic collections."

2.T12 How can you print the jagged array elements in 2.T11 using a `foreach` loop?

Answer:

Here is some sample code that uses the `foreach` loop to print the elements in that array:

```
foreach (int[] rows in jaggedArray)
{
    foreach (int i in rows)
    {
        Console.Write(i + "\t");
    }
    Console.WriteLine();
}
```

2.T13 What is the base class of arrays in C#? Are they value types or reference types?

Answer:

All arrays in C# are derived from the abstract base type `System.Array`. An array in C# is a reference type.

2.T14 When do you prefer a jagged array over a rectangular array?

Answer:

Jagged arrays are an array of arrays. In certain cases, they are better because they support an unequal number of elements in a row. As a result, you do not need to waste any memory storage for an unnecessary allocation.

Programming Skills

Using the following questions, you can test your programming skills in C#. Note that if I do not mention the namespace, you assume that all parts of the program belong to the same namespace.

String Fundamentals

2.P1 Predict the output of the following code segment:

```
string text1= string.Concat("Hello", "World!");
Console.WriteLine("The text is: "+ text1);
Console.WriteLine($"The text is: {text1}");
```

Answer:

You'll get the following output:

```
The text is: HelloWorld!
The text is: HelloWorld!
```

Explanation:

This code segment shows that you can follow different approaches to concatenate two strings.

2.P2 Predict the output of the following code segment:

```
string text2 = "test";
Console.Write($"The length of 'text2' is: {text2.Length}");

for (int i = 0; i < text2.Length; i++)
{
    Console.Write($"\nThe text2[{i}] contains: {text2[i]}");
}
```

Answer:

You'll get the following output:

```
The length of 'text2' is: 4
The text2[0] contains: t
The text2[1] contains: e
The text2[2] contains: s
The text2[3] contains: t
```

Explanation:

This program shows the following points:

- You can use the built-in `Length` method to calculate the number of characters present in a string.
- This program shows you a way to read the individual characters of a string. You may notice that a valid index value starts from 0 and must be less than the length of the string.
- This program also shows how can you print single quotes in the console.

Additional Note:

In Chapter 1, I told you that strings are enumerable. So, you can use a `foreach` loop to print the individual characters of a string. Here is a sample:

```
string text2 = "test";
foreach (char c in text2)
{
  Console.WriteLine(c);
}
```

2.P3 Predict the output of the following code segment:

```
string text3 = @"Welcome to the ""Dream World"" ";
Console.WriteLine(text3);
Console.WriteLine(text3.ToUpper());
Console.WriteLine(text3.ToLower());
```

Answer:

You'll get the following output:

```
Welcome to the "Dream World"
WELCOME TO THE "DREAM WORLD"
welcome to the "dream world"
```

Explanation:

This program shows you that the following:

- You can print double quotes without escape sequence too.
- You can convert a string to uppercase or lowercase using the built-in `ToUpper()` and `ToLower()` methods, respectively.

2.P4 How can you print a URL such as `https://google.com`?

Answer:

Here is a sample code:

```
string url = @"https:\\google.com";
Console.WriteLine(url);
```

POINTS TO REMEMBER

Here you have seen the use of the verbatim identifier (@). You can use this special character for various purposes. One such usage is that you can use this character to enable C# keywords to be used as identifiers. The following code with comments describes this:

// string for="abc"; // compile-time error

string @for= "abc";// ok

2.P5 Predict the output of the following code segment:

```
string text5 = "    This is a sample text. ";
Console.WriteLine($"Original line:'{text5}'");
Console.WriteLine($"Trimmed line:'{text5.Trim()}'");
```

Answer:

You'll get the following output:

```
Original line:'    This is a sample text. '
Trimmed line:'This is a sample text.'
```

Explanation:

The Trim() method can be used to remove all leading and trailing whitespace characters from a string.

2.P6 Predict the output of the following code segment:

```
char[] trimChars = { ' ', 't','.','*' };
string text6 = " ***This is a sample text.*** ";
Console.WriteLine($"Original line:'{text6}'");
Console.WriteLine($"Trimmed line:'{text6.Trim(trimChars)}'");
Console.WriteLine($"New trimmed line:
                              '{text6.TrimEnd(trimChars)}'");
```

Answer:

You'll get the following output:

```
Original line:' ***This is a sample text.*** '
Trimmed line:'This is a sample tex'
New trimmed line:' ***This is a sample tex'
```

Explanation:

This program shows how to use the Trim() method to remove all leading and trailing occurrences of a set of characters (whitespace, t, dot(.), and *) from a string. The TrimEnd() method can do this, but it operates from the end of the current string.

2.P7 Predict the output of the following code segment:

```
string emptyString = String.Empty;
string? nullString = null;
Console.WriteLine("Length of the emptyString is {0}",
                                  emptyString.Length);
Console.WriteLine("Length of the nullString is {0}",
                                  nullString.Length);
string? emptyString = String.Empty;
```

```
string? nullString = null;

Console.WriteLine($"The emptyString's length is:
                                  {emptyString.Length}");
Console.WriteLine($"The nullString's length is:
                                  {nullString.Length}");
```

Answer:

The last line of this code segment will raise an exception. This code shows the difference between an empty string and a null string.

```
The emptyString's length is: 0
Unhandled exception. System.NullReferenceException: Object reference not
set to an instance of an object.
```

Additional Note:

You can test whether a string is null or empty using the `IsNullOrEmpty(...)` method. Here is a sample:

```
Console.WriteLine(string.IsNullOrEmpty(emptyString));//True
Console.WriteLine(string.IsNullOrEmpty(nullString));//True
```

Note I have shown you the use of the nullable strings (see `string?`). Nullable reference types have been allowed since C# 8.0. If you use `string` instead of `string?`, you'll see the following warning message: `CS8600 Converting null literal or possible null value to non-nullable type`.

2.P8 Predict the output of the following code segment:

```
string text8 = "Reviewing the concepts of C#.";
string welcome1 = text8.PadLeft(text8.Length + 2, '*');
string welcome2 = welcome1.PadRight(welcome1.Length + 3, '#');
Console.WriteLine($"Original line:'{text8}'");
Console.WriteLine($"Updated line:'{welcome2}'");
```

Answer:

You'll get the following output:

```
Original line:'Reviewing the concepts of C#.'
Updated line:'**Reviewing the concepts of C#.###'
```

Explanation:

Padding in the string is used to add a space or other character at the beginning or end of a string. This code segment shows you how to pad a specific character at the beginning (or at the end) of a string using the built-in `String` class methods: `PadLeft()` and `PadRight()`. You may note that these methods have overloaded versions too.

Note Remember that in C#, a `String` object is immutable. So, once created, its value cannot be modified again. Methods that appear to modify a `String` object actually return a new `String` object that contains these modifications.

2.P9 A string is a palindrome string if the reverse of it is the same as the original string. Can you write a program to check whether a string is a palindrome?

Answer:

You can reverse the string and then check whether the original string and the reversed strings are the same. Here is a simple program for this:

```
// Console.WriteLine("\n---2.P9---");
Console.WriteLine("Enter the string:");
string? inputStr = Console.ReadLine();
string? reverseStr = ReverseString(inputStr);
Validate(inputStr, reverseStr);

// Reversing a string
static string ReverseString(string str)
{
    char[] tempArray = str.ToCharArray();
    // Reverses the sequence of the elements
    Array.Reverse(tempArray);
    // Change the reversed array to a string
    string reverseStr = new(tempArray);
```

```
    // Return this string
    return reverseStr;
}

// Check for the palindrome string

static void Validate(string str1, string str2)
{
    if (str1.Equals(str2))
    {
        Console.WriteLine($"The string: '{str1}' is a
                          palindrome string.");
    }
    else
    {
        Console.WriteLine($"The string '{str1}' is a not
                          palindrome string.");
    }
}
```

Output:
Here is a sample output (positive case):

```
Enter the string:
abba
The string: 'abba' is a palindrome string.
```

Here is another sample output (negative case):

```
Enter the string:
abcd
The string 'abcd' is a not palindrome string.
```

Author's Note: I know what you are thinking. Yes, you can beautify this program using the exception handling mechanism that you'll learn/test in Chapter 8. For now, let us focus on the core part only. I also want you to note that the Equals method can determine whether two instances of System.String objects have the same value.

2.P10 Can you write a program to demonstrate the distinction between a `String` variable and a `StringBuilder` variable?

Answer:

Let's consider the following program and output. You will see that no new instance is created for StringBuilder.

```
using System.Runtime.Serialization; // For ObjectIDGenerator
using System.Text; // For the StringBuilder uses

Console.WriteLine("***String vs StringBuilder.***");
ObjectIDGenerator idGenerator = new();
bool firstTime = false;

Console.WriteLine("\nWorking with a String instance.");
string text = "Hello";
Console.WriteLine($"The instance id of {text} is
                  {idGenerator.GetId(text, out firstTime)}");
// Creates a new instance ID
text += ",John!";
Console.WriteLine($"The instance id of {text} is
                  {idGenerator.GetId(text, out firstTime)}");
Console.WriteLine("\nWorking with a StringBuilder instance.");
StringBuilder text2 = new("Hello, John!");
Console.WriteLine($"The instance id of {text2} is
                  {idGenerator.GetId(text2, out firstTime)}");
// The following does not create a new instance ID
text2 = text2.Replace("Hello", "Welcome");
Console.WriteLine($"The instance id of {text2} is
                  {idGenerator.GetId(text2, out firstTime)}");
```

Compile and run this code now. You'll get the following output:

```
***String vs StringBuilder.***

Working with a String instance.
The instance id of Hello is 1
The instance id of Hello, John! is 2
```

```
Working with a StringBuilder instance.
The instance id of Hello, John! is 3
The instance id of Welcome, John! is 3
```

2.P11 Can you compile the following code?

```
string strInput = "12";
Console.WriteLine(strInput + 5);
int intInput = int.Parse(strInput);
Console.WriteLine(intInput + 5);
```

Answer:

This code can compile and run successfully. You'll get the following output:

```
125
17
```

Explanation:

The online Microsoft documentation (see `https://docs.microsoft.com/en-us/dotnet/csharp/programming-guide/types/how-to-convert-a-string-to-a-number`) says the following:

> *You use Parse or TryParse methods on the numeric type you expect the string contains, such as the System.Int32 type. The Convert.ToInt32 method uses Parse internally.*

In the first case of this code segment, the + operator performs string concatenation. So, `12+5` becomes `125` (i.e., `"12"+"5"="125"`). In this case, `ToString` is called on the nonstring value. In the second case, you converted the `string` to an int using the `Parse` method. So, this time, you see the result of addition (`12+5=17`).

This online link also suggests the following important point:

> *When calling a Parse method, you should always use exception handling to catch a FormatException when the parse operation fails.*

Since I have not discussed exception handling yet, I have ignored this suggestion in this code segment (2.P11).

2.P12 Predict the output of the following code segment:

```
if (int.TryParse("123", out int input2))
{
   Console.WriteLine("Successfully parsed the string.");
   Console.WriteLine($"The result is: {input2 + 5}");
}
else
{
   Console.WriteLine("Couldn't parse the given string.");
}
```

Answer:

The TryParse method call was successful. So, you'll get the following output:

```
Successfully parsed the given string.
The result is: 128
```

Additional Note:

TryParse and Parse are often used in C# programming. To understand the difference between these two methods, I suggest you read the Microsoft documentation (at the link mentioned in 2.P11). It says the following:

> *The Parse method returns the converted number; the TryParse method returns a boolean value that indicates whether the conversion succeeded, and returns the converted number in an out parameter. If the string isn't in a valid format, Parse throws an exception, but TryParse returns false.*

2.P13 There are four occurrences of the letter "e" in the following string variable:

```
string hello = "Welcome reader!";
```

How can you find the first three index locations of "e"?

Answer:

Here is a sample code segment:

```
string hello = "Welcome reader!";
int firstIndex=hello.IndexOf('e');
int secondIndex = hello.IndexOf('e',firstIndex+1);
int thirdIndex = hello.IndexOf('e', secondIndex + 1);
Console.WriteLine($"The given string: {hello}");
```

```
Console.WriteLine($"The 1st index of 'e' is at location:
                                              {firstIndex}");
Console.WriteLine($"The 2nd index of 'e' is at location:
                                             {secondIndex}");
Console.WriteLine($"The 3rd index of 'e' is at location:
                                              {thirdIndex}");
```

Once you run this code, you'll see the following output:

```
The given string: Welcome reader!
The 1st index of 'e' is at location:1
The 2nd index of 'e' is at location:6
The 3rd index of 'e' is at location:9
```

Author's Note: Alternatively, you can use a for loop to find the concurrences of 'e' and maintain a counter to track how many 'e' you have found. If the counter is 3, you can return the index value. I leave this exercise for you. You may note that if the particular character is not found, the `IndexOf` method returns -1.

Array Fundamentals

2.P14 Predict the output of the following code segment:

```
int row = 2, column = 3;
int[,] elements = new int[row, column];
elements[0, 0] = 2;
elements[0, 1] = 5;
elements[0, 2] = -16;
elements[1, 0] = 6;
elements[1, 2] = 19;

Console.WriteLine("The rectangular array is as follows:");
for (int i = 0; i < row; i++)
{
    for (int j = 0; j < column; j++)
    {
        Console.Write(elements[i, j] + "\t");
    }
    Console.WriteLine();
}
```

Answer:

You'll get the following output:

```
The rectangular array is as follows:
2       5       -16
6       0       19
```

Explanation:

You have seen an example of a rectangular array with the dimensions 2x3. Notice that I have not supplied the value for `elements[1,1]`, so it is initialized with the default value of `int` (because it is an `int` array). In this example, each row has an equal number of columns (three), so it is a rectangular two-dimensional (2D) array.

Note The default values of numeric array elements are zero, but for the reference type elements, these are set to null. So, if you use an array that can hold string elements but you do not supply the required values, you'll see the nulls are set as defaults, instead of zeros.

2.P15 Predict the output of the following code segment:

```
int[][] jaggedArray = new int[3][];
jaggedArray[0] = new int[4] { 1, 2, 3, 4 };
jaggedArray[1] = new int[6] { 5, 6, 7, 8, 9, 10 };
jaggedArray[2] = new int[2] { 11, 12 };
Console.WriteLine($"Element at [0][1]={jaggedArray[0][1]}");
Console.WriteLine($"Element at [1][3]={jaggedArray[1][3]}");
Console.WriteLine($"Element at [2][1]={jaggedArray[2][1]}");
Console.WriteLine($"The last element's index of
        jaggedArray[1] is {jaggedArray[1].GetUpperBound(0)}");
Console.WriteLine($"The first element's index of
        jaggedArray[2] is {jaggedArray[2].GetLowerBound(0)}");
```

Answer:

You'll get the following output:

```
Element at [0][1]=2
Element at [1][3]=8
```

```
Element at [2][1]=12
The last element's index of jaggedArray[1] is 5
The first element's index of jaggedArray[2] is 0
```

Explanation:

The first three lines of output are straightforward. The GetUpperBound and GetLowerBound methods are used to retrieve the last and first element's index of the specified dimension in an array.

2.P16 Suppose the jagged array is the same as in P2.15. Can you predict the output of the following line?

```
Console.WriteLine($"The jaggedArray[2].GetUpperBound(1) is
                    {jaggedArray[2].GetUpperBound(1)}");
```

Answer:

You'll receive the following runtime error:

```
Unhandled exception. System.IndexOutOfRangeException: Array does not have
that many dimensions.
   at System.Array.GetUpperBound(Int32 dimension)
   // The remaining output is skipped.
```

2.P17 Predict the output of the following code segment:

```
int[,] rectArray = new int[3, 4];
Console.WriteLine($"The rectArray.Length=
                              {rectArray.Length}");
```

Answer:

You'll get the following output:

```
The rectArray.Length= 12
```

Explanation:

The Length property gives the total number of elements in all dimensions of the array. Here the number of elements is 3*4=12.

2.P18 Predict the output of the following code segment:

```
int[][] jaggedArray3 = new int[3][];
jaggedArray3[0] = new int[4] { 1, 2, 3, 4 };
jaggedArray3[1] = new int[5] { 5, 6, 7, 8, 9};
jaggedArray3[2] = new int[2] { -2,7 };
Console.WriteLine($"The jaggedArray3.Length=
                    {jaggedArray3.Length}");
Console.WriteLine($"The jaggedArray3[1].Length=
                    {jaggedArray3[1].Length}");
```

Answer:

You'll get the following output:

```
The jaggedArray3.Length= 3
The jaggedArray3[1].Length= 5
```

2.P19 Predict the output of the following code segment:

```
double[] rates = new double[4] { 2.2, 3.3, 1.1, 5.5 };
Console.Write("The original array:");
Display(rates);
Array.Sort(rates);
Console.Write("\nThe sorted array:");
Display(rates);
Console.Write("\nThe reversed array:");
Array.Reverse(rates);
Display(rates);
static void Display(Array rates)
{
    foreach (double rate in rates)
    {
        Console.Write(rate + "\t");
    }

}
```

Answer:

You'll get the following output:

```
The original array:2.2 3.3     1.1     5.5
The sorted array:1.1    2.2     3.3     5.5
The reversed array:5.5 3.3     2.2     1.1
```

Explanation:

The `Sort()` method sorts the elements of an array in ascending order. The `reverse()` method reverses these elements.

2.P20 Predict the output of the following code segment:

```
int[] scores = new int[] { 1, 2, 3, 4, 5 };
scores.SetValue(50, 4);
Console.WriteLine($"scores[3]={scores[3]}");
Console.WriteLine($"scores[4]={scores[4]}");
```

Answer:

The value at index location 4 is changed to 50, but other elements of the array were unchanged. So, you'll get the following output:

```
scores[3]=4
scores[4]=50
```

CHAPTER 3

Enumeration and Structure Types

In the previous two chapters, you saw how to use the built-in simple types as well as other types such as strings and arrays. Now the question is: can we categorize these types? The answer is yes. Broadly, you can divide all C# types into value types and reference types. You can further divide the value types into the following categories:

- Structure types
- Enumeration types

All the simple types are value types in C#. But the strings and arrays are reference types. Part II of this book focuses on object-oriented programming, and classes and objects are the foundation for that. A class is also a reference type. Before you get to that part of this book, in this chapter we will do a quick review of the value types.

POINTS TO NOTE

Note the following points before you read further:

- We often refer to the bool type, char type, integral, and floating-point numeric types as *simple types*. All the simple types are built-in value types in C#.
- In the unified type system of C#, all predefined and user-defined types inherit directly or indirectly from `System.Object`. This applies to any of the value types or reference types. The `object` type is an alias for `System.Object`.

V. Sarcar, *Test Your Skills in C# Programming*, https://doi.org/10.1007/978-1-4842-8655-5_3

- Microsoft says that although string is a reference type, the equality operators == and != are defined to compare the values of string objects, not references. Value-based equality makes testing for string equality more intuitive. You can refer to the online documentation at `https://docs.microsoft.com/en-us/dotnet/csharp/language-reference/builtin-types/reference-types` for more information.

Theoretical Concepts

This section includes the theoretical questions and answers on inheritance.

Enumerations in C#

3.T1 What is an enumeration type in C#? How do you define one?

Answer:

It is a value type. The `enum` keyword is used for the enumeration type in C#. It allows you to specify a set of named numeric constants. To define an enumeration type in C#, you use the `enum` keyword. Here is some sample code to define an enumeration type called `ErrorTypes` that has three members, `NetworkError`, `CodeError`, and `DeviceError`:

```
enum ErrorTypes
{
    NetworkError,
    CodeError,
    DeviceError,
};
```

3.T2 What is the base class of all enumeration types?

Answer:

`System.Enum`. In Visual Studio, you can see the following definition for it:

```
//
// Summary:
//     Provides the base class for enumerations.

public abstract class Enum : ValueType, IComparable, IConvertible,
IFormattable
```

```
{
  // Remaining code skipped
}
```

This definition shows that `Enum` is an abstract class that inherits from `ValueType`. On further investigation, you'll see that `ValueType` is an abstract class that is defined in the `System` namespace.

3.T3 How are the enum members organized?

Answer:

By default, the associated constant values of enum members are of type `int`; they start with zero and increase by one following the definition text order. But you can specify any other integral numeric type as an underlying type. In addition, you can explicitly assign specific values to an enumeration if you want. Here is a sample:

```
enum Values
{
    Val1 = 25,
    Val2 = 52,
    Val3 = 65,
    Val4
};
```

The unassigned enum members keep incrementing from the last explicit value. So, the previous code segment is equivalent to the following:

```
enum Values
{
    Val1 = 25,
    Val2 = 52,
    Val3 = 65,
    Val4 = 66
};
```

Note The word *enumeration* originates from the word *enumerate*. The dictionary definition of enumerate is "to count off, one after the other," which is the intent of enumerations.

3.T4 Why do you think enumeration types are useful in C# programming?

Answer:

Enumeration types are useful for several reasons.

- You can create a custom type.
- Enumerations force you to use only specific and named values. It makes your code less error-prone.
- You saw an enum declaration in 3.T1. Now consider the case when you read something like this:

  ```
  int errorType=(int)ErrorTypes.NetworkError;
  ```

  This is very clear. But when you read something like `int errorType=0;`, it is not so clear. In this case, you need to go through the previous code carefully. So, enumerations make your code more readable.

3.T5 How can you apply casting in enumeration conversions?

Answer:

Suppose you have the following enum types:

```
public enum Measurement : int
{
    Left,
    Middle,
    Right
}
public enum Alignment : uint
{
    TowardsLeft= 1,
    TowardsRight= 2,
}
```

In this case, you can explicitly cast one enum type to another as follows:

```
Measurement position = (Measurement)Alignment.TowardsLeft;
```

Now the following segment of code:

```
Console.WriteLine($"The current position is {position}");
Console.WriteLine($"Its integral value is {(int)position}");
```

will produce the following output:

```
The current position is Middle
Its integral value is 1
```

Structures in C#

3.T6 What is a struct type in C#? How do you define one?

Answer:

A struct type is a value type that can encapsulate data and related functionality. You use the `struct` keyword to define a structure in C#. Here is a sample:

```
struct Employee
{
    public int Id;
    public string Name;
    public Employee(int id, string name)
    {
        this.Id = id;
        this.Name = name;
    }
}
```

POINTS TO REMEMBER

The structures in C# follow the value semantics. This means that in the case of a struct variable, an instance of the type is copied. See `https://docs.microsoft.com/en-us/dotnet/csharp/language-reference/builtin-types/struct`. Here you'll find that Microsoft recommends you use immutable struct types in general. So, the question is how to make a structure immutable. One possible option is to make proper use of `readonly` modifiers. Starting with C# 7.2, this can be done.

But there are cases when you cannot declare the whole structure as `readonly`. What to do then? You can use the `readonly` modifier to mark the instance members that should not modify the state of the `struct`.

3.T7 It looks like immutability is an important concept in programming. Why is it important?

Answer:

In simple language, an immutable object is an object that cannot be changed after its birth. These objects are inherently thread-safe; as a result, in a multithreaded environment, they can help you a lot. Also, these objects help you to avoid race conditions.

3.T8 How can you make a structure read-only? What is the benefit of making a structure read-only?

Answer:

You can make a structure read-only when you tag the `readonly` keyword to its data members such as fields and properties. This activity guarantees that no member of this structure can modify its state. The use of the `readonly` modifier can help the compiler during performance optimizations too.

3.T9 How can you instantiate a structure variable in C#?

Answer:

You can do this in various ways. Here is some sample code to demonstrate this:

```
Employee emp1 = new(1, "Sam");
Console.WriteLine($"Name: {emp1.Name}, ID:{emp1.Id}");

Employee emp2 = new();
emp2.Name = "Jack";
emp2.Id = 2;
Console.WriteLine($"Name: {emp2.Name}, ID:{emp2.Id}");

Employee emp3;
emp3.Name = "Kate";
emp3.Id = 3;
Console.WriteLine($"Name: {emp3.Name}, ID:{emp3.Id}");

struct Employee
{
    public int Id;
    public string Name;
    public Employee(int id, string name)
    {
```

```
        this.Id = id;
        this.Name = name;
    }
}
```

Once you compile and run this program, you'll see the following output:

```
Name: Sam, ID:1
Name: Jack, ID:2
Name: Kate, ID:3
```

3.T10 Can you highlight some differences between structures and class in C#? When should I prefer structures over classes?

Answer:

Structures are value types, but classes are reference types. A structure type can't inherit from another class or structure type, and it can't be the base of a class. Also, you cannot have a default constructor (explicit parameterless constructor) for a structure before C# 10.0.

For lightweight objects, you should prefer structures. Microsoft's online documentation (`https://docs.microsoft.com/en-us/dotnet/csharp/language-reference/builtin-types/struct`) suggests the following:

> *Typically, you use structure types to design small data-centric types that provide little or no behavior. For example, .NET uses structure types to represent a number (both integer and real), a Boolean value, a Unicode character, a time instance. If you're focused on the behavior of a type, consider defining a class. Class types have reference semantics. That is, a variable of a class type contains a reference to an instance of the type, not the instance itself.*

3.T11 Fill in the blank: In C#, structures are inherited from___________.

Answer:

`System.ValueType`. To verify this, you can look at the IL code of a structure. For example, in 3.T9, you saw the following structure:

```
struct Employee
{
    public int Id;
    public string Name;
```

```
    public Employee(int id, string name)
    {
        this.Id = id;
        this.Name = name;
    }
}
```

Let me break down this IL code. Figure 3-1 shows a partial snapshot (follow the arrow).

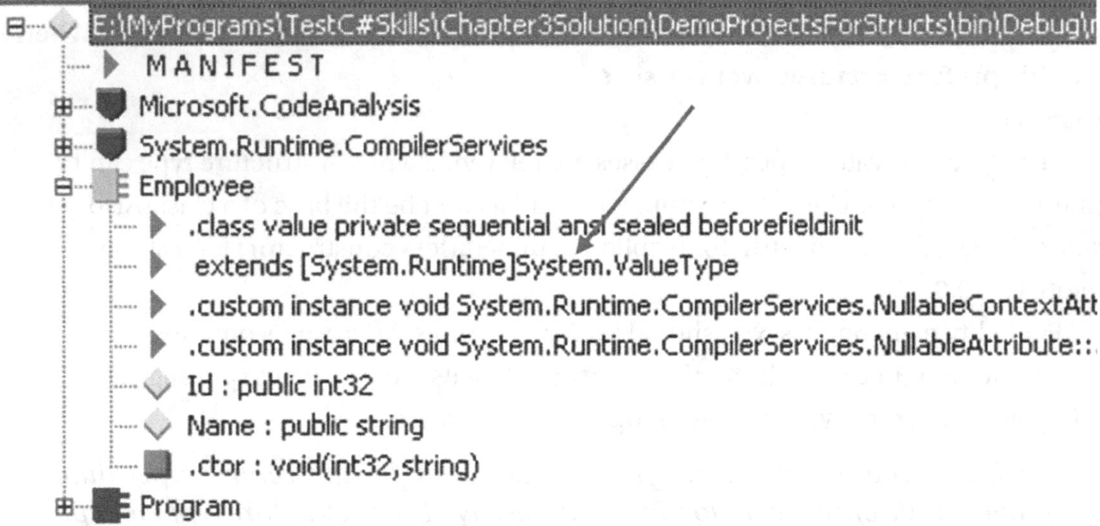

Figure 3-1. *IL code for the Employee structure*

It is also important to remember what Microsoft says about this (see `https://docs.microsoft.com/en-us/dotnet/api/system.valuetype?view=net-6.0`):

> *Although ValueType is the implicit base class for value types, you cannot create a class that inherits from ValueType directly.*

Note The structures in C# are not great promoters of inheritance. You will learn that a structure type can't inherit from another class or structure type and it can't be the base of a class. However, a structure type can implement interfaces. But from Figure 3-1, you can see that they implicitly derive from `System.ValueType`. I want you to note this fact. I discuss inheritance in detail in Chapter 5.

Limitations of Using Structures in C#

3.T12 Can you mention some limitations of using a structure?

Answer:

You will see many of them in the upcoming "Programming Skills" section. For now, here are some limitations:

- Before C# 10.0, you cannot declare a parameterless constructor for a structure. See 3.P17 and 3.P18 for an example. Also, 3.P18 shows that to avoid the compile-time error CS8958, the parameterless struct constructor must be `public` in C#10.0. Every structure type has an implicit parameterless constructor that produces the default value of the type.
- Before C# 10.0, you can't initialize an instance field (or property) in its declaration. See P3.16 for an example.
- A constructor of a structure type must initialize all instance fields of the type. See 3.P21 for an example.
- A structure type can't inherit from another class or structure type, and it can't be the base of a class. However, a structure type can implement interfaces. See 3.P15 for an example.
- The structures in C# do not support inheritance. So, the concept of a protected member in a struct makes no sense.
- You can't declare a finalizer within a structure type.

Note I have intentionally reduced the use of object-oriented features such as class, inheritance, and encapsulations (using properties) in this chapter because Part II of this book discusses them in detail. In some places, I needed to mention them for the sake of completeness in this chapter. In fact, this comment applies to the first three chapters of this book.

Programming Skills

Using the following questions, you can test your programming skills in C#. Note that if I do not mention the namespace, you can assume that all parts of the program belong to the same namespace.

The enum Type Fundamentals

3.P1 Predict the output of the following code segment:

```
Console.WriteLine($"Type1= {(int)Codes.Type1}");
Console.WriteLine($"Type2= {Codes.Type2}");
Console.WriteLine($"Type3= {(int)Codes.Type3}");
enum Codes
{
    Type1,
    Type2,
    Type3,
};
```

Answer:

This code can compile and run successfully. You'll get the following output:

```
Type1= 0
Type2= Type2
Type3= 2
```

Explanation:

Microsoft (`https://docs.microsoft.com/en-us/dotnet/csharp/language-reference/builtin-types/enum`) says the following:

> *By default, the associated constant values of enum members are of type int; they start with zero and increase by one following the definition text order. You can explicitly specify any other integral numeric type as an underlying type of an enumeration type. You can also explicitly specify the associated constant values.*

The documentation also says the following:

For any enumeration type, there exist explicit conversions between the enumeration type and its underlying integral type. If you cast an enum value to its underlying type, the result is the associated integral value of an enum member.

I did not apply casting to the second member before I printed it to the console; so it has appeared as shown.

3.P2 Predict the output of the following code segment:

```
Console.WriteLine($"Val4={(int)Values.Val4}");
enum Values
{
    Val1 = 25,
    Val2 = 52,
    Val3 = 65,
    Val4
};
```

Answer:

You'll get the following output:

```
Val4=66
```

Explanation:

The previous constant value was 65, so it is increased by 1 for the next member.

3.P3 Predict the output of the following code segment:

```
TrafficLight light0 = TrafficLight.Red;
Console.WriteLine($"The integral value of {light0} is
                                        {(int)light0}");

var light1 = (TrafficLight)1;
Console.WriteLine($"The light1 is {light1}");
var light2 = (TrafficLight)2;
Console.WriteLine($"The light2 is {light2}");
var light3 = (TrafficLight)3;
Console.WriteLine($"The light3 is {light3}");
var light75 = (TrafficLight)75;
Console.WriteLine($"The light75 is {light75}");
```

```
enum TrafficLight : byte
{
    Red,
    Green,
    Yellow
};
```

Answer:

You'll get the following output:

```
The integral value of Red is 0
The light1 is Green
The light2 is Yellow
The light3 is 3
The light75 is 75
```

Explanation:

See the explanation of 3.P1. You can also see why the integral value of `TrafficLight.Green` is 1 and `TrafficLight.Yellow` is 2. So, for the constants 0, 1, and 2, you have corresponding enum members. But for other constants, you do not have any such members.

3.P4 Can you compile the following code?

```
Console.WriteLine($"Val2= {(byte)Values.Val2}");
enum Values : byte
{
    Val1,
    Val2,
    Val3
};
```

Answer:

This code can compile and run successfully. You'll get the following output:

```
Val2= 1
```

Explanation:

The code explanation of 3.P1 shows you that Microsoft allows you to use any integral type such as byte here.

3.P5 Can you compile the following code?

```
enum Colors : string
{
    Red,
    Green,
    Blue
};
```

Answer:

No. You'll receive the following compile-time error:

```
CS1008   Type byte, sbyte, short, ushort, int, uint, long, or ulong
expected
```

3.P6 Predict the output of the following code segment:

```
Console.WriteLine($"The members of BigNumbers are:
        {Enum.GetUnderlyingType(typeof(BigNumbers))}");
Console.WriteLine($"The members of Numbers are:
        {Enum.GetUnderlyingType(typeof(SmallNumbers))}");
enum BigNumbers
{
    Num1=1001,
    Num2 = 7005,
    Num3 = 3005
};
enum SmallNumbers:short
{
    Num1 = 10,
    Num2 = 7,
    Num3 = 21
};
```

Answer:

You'll get the following output:

```
The 'BigNumbers' members are System.Int32
The 'SmallNumbers' members are System.Int16
```

Explanation:

System.Int16 is an alias for the short type. This example shows you how you can retrieve the underlying type of an enumeration.

3.P7 Predict the output of the following code segment:

```
foreach (Numbers num in Enum.GetValues(typeof(Numbers)))
{
    Console.WriteLine($"{num} has stored {(int)num}");
}

enum Numbers
{
    Num1 = 75,
    Num2 = -17,
    Num3,
    Num4=0,
    Num5=95

};
```

Answer:

You'll get the following output:

```
Num4 has stored 0
Num1 has stored 75
Num5 has stored 95
Num2 has stored -17
Num3 has stored -16
```

Explanation:

The GetValues method in the abstract class Enum returns an array that contains the values of the constants in the enum type. But have you noticed the order? The Microsoft documentation at https://docs.microsoft.com/en-us/dotnet/api/system.enum.getvalues?view=net-6.0 describes this:

> *The elements of the array are sorted by the binary values of the enumeration constants (that is, by their unsigned magnitude).*

For example, consider the values -1, 0, and 1. As per this documentation, these values will be sorted as 0, 1, and -1. In addition, probably you have noticed the value of Num3. You can see that it is increased by 1 from its previous value.

3.P8 Predict the output of the following code segment:

```
foreach (Numbers num in Enum.GetValues(typeof(Numbers)))
{
    Console.WriteLine($"{num} is storing {(int)num}");
}

enum TrafficLight : byte
{
    Red,
    Green = (byte)Numbers.Num3,
    Yellow
};
enum Numbers
{
    Num1 = -12,
    Num2 = TrafficLight.Red,
    Num3,
    Num4 = 100
};
```

Answer:

This code can compile and run successfully. You'll get the following output:

```
Num2 is storing 0
Num3 is storing 1
Num4 is storing 100
Num1 is storing -12
```

Explanation:

The output is straightforward. The order of this kind of output is described in the previous explanation (see 3.P7).

3.P9 Predict the output of the following code segment:

```
foreach (Numbers num in Enum.GetValues(typeof(Numbers)))
```

```
{
    Console.WriteLine($"{num} is storing {(int)num}");
}
enum TrafficLight : byte
{
    Red,
    Green = (byte)Numbers.Num3,
    Yellow
};
enum Numbers
{
    Num1 = -12,
    Num2 = TrafficLight.Green,
    Num3,
    Num4 = 100
};
```

Answer:

You'll receive the following compile-time error:

```
CS0110   The evaluation of the constant value for 'TrafficLight.Green'
involves a circular definition
```

Explanation:

The reason for this circular definition is as follows: Num2 is getting values from TrafficLight.Green. So, you understand that Num3 is dependent on that value (since it will be incremented by 1). But again, TrafficLight.Green is dependent on Num3.

3.P10 Predict the output of the following code segment:

```
class Test
{
    int flag = 2;

    enum Codes
    {
        Code1 = 1,
        Code2 = flag,
```

```
        Code3 = 3
    };
}
```

Answer:

No. You'll receive the following compile-time error:

```
CS0120   An object reference is required for the non-static field, method,
or property 'Test.flag'
```

Additional Note:

The enum members must be constant. If you make the `flag` variable `static readonly` and use the following code:

```
class Test
{
    static readonly int flag = 2;
    enum Codes
    {
        Code1 = 1,
        Code2 = flag, // Error :CS0133
        Code3 = 3
    };
}
```

you'll again receive the following compile-time error:

```
CS0133   The expression being assigned to 'Test.Codes.Code2' must be
constant
```

A possible fix is as follows:

```
class Test
{
    const int flag = 2;
    enum Codes
    {
        Code1 = 1,
        Code2 = flag, // OK now
```

```
        Code3 = 3
    };
}
```

3.P11 Can you compile the following code?

```
Console.WriteLine($"Type0=
            {(int)Sample.ErrorTypes.NetworkError}");
Console.WriteLine($"Type2= {(Sample.ErrorTypes)2}");

class Sample
{
    public enum ErrorTypes
    {
        NetworkError,
        CodeError,
        DeviceError,
    }

}
```

Answer:

Yes, this code can compile and run successfully. You'll get the following output:

```
Type0= 0
Type2= DeviceError
```

Additional Note:

This code shows that you can define an enum type inside a class.

3.P12 Can you compile the following code?

```
Sample sample = new Sample();
Console.WriteLine($"Type0=
              {(int)sample.ErrorTypes.NetworkError}");

class Sample
{
    public enum ErrorTypes
    {
```

```
        NetworkError,
        CodeError,
        DeviceError,
    }
}
```

Answer:

No. You'll receive the following compile-time error:

```
CS0572 'ErrorTypes': cannot reference a type through an expression; try
'Sample.ErrorTypes' instead
```

Additional Note:

Instead of the nested enum, if you use a nested class, you'll get a similar compile-time error.

Reviewing the Flags Enumeration

3.P13 Predict the output of the following code:

```
Console.WriteLine(ErrorTypes.NetworkError &
                  ErrorTypes.CodeError);

Console.WriteLine(ErrorTypes.DeviceError |
                  ErrorTypes.CodeError |
                  ErrorTypes.NetworkError);

[Flags]
public enum ErrorTypes
{
    NoError = 0,
    NetworkError = 1,
    CodeError = 2,
    DeviceError = 4,

}
```

Answer:

You'll get the following output:

```
NoError

NetworkError, CodeError, DeviceError
```

Explanation:

You have seen an example of a flag enum usage (notice the attribute `[Flags]` before the class definition). It is useful to combine enum members. Microsoft says the following (see `https://docs.microsoft.com/en-us/dotnet/csharp/language-reference/builtin-types/enum`):

> *If you want an enumeration type to represent a combination of choices, define enum members for those choices such that an individual choice is a bit field. That is, the associated values of those enum members should be the powers of two. Then, you can use the bitwise logical operators | or & to combine choices or intersect combinations of choices, respectively. To indicate that an enumeration type declares bit fields, apply the Flags attribute to it.*

If you remove the `Flag` attribute from this code segment, you'll get the following output:

NoError
7

Can you tell me the reason? See the result of the following expressions:

1&2=0
4|2|1=7

Now notice that there is a named enum member defined for the number 0, but there is no such named member for the number 7. So, you see `NoError` and `7` in this output.

The struct Type Fundamentals

3.P14 Can you compile the following code?

```
Employee emp1= new Employee();
emp1.Name = "Jack";
Console.WriteLine($"{emp1.Name} is a {emp1.Occupation()}");
```

```
interface IPerson
{
    string Occupation();
}

struct Employee : IPerson
{
    public string Name;
    public string Occupation()
    {
        return "salaried person.";
    }
}
```

Answer:

Yes, this code can compile and run successfully. You'll get the following output:

```
Jack is a salaried person.
```

Additional Note:

You could use the simplified new statement (`Employee emp1 = new ();`) to get the same output.

3.P15 Can you compile the following code?

```
Employee emp1 = new();
emp1.Name = "Jack";
Console.WriteLine($"{emp1.Name} is a {emp1.Occupation()}");

struct Person
{
    string Occupation()
    {
        return String.Empty;
    }
}

struct Employee : Person
{
    public string Name;
```

```
    public string Occupation()
    {
        return "salaried person.";
    }
}
```

Answer:

No. You'll receive the following compile-time error:

```
CS0527   Type 'Person' in interface list is not an interface.
```

Explanation:

The Microsoft documentation (see `https://docs.microsoft.com/en-us/dotnet/csharp/language-reference/builtin-types/struct`) says the following:

> *A structure type can't inherit from other class or structure type and it can't be the base of a class. However, a structure type can implement interfaces.*

This is the reason you'll see the same error for the following code:

```
class Person
{
    // Some code
}

struct Employee : Person //Error CS0527
{
 // Some code
}
```

3.P16 Can you compile the following code?

```
struct Codes
{
    int _error1 = 1;
}
```

Answer:

This code is interesting. Before C# 10.0, you'll receive a compile-time error for this code. For example, if you use this code in C# 9.0, you'll see the following error:

```
CS8773	Feature 'struct field initializers' is not available in C# 9.0. 
Please use language version 10.0 or greater.
```

When I documented this Q&A, this code was working fine in C# 10. But once I updated Visual Studio to version 17.2.3, I was seeing the following compile-time error:

```
CS8983	A 'struct' with field initializers must include an explicitly 
declared constructor.
```

So, I raised a ticket about it: `https://github.com/dotnet/docs/issues/29930`. I came to learn about the breaking changes that are documented here: `https://docs.microsoft.com/en-us/dotnet/csharp/whats-new/breaking-changes/compiler%20breaking%20changes%20-%20dotnet%207#6`. The following is the key takeaway:

> *We added field initializers for structs in C# 10. Field initializers are executed only when an explicitly declared constructor runs. Significantly, they don't execute when you use default or create an array of any struct type.*
>
> *In 17.0, if there are field initializers but no declared constructors, a parameterless constructor is synthesized that runs field initializers. However, that meant adding or removing a constructor declaration may affect whether a parameterless constructor is synthesized, and as a result, may change the behavior of new().*
>
> *To address the issue, in .NET SDK 6.0.200 (VS 17.1) the compiler no longer synthesizes a parameterless constructor. If a struct contains field initializers and no explicit constructors, the compiler generates an error. If a struct has field initializers it must declare a constructor, because otherwise the field initializers are never executed.*

3.P17 Can you compile the following code?

```
struct Codes
{
    public Codes()
    {
        // Some code
    }
}
```

Answer:

Starting with C# 10, you won't see any compile-time error. But before C# 10, you'll receive a compile-time error. For example, if you use this code in C# 9.0, you'll see the following error:

```
CS8773   Feature 'parameterless struct constructors' is not available in C#
9.0. Please use language version 10.0 or greater.
```

3.P18 Can you compile the following code?

```
struct Codes
{
    Codes()
    {
        // Some code
    }
}
```

Answer:

No. You'll receive the following compile-time error:

```
CS8958   The parameterless struct constructor must be 'public'.
```

Explanation:

See the online documentation at `https://docs.microsoft.com/en-us/dotnet/csharp/language-reference/proposals/csharp-10.0/parameterless-struct-constructors`. It confirms this behavior by saying the following:

> *A parameterless instance struct constructor must be declared public.*

For an immediate reference, you can refer to the following code with the supporting comments:

```
struct S1 { }                        // OK
struct S2 { public S2() { } }    // OK
struct S3 { internal S3() { } } // Error CS8958
```

3.P19 Can you compile the following code?

```
struct Codes3
{
    protected int _error;
}
```

Answer:

No. You'll receive the following compile-time error:

```
Error    CS0666    'Codes3._error': new protected member declared in struct
```

Explanation:

The Microsoft documentation (see `https://docs.microsoft.com/en-us/dotnet/csharp/misc/cs0666?f1url=%3FappId%3Droslyn%26k%3Dk(CS0666)` confirms this behavior by saying the following:

> *A struct cannot be abstract and is always implicitly sealed. Because structs do not support inheritance, the concept of a protected member in a struct makes no sense.*

Additional Note:

For the same reason, you cannot use virtual members in a structure. The following code:

```
struct Codes3
{
    public virtual void SomeMethod() { }
}
```

will raise the compile-time error:

```
Error    CS0106    The modifier 'virtual' is not valid for this item
```

Now, it is easy to guess that if you try to use an `abstract` method inside a structure, you'll also see the compile-time error. For example, the following code:

```
struct Codes3
{
    public abstract void SomeMethod(); // Error CS8958
}
```

will raise the following compile-time error:

```
Error   CS0106   The modifier 'abstract' is not valid for this item
```

3.P20 Can you compile the following code?

```
struct Employee
{
    public string Name;
    public int Id;
    public Employee(string name, int id)
    {
        Name = name;
    }
    public override string ToString()
    {
        string emp = Name + " has ID " + Id;
        return emp;
    }
}
```

Answer:

You'll see the following output:

```
Error   CS0171   Field 'Employee.Id' must be fully assigned before control
is returned to the caller
```

Explanation:

This is expected behavior now. Microsoft (`https://docs.microsoft.com/en-us/dotnet/csharp/language-reference/builtin-types/struct`) confirms this by saying the following:

A constructor of a structure type must initialize all instance fields of the type.

Testing the Default Value Expression

3.P21 Can you compile the following code?

```
Point point1 = new Point();
Console.WriteLine($"Point_1: {point1}");
```

```
Point point2 = default (Point);
Console.WriteLine($"Point_2: {point2}");
struct Point
{
    int _xCoordinate = 1;
    int _yCoordinate;

    public Point()
    {
        _yCoordinate = 2;
    }
    public override string ToString()
    {
        string temp= "(" + _xCoordinate + "," + _yCoordinate +
                        ")";
        return temp;
    }
}
```

Answer:

You'll receive the following compile-time error:

```
Point_1: (1,2)
Point_2: (0,0)
```

Explanation:

In 3.P17, you saw that C# 10 allows you to place a public parameterless constructor. So, this also does not cause any compile-time error. In 3.P16, you saw that C# 10 allows you to perform field initialization inside a structure, but in that case, you must have an explicitly defined constructor. This condition is also met in this example. So, when you initialized the x coordinate, there is no compile-time error.

Now all instance fields of the structure are assigned. So, this code is free from compile-time errors.

So, the first line of output is expected. There is no magic. But the second line of the output makes the program interesting. It is because you see the default values of an int as the coordinate value. How is this possible? To understand this, you have to read the online documentation (`https://docs.microsoft.com/en-us/dotnet/csharp/language-reference/builtin-types/struct`) that says the following:

> *The default value expression ignores a parameterless constructor and produces the default value of a structure type, which is the value produced by setting all value-type fields to their default values (the 0-bit pattern) and all reference-type fields to null. Structure-type array instantiation also ignores a parameterless constructor and produces an array populated with the default values of a structure type.*

Additional Note:

You can use the simplified expressions here. For example,

- You can replace the line `Point point1 = new Point();` with `Point point1 = new ();`
- In the same way, you can use the simplified default expression as `Point point2 = default;`
- Lastly, the `ToString` method also can be written as follows:

```
public override string ToString() =>
    "(" + _xCoordinate + ","+ _yCoordinate + ")";
```

Note In the upcoming chapters, you'll see me using lots of simplified expressions.

Discussion About a C# 11 Feature

Refer to `https://docs.microsoft.com/en-us/dotnet/csharp/language-reference/builtin-types/struct` where Microsoft says the following:

> *Beginning with C# 11 if you don't initialize all fields in a struct, the compiler adds code to the constructor that initializes those fields to the default value.*

But, in 3P.16, you came to know about the breaking changes, which is an important point. You'll see the discussions on autodefault structs in Chapter 15.

Testing a Nondestructive Mutation

3.P22 Can you compile the following code?

```
Employee emp1 = new Employee("Sam",1);
Console.WriteLine(emp1);

Employee emp2 = emp1 with { Id=2};
Console.WriteLine(emp2);

Employee emp3 = emp1 with { Name = "Kate", Id = 2 };
Console.WriteLine(emp3);

struct Employee
{
    public string Name;
    public int Id;
    public Employee( string name, int id)
    {
        Name = name;
        Id = id;
    }
    public override string ToString()
    {
        string emp= Name+ " has ID " +Id;
        return emp;
    }
}
```

Answer:

Yes, this code can compile and run successfully. You'll get the following output:

```
Sam has ID 1
Sam has ID 2
Kate has ID 2
```

Explanation:

You saw an example of using the `with` expression. It helps you to produce a copy of a structure-type instance with the specified properties and fields modified. You can use object initializer syntax to modify a member with the new values. This whole process is also known as *nondestructive mutation*. You use this technique when you need to copy an instance with some modifications.

Additional Note:

The `with` expression can produce a copy of its operand with the specified properties and fields modified. This feature has been available since C# 9.0. But you can apply this feature to a structure instance since C# 10.

PART II

Object-Oriented Programming

Once you learn the fundamentals of programming, your coding life is easy. Let me show you some interesting quotes from the book- *The Almanack of Naval Ravikant(ISBN-13: 978-1544514222)*:

> *The really smart thinkers are clear thinkers. They understand the basics at a very, very fundamental level. I would rather understand the basics really well than memorize all kinds of complicated concepts I can't stitch together and can't rederive from the basics. If you can't rederive concepts from the basics as you need them, you're lost. You're just memorizing.*

C# is a powerful object-oriented programming (OOP) language. You must understand OOP in detail. This part reviews the concepts of classes, objects, inheritance, polymorphism, abstraction, and encapsulation.

Error-free, efficient code is the hallmark of good software. So, in addition to the OOP concepts, this part covers exception handling and some other useful coding concepts.

CHAPTER 4

Classes and Objects

Object-oriented programming (OOP) primarily depends on two concepts—classes and objects. These are the building blocks for the rest of the book. Typically, a class can contain different members such as fields, methods, constructors, finalizers, constants, properties, events, operators, indexers, and nested types. In addition, C# supports different kinds of access modifiers for a type and its members. To make the chapter short and simple, this chapter primarily focuses on the following topics:

- Class and object creations
- Instance fields and methods
- Constructors and their usage
- Optional parameters
- Object initializers
- Nested classes
- The uses of private, internal, and public modifiers inside a class

Let's review and test your understanding of these topics now. You can review the usage of the remaining members in the subsequent chapters of this book.

Theoretical Concepts

This section includes the theoretical questions and answers on classes and objects.

Class and Object

4.T1 What do you mean by a class and an object?

Answer:

V. Sarcar, *Test Your Skills in C# Programming*, https://doi.org/10.1007/978-1-4842-8655-5_4

A class is a template or blueprint, and an object is an instance of that. An object can have states and behaviors. For example, if you are familiar with the game of football (or soccer, as it's known in the United States), you can say that Ronaldo or Beckham are objects from the `Footballer` class. You may notice that they have states like "playing state" or "nonplaying state." In the playing state, they can show different skills (or, behaviors)—they can run, they can kick, they can pass the ball, and so forth. To begin with object-oriented programming, you can ask the following questions:

- What are the possible states of my objects?
- What are the different functions (behaviors) that they can perform in those states?

Note It may appear to you that it is a chicken-or-egg type of dilemma. You can argue that if I say, "X is playing like Ronaldo," then, in that case, Ronaldo is acting as a class. Yes, that is also correct. So, there is no right or wrong in this type of thinking. But the key takeaway is: each class of objects has certain properties in common, and they have some common behavior. So, in object-oriented design, you make things simple by deciding who comes first, and you decide that guy is the class in your application. And based on a class definition, you create objects in an application.

4.T2 Demonstrate a simple example of a class and objects in C#.

Answer:

In the following code fragment, `Sample` is a class, and `sample1` is its object:

```
Console.WriteLine("***Class and Object Demo in C#.***");
// Creating an object of Sample
Sample sample1 = new Sample(5);
Console.WriteLine($"sample1._id={sample1._id}");

class Sample
{
    internal int _id;
    public Sample(int id)
    {
```

```
            this._id = id;
        }
}
```

This program can produce the following output:

```
***Class and Object Demo in C#.***
sample1._id=5
```

It is interesting to note that now you can type less to create an object in C#. Here the type Sample is apparent. So, you can use the following line to create an object and get the same output:

```
Sample sample1 = new (5); // Ok
```

Note In general, I do not like to use an underscore as a prefix before a variable name. But Microsoft suggests the following coding convention: "Use camel casing when naming private or internal fields, and prefix them with _." You can refer to the following link to learn about coding conventions: https://docs.microsoft.com/en-us/dotnet/csharp/fundamentals/coding-style/coding-conventions.

Constructor

4.T3 Why do you need constructors? How do you use them in your program?

Answer:

We use constructors to initialize objects. Here are some important points about them:

- The class name and corresponding constructor's names must be the same.
- They do not have any return types.
- You can say that there are two types of constructors: parameterless constructors (sometimes referred to as constructors with no argument or default constructor) and constructors with parameters

(termed *parameterized constructors*). In C# parlance, it does not matter whether you create a parameterless constructor or if it is created by the C# compiler. In both cases, we generally call it a default constructor.

- You can also distinguish constructors based on whether it is a static constructor or nonstatic constructor (or instance constructor). You'll see the use of instance constructors in this chapter. We use instance constructors to initialize instances (objects) of the class, whereas static constructors are used for initializing the class itself when it comes into the picture for the first time. I'll discuss the meaning of *static* in Chapter 9 of this book.
- In general, common tasks like initialization of all the variables inside a class are achieved through constructors.

4.T4 How can you differentiate a constructor from a method?
Answer:

There are two important things to remember:

- A class and its constructors have the same name.
- Constructors do not have a return type.

4.T5 "Constructors do not have a return type." Using this statement, did you mean that their return type is void?
Answer:

No. Implicitly a constructor's return type is the same as its class type. You should not forget that even `void` is considered a return type.

4.T6 I am a little bit confused about the use of a user-defined parameterless constructor and a C#-provided default constructor. Both appear the same to me. Is there any key difference between them?
Answer:

In C# parlance, it does not matter whether you create your parameterless constructor or if it is created by the C# compiler. In both cases, we generally call it the default constructor. Sometimes both may appear to be the same. But with a user-defined constructor, you can have some flexibility; you can use your own logic and have some additional control on object creation.

Consider the following code segment:

```
Sample sample = new Sample();
Console.WriteLine($"The variable _flag is initialized with {sample._
  flag}.");

class Sample
{
    internal int _flag;
    internal Sample()
    {
        this._flag = 10;
    }

}
```

Compile and run this program. You'll get the following output:

```
The variable _flag is initialized with 10.
```

Now comment out (or remove) the constructor. Compile and run the program again. This time you'll see the following output:

```
The variable _flag is initialized with 0.
```

You can recognize that in this case, the variable `_flag` is initialized with the default value of an int.

Let us refer to the Microsoft documentation in this context (see `https://docs.microsoft.com/en-us/dotnet/csharp/programming-guide/classes-and-structs/instance-constructors`). Refer to the following points:

- If a class has no explicit instance constructors, C# provides a parameterless constructor that you can use to instantiate an instance of that class.
- That parameterless constructor initializes instance fields and properties according to the corresponding initializers. If a field or property has no initializer, its value is set to the default value of the field's or property's type.

- If you declare at least one instance constructor in a class, C# doesn't provide a parameterless constructor.

If you are familiar with inheritance, then you will also understand the importance of the following point, which I picked up from the C# language reference:

- If the class is abstract, then the declared accessibility for the default constructor is protected. Otherwise, the declared accessibility for the default constructor is public.

So, you understand that for a C#-provided default constructor, you cannot change the access modifier, but for a user-defined constructor, you can choose the access modifier too.

Bonus Q&A

4.T7 I often hear about objects and instances. Are they the same?

Answer:

Yes. We often use the terms *object* and *instance* interchangeably.

4.T8 What is the use of the `this` keyword?

Answer:

Sometimes you need to refer to the current object, and to do that, you use the keyword `this`. It is because the `this` reference refers to the instance itself. To understand this better, consider the following code and discussion:

```
class Sample
{
   internal int id; // instance variable
   public Sample(int sampleId) // sampleId is a local variable
   {
       id = sampleId;
   }
}
```

You are familiar with code like this: `a=25`. Here you are assigning 25 into `a`. But are you familiar with code like this: `5=a;`? No. The compiler will raise an issue; it also assumes that the left-hand side of an assignment is a variable.

In the previous example, `sampleId` was our local variable (these are seen inside methods, blocks, or constructors), and `id` was our instance variable (these are declared inside a class but outside a method, block, or constructor).

So, instead of the `sampleId`, if you use `id`, you need to tell the compiler about your direction of the assignment. It should not be confused about "which value is assigned where." Here I am assigning the value of the local variable to the instance variable, and the compiler should clearly understand the intention. With `this.id=id;`, the compiler will clearly understand that the instance variable `id` should be initialized with the value of the local variable `id`.

Suppose, by mistake, you wrote something like `id=id;` in the previous scenario. Then there will be confusion from the compiler's point of view. That's because, in that case, it interprets that you are dealing with the same two local variables. (Though your intention was different, you meant that the `id` on the left side is the field and the other one is the method parameter.) In this case, you'll see the following warning:

```
CS1717 Assignment made to same variable; did you mean to assign
something else?
```

I hope you understand the use of the `this` keyword. In short, remember that a variable in a smaller scope hides the variable in a larger scope (we call it *name hiding*). The `this` keyword helps you resolve this kind of scenario. It is a special reference to the current instance and helps you write better readable code.

4.T9 How should you choose among private, public, and internal accessibility levels?

Answer:

The general guideline is that you should make everything as restricted as possible, which means you should prefer `private` over `internal`, and `internal` over `public`, but still allow everything to work properly.

Let me give you an elaborate answer: you should protect the class data in general. So, you make class-level variables `private` in most cases. How can you decide between public and internal? Well, you ask yourself the question: how do you want to reuse the class? If you want your class to be used only inside a single project, it should be `internal`. But if you want it to be reused across many projects, you need to mark it with the `public` keyword.

You can apply the same rule for methods as well.

4.T10 Can we say that class is a custom type?

Answer:

Yes. When you're familiar with memory management, you'll also say that a class is a reference type.

4.T11 What are the different types of members that a class can have?
Answer:

A class can contain different kinds of members such as fields, methods, constructors, finalizers, constants, properties, events, operators, indexers, and nested types.

Author's Note: As mentioned, in this chapter, you'll see some of these types. The usage of the remaining members will be discussed in subsequent chapters.

4.T12 It appears to me that we can call some methods to initialize those variables. Then why do we choose constructors?
Answer:

From that point of view, to do that job, you need to call the method explicitly; i.e., in simple language, the call is not automatic. But with constructors, we are performing automatic initialization each time we are creating objects.

4.T13 Which initializations occur first, field initializations or initialization through a constructor?
Answer:

Field initializations occur first. But when a constructor assigns the value of a field, it overwrites any value given during field declaration.

Programming Skills

Using the following questions you can test your programming skills in C#. Note that if I do not mention the namespace, you can assume that all parts of the program belong to the same namespace.

Basic Concepts and Use of Constructors

4.P1 Predict the output of the following code segment:

```
Sample sample = new();
Console.WriteLine($"sample.i={sample.i}");
Console.WriteLine($"sample.d={sample.d}");
class Sample
```

```
{
    internal int i=5;
    internal double d;
    internal Sample()
    {
        Console.WriteLine($"Current value of i is: {i}");
        Console.WriteLine($"Current value of d is: {d}");
        // Changing the values
        i += 2;
        d++;

    }
}
```

Answer:

```
Current value of i is: 5
Current value of d is: 0
sample.i=7
sample.d=1
```

Explanation:

The field values were initialized first. So, you can see that the initial values of the variables i and d were 5 and 0, respectively. There was no initial value for d; so, this program considered the default value for a double data type. Later, inside the constructor, you changed these values (incremented i by 2 and d by 1). So, the final instance values appeared as 7 and 1, respectively.

It is interesting to note that in C# 7.1, you write something like the following to initialize a variable with the default value of its type:

`internal double d=` **default**;

4.P2 Predict the output of the following code segment:

```
Sample sample = new();
Console.WriteLine($"sample._i={sample._i}");

class Sample
{
```

```
    internal int _i;
    internal Sample(int i)
    { this._i = i; }
}
```

Answer:

This program will not compile. You will see the following error:

```
Error   CS7036   There is no argument given that
corresponds to the required formal parameter''' of ''Sample.Sample(int''
```

Explanation:

The error message is self-explanatory. The only question that may come into your mind is: where is the default parameterless constructor that C# provides automatically for you? The answer is: if you do not supply any explicit instance constructor in a class, then only C# supplies you with a parameterless constructor to instantiate an instance of that class. (You can refer to `https://docs.microsoft.com/en-us/dotnet/csharp/programming-guide/classes-and-structs/instance-constructors`.) But in this case, you are specific: you are using a constructor that can accept an integer argument. So, the compiler expects you to supply the required argument.

4.P3 Predict the output of the following code segment:

```
Sample sample = new();
Console.WriteLine($"sample._flag={sample._flag}");
Console.WriteLine($"sample._number={sample._number}");

class Sample
{
    internal int _flag;
    internal double _number;
    internal Sample() : this(5) { }
    internal Sample(int i)
    {
        this._flag = i;
        this._number = _flag * 2;
    }
}
```

Answer:

```
sample._flag=5
sample._number=10
```

Explanation:

Inside the client code, you used a parameterless constructor. But notice that this constructor calls the second constructor with an argument 5. This argument value sets the `_flag` value now. The `_flag` value is then multiplied by 2 to set the value of the `_number`.

Optional Parameters and Object Initializers

4.P4 Can you compile the following code?

```
Employee emp1 = new();
Employee emp2 = new("Bob");
Employee emp3 = new("Sumit", 2);

Console.WriteLine("Employee Details:");
Console.WriteLine($"Name: {emp1.Name}, Id: {emp1.Id}");
Console.WriteLine($"Name: {emp2.Name}, Id: {emp2.Id}");
Console.WriteLine($"Name: {emp3.Name}, Id: {emp3.Id}");

class Employee
{
    public string Name;
    public int Id;

    public Employee(string name = "Anonymous", int id = 0)
    {
        this.Name = name;
        this.Id = id;
    }
}
```

Answer:

Yes. It is a valid code segment. It can produce the following output:

```
Employee Details:
Name: Anonymous, Id: 0
Name: Bob, Id: 0
Name: Sumit, Id: 2
```

Explanation:

Here you have used the concepts of optional parameters in a constructor. This constructor needs two arguments: one for the employee's name and one for the employee's `Id`. If you pass a fewer number of arguments, the compiler will not complain at all. This is because this application can pick the default values that are already set in the optional parameter's list.

For example, notice the second line of output: you can see the default values of an employee object were `Anonymous` and `0` (corresponding to the employee's name and ID). But in the next line, you can see that the program picked the employee name as Bob, but since there was no ID associated with this object, it supplied the default ID of 0. The final line of this output confirms that when you pass all the required arguments, the program can accept all those values.

4.P5 Can you compile the following code?

```
Employee emp1 = new() { Name = "Bob", Id = 1 };
Employee emp2 = new("Kate") { Id = 3};
Console.WriteLine("Employee Details:");
Console.WriteLine($"Name: {emp1.Name}, Id: {emp1.Id}");
Console.WriteLine($"Name: {emp2.Name}, Id: {emp2.Id}");
class Employee
{
    public string Name;
    public int Id;
    public Employee() { }
    public Employee(string name)
    {
        this.Name = name;
    }
}
```

Answer:

Yes. It is a valid code segment. It will produce the following output:

```
Employee Details:
Name: Bob, Id: 1
Name: Kate, Id: 3
```

Explanation:

This program demonstrates the use of object initializers. You can see that a single line of code was sufficient to instantiate the objects emp1 and emp2. You have also experimented with the different types of constructors in this program. But it is evident that in all cases, object initializers simplify the instantiation process.

Visibility Control Basics

4.P6 Can you compile the following code?

```
Sample sample = new();
Console.WriteLine($"sample._flag={sample._flag}");

class Sample
{
    int _flag;
    internal Sample(int i = 0)
    {
        this._flag = i;
    }

}
```

Answer:

No. You will see the following error:

```
Error   CS0122   'Sample._flag' is inaccessible due to its
protection level
```

Explanation:

In a namespace, internal is the default access modifier for a class, but the class members have private visibility. In this context, the Microsoft documentation (https://docs.microsoft.com/en-us/dotnet/csharp/programming-guide/classes-and-structs/access-modifiers) says the following:

> *Classes, records, and structs declared directly within a namespace (in other words, that aren't nested within other classes or structs) can be either public or internal. internal is the default if no access modifier is specified. Class and struct members, including nested classes and structs, have private access by default.*

So, in this case, if you can make the instance variable `internal` or `public`, there is no compile-time error. You have seen the use of the internal instance variables already in different code segments in this chapter.

Nested Classes

4.P7 Predict the output from the following code segment:

```
Sample.NestedSample nested = new();
Console.WriteLine($"Flag2={nested.Flag2}");

class Sample
{
    public int Flag1;
    public Sample()
    {
        Flag1 = 1;
        Console.WriteLine("Sample is initialized.");
    }
    public class NestedSample
    {
        public int Flag2;
        public NestedSample()
        {
            Flag2 = 2;
            Console.WriteLine("NestedSample is initialized.");
        }
    }
}
```

Answer:

```
NestedSample is initialized.
Flag2=2
```

Explanation:

You saw an example of a nested class in C#.

Additional Note:

The public field inside the `NestedSample` class is named `Flag2` following Microsoft's naming conventions for the public members of a type. If interested, you can refer to `https://docs.microsoft.com/en-us/dotnet/csharp/fundamentals/coding-style/coding-conventions` for your reference.

4.P8 Can you compile the following code?

```
Console.WriteLine("---4.P8---");
Sample.NestedSample nested = new();
class Sample
{
    class NestedSample
    {
        public NestedSample()
        {
            Console.WriteLine("NestedSample is initialized.");
        }
    }
}
```

Answer:

No. You will see the following error:

```
Error   CS0122   'Sample.NestedSample' is inaccessible due to its
protection level
```

Explanation:

In 4.P6, you have seen already that in a namespace, `internal` is the default access modifier for a class, but the class members including nested classes and structs have `private` access by default.

Use of Instance Methods

4.P9 Can you predict the output of the following code segment?

```
Sample sample = new();
class Sample
{
    internal int _flag1,_flag2;
    internal Sample(int i = 5)
    {
        this._flag1 = i;
        this._flag2 = 0;
        Increment();
    }
    public void Increment()
    {
        _flag1++;
        _flag2++;
        Console.WriteLine($"_flag1={_flag1}");
        Console.WriteLine($"_flag2={_flag2}");
    }
}
```

Answer:

```
_flag1=6
_flag2=1
```

Explanation:

This code uses a default constructor that can accept an optional argument. When you do not pass the argument, it sets the flag values 5 and 0, respectively, and invokes the instance method `Increment()` to increase these values by 1.

4.P10 Predict the output of the following code segment:

```
Sample sample = new();
sample.AddTwoNumbers(5,10.7);
class Sample
{
```

```
    public void AddTwoNumbers(int num1,double num2)
    {
        var number1 = num1;
        var number2 = num2;
        Console.WriteLine($"Result: { number1 + number2}");
    }
}
```

Answer:

This program can compile and run successfully. You will receive the following output:

```
Result: 15.7
```

4.P11 Predict the output of the following code segment:

```
class Sample
{
    int _flag1=5;
    var _flag2=7;

    public void AddTwoNumbers()
    {
        var number1 = _flag1;
        var number2 = _flag2;
        Console.WriteLine(number1 + number2);
    }

}
```

Answer:

You will receive the following compile-time error:

```
Error   CS0825   The contextual keyword 'var' may only appear within a
local variable declaration or in script code
```

Explanation:

The error message is self-explanatory. So, you cannot use var for instance variables.

4.P12 Predict the output of the following code segment:

```
Sample sample = new();
Console.WriteLine($"sample._flag = {sample._flag}");

class Sample
{
    internal double _flag;
    private Sample()
    {
        _flag = 5.75;
    }
}
```

Answer:

You will receive the following compile-time error:

```
Error   CS0122   'Sample.Sample()' is inaccessible due to its
protection level
```

Explanation:

The constructor is private, so you cannot create an object using `new()`. This is useful when you want to prevent inheritance or you need to follow the Singleton design pattern. (A Singleton design pattern ensures that a class can have a maximum of one instance.)

So, is there any way to access the `_flag` variable? Yes. If you are familiar with the `static` keyword, you can use the following code to access the `_flag` variable of `Sample`:

```
Sample sample=Sample.GetInstance();
Console.WriteLine($"sample._flag = {sample._flag}");

class Sample
{
    internal double _flag;
    private Sample()
    {
        _flag = 5.75;
    }
```

```
    public static Sample GetInstance()
    {
        return new Sample();
    }
}
```

This code can produce the following output:

```
sample._flag = 5.75
```

CHAPTER 5

Inheritance

No one likes to write the same code repeatedly to create an application. In fact, novice programmers often like to copy and paste existing code and then modify that code to fulfill a need. An expert programmer knows that this is not a recommended practice. Why? The short and simple answer is that you inherit any existing bugs. In addition, when you copy and paste a code segment and start using it in different parts of your application, you introduce lots of duplicate code. As a result, the overall maintenance becomes tough, because an update required in one place demands you find and update all other places that code appears. So, what are the alternatives? You know one possible answer: inheritance. This chapter covers the following topics:

- Inheritance and types
- Method and constructor overloading
- Method overriding
- Use of the `virtual`, `override`, and `new` keywords
- Use of the `sealed` keyword
- Introductory discussion of covariance and contravariance

Let us review and test your understanding of these topics now.

Theoretical Concepts

This section includes theoretical questions and answers on inheritance.

V. Sarcar, *Test Your Skills in C# Programming*, https://doi.org/10.1007/978-1-4842-8655-5_5

Basic Concepts

5.T1 What do you mean by inheritance?

Answer:

The main objective of inheritance is to promote reusability and eliminate redundancy of code. By using this concept, you can reuse a class by expanding it into a more specific type of that class. As a result, this child class can obtain the features/characteristics of its parent class. In programming terms, you say that a child class is *derived* from another class, called its *parent class* (or *base class*). Therefore, the parent class is placed at a higher level in the class hierarchy.

In general, you deal with four types of inheritance.

- *Single inheritance*: A child class is derived from a single base class.
- *Hierarchical inheritance*: Multiple child classes can be derived from a single base class.
- *Multilevel inheritance*: The parent class has a grandchild.
- *Multiple inheritance*: A child can derive from multiple parents.

POINTS TO REMEMBER

- C# does not support multiple inheritance through class; that is, a child class cannot derive from more than one parent class. To deal with this type of situation, you can use interfaces.
- There is another type of inheritance known as *hybrid inheritance*. It is a combination of two or more types of inheritances.

Types of Inheritance

5.T2 Can you demonstrate each type of inheritance with code examples?

Answer:

For your reference, here I summarize each type of inheritance.

Single Inheritance

A child class is derived from one parent class. Figure 5-1 shows this type of inheritance.

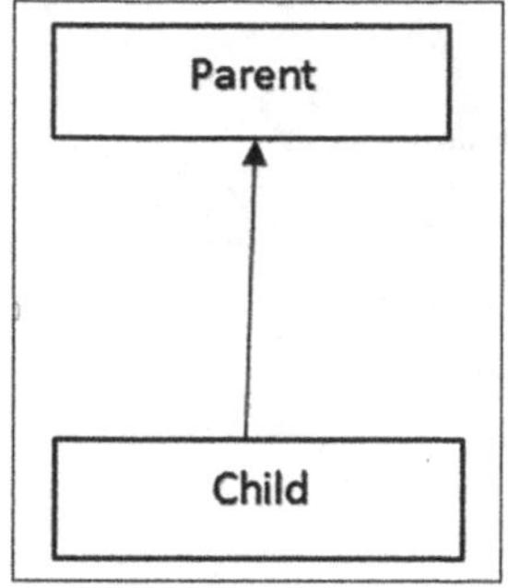

Figure 5-1. *Single inheritance*

Here is some sample code:

```
// Single inheritance demo
class Parent
{
    // Some code
}
class Child : Parent
{
    // Some code
}
```

Hierarchical Inheritance

Multiple child classes can be derived from one parent class. Figure 5-2 shows this type of inheritance.

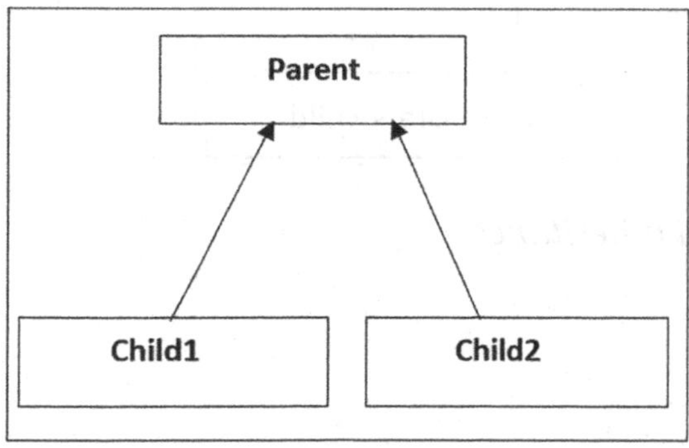

Figure 5-2. *Hierarchical inheritance*

Here is some sample code:

```
// Hierarchical inheritance demo
class Parent
{
    // Some code
}
class Child1 : Parent
{
    // Some code
}
class Child2 : Parent
{
    // Some code
}
```

Multilevel inheritance

The parent class can have a grandchild. Figure 5-3 shows this type of inheritance.

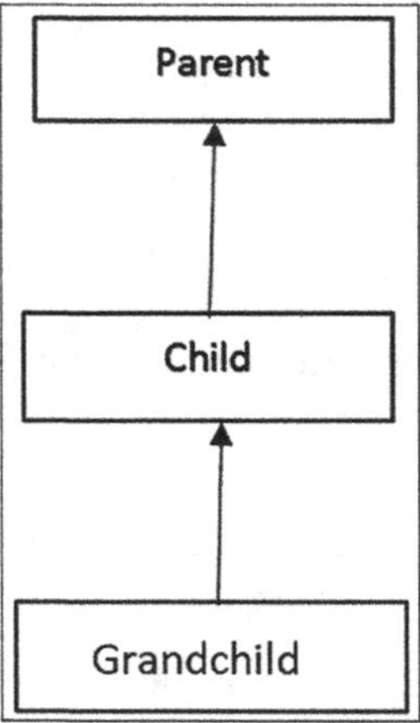

Figure 5-3. *Multilevel inheritance*

Here is some sample code:

```
// Multilevel inheritance demo

class Parent
{
    // Some code
}
class Child : Parent
{
    // Some code
}

class Grandchild : Child
{
    // Some code
}
```

Multiple Inheritance

A child can derive from multiple parents. But this type of inheritance is not supported in C# through classes. You need to learn about interfaces. Figure 5-4 shows this type of inheritance.

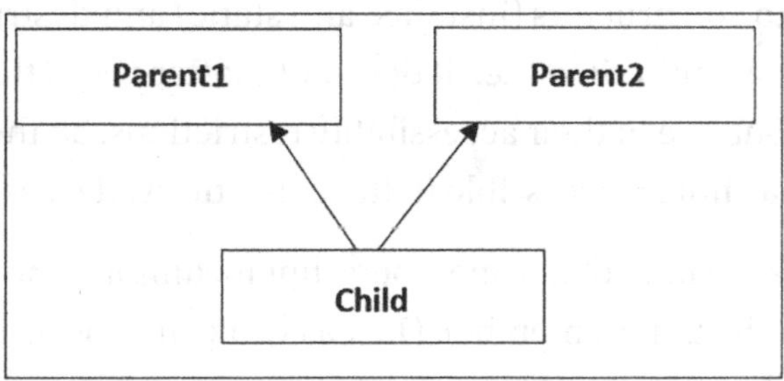

Figure 5-4. *Multiple inheritance*

Here is some sample code:

```
// Multiple inheritance demo.
interface IParent1
{
    // Some Code
}
```

```
interface IParent2
{
    // Some code
}
class MyClass : IParent1, IParent2
{
    // Some code
}
```

Author's Note: Since C# does not support multiple inheritance through classes, I show how to use interfaces to demonstrate this type of inheritance in Chapter 6.

Different Aspects of Inheritance

5.T3 What do you need to know when using inheritance in C# programming?

Answer:

Here are some typical points:

- In C#, `Object` is the root for all classes in the .NET Framework. In other words, `System.Object` is the ultimate base class in the type hierarchy.
- In addition to constructors (instance and static) and destructors, all members are inherited (i.e., it does not matter about the access specifiers). But due to their accessibility restrictions, all the inherited members may not be accessible in the child/derived class.
- The child class can add new members, but it cannot remove the definition of the parent member. (Just as you can choose a new name for yourself, but you cannot change the surname of your parents.)
- The inheritance hierarchy is transitive; that is, if class C inherits class B, which in turn is derived from class A, then class C contains all the members from class B and class A.

5.T4 You have said that private members also inherited. Is this correct?

Answer:

Yes.

5.T5 How can I examine the fact that private members are also inherited?

Answer:

You can refer to the following program and analyze the output:

```
B obB = new B();

// This is the proof that 'a' is also inherited.
// See the error message.
Console.WriteLine(obB._flag1); // 'A._flag1' is inaccessible
                               // due to its protection level
Console.WriteLine(obB._flag2); // 'B' does not contain a
                               // definition for '_flag2' etc.
class A
{
    private int _flag1;
}
class B : A
{
}
```

Once you try to compile the previously shown program, you can see the error messages:

```
Error   CS0122   'A._flag1' is inaccessible due to its protection level
Error   CS1061   'B' does not contain a definition for '_flag2' and no
accessible extension method '_flag2' accepting a first argument of type
'B' could be found (are you missing a using directive or an assembly
reference?)
```

You can see that there are two different types of errors: CS0122 and CS1061.

- CS0122: This indicates that the private member _flag1 from class A is inherited in child class B.
- CS1061: You also examined this case study with a field that was not present in this class hierarchy (i.e., the field is not present—neither in A nor in B). When you tried to access the member with a B-type object, you encountered a different error. Therefore, if _flag1 is absent in class B, then you should get a similar error.

5.T6 Why doesn't C# support multiple inheritance through classes?

Answer:

The main reason is to avoid ambiguity. It can cause confusion in typical scenarios; for example, let's suppose that you have a method named Show() in your parent class. Let us further assume that the parent class has multiple children—Child1 and Child2, who are redefining (in programming terms, overriding) the method as per their needs. The code may look like the following:

```
class Parent
{
        public void Show()
        {
                Console.WriteLine("I am in Parent");
        }
}

class Child1 : Parent
{
        public void Show()
        {
              Console.WriteLine("I am in Child-1");
        }
}

class Child2 :Parent
{
        public void Show()
        {
              Console.WriteLine("I am in Child-2");
        }
}
```

Now, let's say a new class, GrandChild, derives from both Child1 and Child2, but it has not overridden the Show() method. See Figure 5-5.

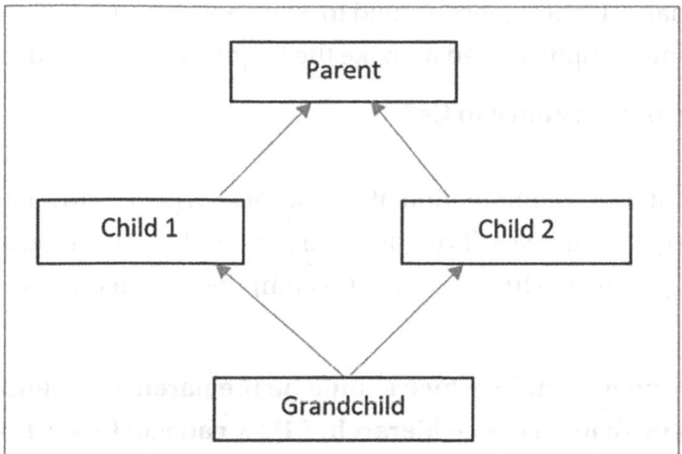

***Figure 5-5.** A typical multiple inheritance example*

Now you have an ambiguity: from which class will the grandchild inherit/call the `Show()` method—`Child1` or `Child2`? To avoid this type of ambiguity, C# does not support multiple inheritance through classes. This is known as the *diamond problem*.

So, if you code like this:

```
class Grandchild : Child1, Child2 // Error
{
    public void Show()
    {
        Console.WriteLine("Inside the Grandchild class.");
    }
}
```

the C# compiler will show the following error:

```
CS1721  Class 'Grandchild' cannot have multiple base classes: 'Child1' and
'Child2'
```

5.T7 Why do C++ designers support multiple inheritance? It seems that the diamond problem can impact them too.

Answer:

I can share my point of view: they probably did not want to discard multiple inheritance (i.e., they wanted the feature to be included to make the language rich). They gave developers this feature but left the control of proper usage up to them.

On the other hand, C# designers wanted to avoid any unwanted outcomes due to this kind of support. They simply wanted to make the language simple and less error-prone.

5.T8 Is there hybrid inheritance in C#?
Answer:

Hybrid inheritance is a combination of two or more types of inheritance. So, the answer to this question is yes, if you do not try to combine any type of multiple inheritance through classes. Otherwise, the C# compiler will raise its concern immediately.

5.T9 Sometimes I am uncertain: which should be the parent class and which should be the child class in an inheritance hierarchy? How can you tackle this scenario?
Answer:

You can try to remember a simple statement: a football player is an athlete, but the reverse is not necessarily true. Or, a bus is a vehicle, but the reverse is not necessarily true. This type of "is-a" test can help you to decide who should be the parent; for example, "athlete" is the parent class, and "football player" is the child class.

You can also apply this "is-a" test to determine in advance whether you can place a class in the same inheritance hierarchy.

5.T10 It appears to me that a subclass can use its base class methods. But is there any way by which a superclass can use its child class methods?
Answer:

No. You can acknowledge the fact that a parent/base class is ready before its subclass, so it should not have any idea about its subclass methods. It only announces something (think about some contract/methods) that can be used by its children. It is only given without any expectation to get anything returned from its children.

If you notice carefully, you will find that the "is-a" test is one-way (e.g., a football player is always an athlete, but the reverse is not necessarily true, so there is no concept of backward inheritance).

5.T11 In object-oriented programming (OOP), inheritance is helping us reuse the behavior. Is there any other way to achieve this?
Answer:

Yes. Although the concept of inheritance is used in many places, it cannot provide the best solution in every possible case. To understand it better, you need to understand the concept of design patterns. In this context, a common alternative is to use the concept of composition, which you may notice in various applications.

5.T12 It appears that when a developer makes a method for an application, they should always reuse the same method through the concept of inheritance to avoid duplicate efforts. Is this understanding correct?

Answer:

Not at all. You cannot generalize inheritance in this manner. It depends on the nature of the application. For example, let us assume that someone has already made a `Show()` method to describe the details of a `Car` class. Now let's say that you have also created a class called `Animal` and you also need to describe the characteristics of an animal with a method. Suppose that you also believe that the name `Show()` best suits your method.

In this case, since you already have a `Show()` method in a class called `Car` and if you think that you need to reuse the method for your `Animal` class, you'd write something like this: `class Animal : Car{...}`.

Now think for a moment: is this a good design? You must agree that there is no relationship between a car and an animal. So, you should not relate them in the same inheritance hierarchy.

5.T13 Why do you use the sealed keyword?

Answer:

This keyword can help you to prevent a class (or, a method) from being inherited.

5.T14 How can we inherit a constructor or a destructor?

Answer:

The constructors and destructors are not inherited.

Author's Note: In this context, it'll be useful for you to note that using the `base` keyword, a derived class constructor, can call the parent class constructor. In 5.P3, you'll see an example of this.

T5.15 What do you mean by method overloading?

Answer:

Method overloading means that you can have multiple methods with the same name, but a different signature. Ideally, a method name with the number, types of the parameters, and order of the parameters consist of its signature. A C# compiler can distinguish among methods with the same name, but with a different parameters. For example, a C# compiler can distinguish that `double Add(double x){..}` is different from `int Add(int x) {..}` or `double Add(double x, double y){...}`. You also remember that method overloading does not include the parameters' names, just their types.

T5.16 What do you mean by method signature?

Answer:

The MSDN documentation (`https://docs.microsoft.com/en-us/dotnet/csharp/programming-guide/classes-and-structs/methods#:~:text=see%20Lambda%20expressions.-,Method%20signatures,method%2C%20and%20any%20method%20parameters.`) says the following:

> *Methods are declared in a class, struct, or interface by specifying the access level such as public or private, optional modifiers such as abstract or sealed, the return value, the name of the method, and any method parameters. These parts together are the signature of the method.*

MSDN also says the following:

> *A return type of a method is not part of the signature of the method for the purposes of method overloading. However, it is part of the signature of the method when determining the compatibility between a delegate and the method that it points to.*

Author's Note: You will see the discussions on delegates in Chapter 10.

Programming Skills

Using the following questions, you can test your programming skills in C#. Note that if I do not mention the namespace, you can assume that all parts of the program belong to the same namespace.

Fundamentals

5.P1 Predict the output of the following code segment:

```
GrandChild grandChild = new GrandChild();

class Parent
{
    public Parent()
    {
        Console.WriteLine("The parent class constructor is
                          called.");
    }
```

```
}

class Child : Parent
{
    public Child()
    {
        Console.WriteLine("The child class constructor is
                           called.");
    }
}

class GrandChild : Child
{
    public GrandChild()
    {
        Console.WriteLine("The grandchild class constructor is
                           called.");
    }
}
```

Answer:

```
The parent class constructor is called.
The child class constructor is called.
The grandchild class constructor is called.
```

Explanation:

The constructor's calls follow the path from the parent class to the child class.

Author's Note:

If you are aware of the expression-body definitions in C#, you know that I could rewrite the previous code as follows:

```
GrandChild grandChild = new GrandChild();

class Parent
{
    public Parent()=> Console.WriteLine("The parent class
                              constructor is called.");
```

```
}

class Child : Parent
{
    public Child()=> Console.WriteLine("The child class
                                constructor is called.");
}

class GrandChild : Child
{
    public GrandChild()=> Console.WriteLine("The grandchild
                                class constructor is called.");
}
```

Note The expression-body definitions help you write concise and more readable code. Many entry-level programmers are unsure about them. So, in this book, I have used a mixed approach: in some code segments they are present, and in other segments they are absent. This approach can help you understand both types of code.

5.P2 Predict the output of the following code segment:

```
B obB=new B();
Console.WriteLine($"x={obB.x}");
Console.WriteLine($"y={obB.y}");

class A
{
    internal int x = 1;
}

class B : A
{
    internal int y = x + 2;
}
```

Answer:

This program will not compile. You will see the following error:

```
Error   CS0236   A field initializer cannot reference the non-static field,
method, or property 'A.x'
```

Author's Note: There are many discussions on this topic. The statement `y=x+2;` in the preceding example is equivalent to `y=this.x+2`; `this` means the current object. So, if we want to make a call like `this.x`, the current object needs to be completed first. But the current object may not be completed at this point in some situations (e.g., if `x` is a property, instead of a field, that is not created yet or it is a part of another instance, etc.). You should also remember that the constructors are created to handle this kind of initialization. So, if these types of constructs are allowed, they can also question the purpose of constructors.

I believe that it's worth reading the following MSDN resources:

- `https://blogs.msdn.microsoft.com/ericlippert/2008/02/15/why-do-initializers-run-in-the-opposite-order-as-constructors-part-one/`
- `https://blogs.msdn.microsoft.com/ericlippert/2008/02/18/why-do-initializers-run-in-the-opposite-order-as-constructors-part-two/`

5.P3 Predict the output of the following code segment:

```
Child child = new Child(1, 2);
child.Display();

class Parent
{
    protected int a;
    public Parent() { }
    public Parent(int a)
    {
        this.a = a;
    }
}
```

```
class Child : Parent
{
    internal int b;
    public Child(int a, int b) : base(a)
    {
        this.b = b;
    }
    public void Display()
    {
        Console.WriteLine("Initialized values are:");
        Console.WriteLine($"a={a}");
        Console.WriteLine($"b={b}");
    }
}
```

Answer:

```
The initialized values are as follows:
a=1
b=2
```

Explanation:

You have seen one usage of the base keyword where you use it to invoke the parent class constructor. It is useful to decide which base class constructor should be invoked before you create an instance of the derived class.

5.P4 Predict the output of the following code segment:

```
Employee emp = new ();
emp.DisplayInfo();

class Person
{
    protected string ssn = "123-45-6789";
    protected string name = "K. Peterson";

    protected void GetInfo()
```

```
    {
        Console.WriteLine($"Name: {name}");
        Console.WriteLine($"SSN: {ssn}");
    }
}

class Employee : Person
{
    private string id;
    public Employee() => id = "E001";

    public void DisplayInfo()
    {
        base.GetInfo();
        Console.WriteLine($"ID: {id}");
    }

}
```

Answer:

```
Name: K. Peterson
SSN: 123-45-6789
ID: E001
```

Explanation:

You have seen another usage of the base keyword where you use it to access the base class method that is overridden by a derived class method.

POINTS TO REMEMBER

- As per the language specification, base class access is permitted only in a constructor, an instance method, or an instance property access.
- The keyword base should not be used in a static method context.

- It is similar to the `super` keyword in Java and the `base` keyword in C++. It is almost identical to C++'s base keyword, from which it was adopted. However, in Java, there is a restriction. You can refer to `https://docs.oracle.com/javase/tutorial/java/IandI/super.html` where it says that the invocation of a superclass constructor must be the first line in the subclass constructor.
- Instead of using `base.GetInfo()`, you could use `GetInfo()` to produce the same output in this program. Why? Notice that there is only one method named `GetInfo()` in this inheritance hierarchy.

Analyzing the sealed Keyword

5.P5 Can you compile the following code?

```
Console.WriteLine("Case-Study: 5.P5");

sealed  class Parent
{
    public void ShowClassName()=>
        Console.WriteLine("Inside the Parent class");

}

class ChildClass : Parent // Error
{
    // Some code
}
```

Answer:

No. You'll receive the following compile-time error:

```
Error   CS0509   'ChildClass': cannot derive from sealed type 'Parent'
```

5.P6 Can you compile the following code?

```
Polygon polygon = new Square();

class Polygon
{
```

```
    public Polygon() => Console.WriteLine("Polygon class
                                   constructor.");
}

sealed class Square : Polygon
{
    public Square() => Console.WriteLine("Square class
                                  constructor.");
}
```

Answer:

Yes. This code will produce the following output:

```
Polygon class constructor.
Square class constructor.
```

Explanation:

Notice that the sealed keyword is applied to the Square class, but not to the Polygon class. So, you can inherit the Polygon class, but not the Square class. I also believe that you remember the calling sequence of the constructors. So, when you instantiate a Square instance, the base class constructor was called first. This is why you could use the following line inside the derived class to get the same output:

```
public Square():base() =>
               Console.WriteLine("Square class constructor.");
```

5.P7 Can you compile the following code?

```
class Polygon
{
   sealed int _flag = 1;
   sealed Polygon()=> Console.WriteLine("Polygon class
                              constructor.");
}
```

Answer:

No, you'll see two error messages of the same kind:

```
Error   CS0106   The modifier 'sealed' is not valid for this item
Error   CS0106   The modifier 'sealed' is not valid for this item
```

Explanation:

You cannot apply the sealed keyword to a field or a constructor. You have also learned that constructors are not inherited at all.

Method Overloading

5.P8 Predict the output of the following code segment:

```
Sample sample = new Sample();
Console.WriteLine(sample.Add(2, 3));
Console.WriteLine(sample.Add("Mike", "Proctor"));

class Sample
{
    public int Add(int x, int y)
    {
        return x + y;
    }
    public string Add(string s1, string s2)
    {
        return string.Concat(s1,",",s2);
    }
}
```

Answer:

```
5
Mike,Proctor
```

Explanation:

You have seen an example of method overloading in the Sample class definition.

Additional Note:

Using the expression-body definitions in C#, you can rewrite the previous code as follows (note that the return keyword is absent in the expression body definition):

```
Sample sample = new Sample();
Console.WriteLine(sample.Add(2, 3));
Console.WriteLine(sample.Add("Mike", "Proctor"));
```

```
class Sample
{
    public int Add(int x, int y) => x + y;

    public string Add(string s1, string s2) =>
                        string.Concat(s1, ",", s2);
}
```

5.P9 Can you compile the following code?

```
class Sample
{
    public int Sum(int x, int y)
    {
        return x + y;
    }
    public double Sum(int x, int y)
    {
        return x + y;
    }
}
```

Answer:

No, you'll see the following error:

```
Error   CS0111   Type 'Sample' already defines a member called 'Sum' with
the same parameter types.
```

Explanation:

The compiler does not consider the "return type" to differentiate these methods. Earlier (see 5.T16) I mentioned the MSDN reference, which says the following:

> *A return type of a method is not part of the signature of the method for the purposes of method overloading.*

5.P10 Predict the output of the following code segment:

```
Employee employee = new Employee();
Employee employee2 = new Employee("Jim", 2);
Employee employee3 = new Employee(3);
```

```
class Employee
{
    public Employee() =>
        Console.WriteLine("Employee name: Unknown,
                           ID: Not given");

    public Employee(int id) =>
        Console.WriteLine($"Employee name: Unknown,
                           ID: {id}");

    public Employee(string name, int id) =>
        Console.WriteLine($"Employee name: {name},
                           ID: {id}");
}
```

Answer:

```
Employee name: Unknown, ID: Not given
Employee name: Jim, ID: 2
Employee name: Unknown, ID: 3
```

Explanation:

You have seen an example of constructor overloading now.

Author's Note: What is the difference between a method and a constructor? A constructor has the same name as a class, and also it has no return type. So, you can consider a constructor as a special kind of method that has the same name as a class and no return type. But there are many other differences: the main focus of a constructor is to initialize objects. You cannot call them directly.

5.P11 Can you compile the following code?

```
Console.WriteLine("Overloading the Main() method.");
Main(5);

static void Main(int a)
{
    Console.WriteLine("I am inside Main(int a) now.");
}
```

Answer:

Yes. When you run this code, you can get the following output:

```
Overloading the Main() method.
I am inside Main(int a) now.
```

Explanation:

I have used one of the latest features of C# top-level statements. So, the previous code segment is equivalent to writing the following:

```
class Program
{
    static void Main(string[] args)
    {
       Console.WriteLine("Overloading the Main() method.");
       Main(5);
       static void Main(int a)
       {
         Console.WriteLine("I am inside Main(int a) now.");
       }
   }
}
```

5.P12 Can you compile the following code?

```
Console.WriteLine("Overloading the Main() method.");
Main();
static void Main() => Console.WriteLine("I am inside Main() now.");
```

Answer:

You can compile and run this code, but you'll see this warning message:

```
CS7022   The entry point of the program is global code; ignoring 'Main()'
entry point.
```

When you run this code, you can get the following output:

```
Overloading the Main() method.
I am inside Main() now.
```

Explanation:

You can refer to the latest documentation at `https://docs.microsoft.com/en-us/dotnet/csharp/fundamentals/program-structure/top-level-statements#:~:text=CS7022%20The%20entry%20point%20of,one%20or%20more%20Main%20methods`, where you can see the following information:

> *You can write a Main method explicitly, but it can't function as an entry point. The compiler issues the following warning:*
>
> *CS7022 The entry point of the program is global code; ignoring 'Main()' entry point.*
>
> *In a project with top-level statements, you can't use the -main compiler option to select the entry point, even if the project has one or more Main methods.*

5.P13 Can you compile the following code?

```
class Sample
{
    public Sample()
    {
        // Some code
    }
    public void Sample()
    {
        // Some code
    }
}
```

Answer:

No. In C#, it is not allowed. You'll receive the following error:

```
CS0542   'Sample': member names cannot be the same as their enclosing type
```

In this context, Java programming lovers can note that Java (tested in JDK 17.0.1) allows the following code to compile and execute:

```
public class MyClass {
    public static void main(String args[]) {
      Sample sample=new Sample();
```

```
            sample.Sample();
        }
}
class Sample
{
        public Sample()
        {
            System.out.println("Inside the Sample class
                                constructor.");
        }
        public void Sample()
        {
            System.out.println("Inside the Sample() method.");
        }
}
```

POINT TO REMEMBER

If possible, try to be consistent with parameter names and their corresponding order for overloaded methods. For example, the following code shows an example of a good design:

public void ShowMe(int a) {..}
public void ShowMe(int a, int b){…}

Note that in the second method, the position of `int a` is the same as in the first method.

The following code is *not* recommended:

public void ShowMe(int a) {..}
public void ShowMe(int x, int b){…} // Try to use ‘a’ instead of ‘x’

Note that in the second method, you start with `int x` instead of `int a`.

Method Overriding

5.P14 Predict the output of the following code segment:

```
Derived derived = new Derived();
derived.DoNotChangeMe();
derived.ChangeMe();

class Parent
{
    public virtual void ChangeMe()
    {
        Console.WriteLine("Initial version of the
                                   ChangeMe().");
    }

    public void DoNotChangeMe()
    {
        Console.WriteLine("Initial version of the
                                   DoNotChangeMe().");
    }
}

class Derived : Parent
{
    public override void ChangeMe()
    {
        Console.WriteLine("Updated version of the
                                   ChangeMe().");
    }
}
```

Answer:

You have seen an example of method overriding in C#. Here is the output from the previous segment:

```
Initial version of the DoNotChangeMe().
Updated version of the ChangeMe().
```

Explanation:

The presence of the `virtual` keyword in the base/parent class indicates that you can change the method to behave differently inside a derived class using the `override` keyword. You can interpret this as follows: the `virtual` keyword in the base class says "You can provide an alternative implementation of this method," while the `override` keyword in the derived class says "You gave me permission, so I'm going to take this opportunity and apply a change to it as per my needs."

Note It is important to understand that you are *not* forced to override the `virtual` methods, but you're allowed to do so. If a class has more than one virtual method, you can override some of them in the derived classes as per your needs.

5.P15 Can you compile the following code?

```
class Parent
{
    public void DoNotChangeMe()
    {
        Console.WriteLine("Initial version of the
                                DoNotChangeMe().");
    }
}

class Derived : Parent
{
    public override void DoNotChangeMe()
    {
        Console.WriteLine("Updated version of the
                                ChangeMe().");
    }
}
```

Answer:

No. You'll receive the following compile-time error:

```
Error CS0506 'Derived.DoNotChangeMe()': cannot override inherited member
'Parent.DoNotChangeMe()' because it is not marked virtual, abstract, or
override
```

Explanation:

The error message is self-explanatory. You understand that since you have not marked the parent class method with the `virtual` keyword, you cannot override it inside the `Derived` class.

5.P16 Can you compile the following code?

```
Derived derived = new Derived();
derived.ShowMe();

class Parent
{
    public void ShowMe() =>
        Console.WriteLine("The ShowMe() of Sample.");
}
class Derived : Parent
{
    public void ShowMe() =>
        Console.WriteLine("The ShowMe() of Derived.");
}
```

Answer:

This code did not use either the `virtual` or `override` keyword. Still, this code can compile and run to produce the following output:

```
The ShowMe() of Derived.
```

But you'll see a warning message saying this:

```
CS0108   'Derived.ShowMe()' hides inherited member 'Parent.ShowMe()'. Use
the new keyword if hiding was intended.
```

5.P17 Can you compile the following code?

```
Derived derived = new Derived();
derived.ShowMe();

class Parent
{
    public virtual void ShowMe() =>
        Console.WriteLine("The ShowMe() of the parent
                               class.");
}

class Derived : Parent
{
    public void ShowMe() =>
        Console.WriteLine("The ShowMe() of the derived
                              class.");
}
```

Answer:

Yes. The C# compiler allows you to compile and run this program, and it can produce the following output:

```
The ShowMe() of the derived class.
```

But you'll see a warning message saying this:

```
CS0114    'Derived.ShowMe()' hides inherited member 'Parent.ShowMe()'. To
make the current member override that implementation, add the override
keyword. Otherwise, add the new keyword.
```

5.P18 Can you compile the following code?

```
class Parent
{
    public virtual int GetNumber(int i)
    {
        Console.WriteLine("I am inside the Parent class.");
        return i;
    }
}
```

```
class Child : Parent
{
    public override int GetNumber(int i, int j)
    {
        Console.WriteLine("I am inside the Child class");
        return i + 10;
    }
}
```

Answer:

No. You'll receive the following compile-time error:

```
CS0115   'Child.GetNumber(int, int)': no suitable method found to override
```

Explanation:

The method signatures of the Parent class method and Child class method are not the same. So, you cannot use the override keyword for the Child class method.

5.P19 Predict the output of the following code segment:

```
Parent parent = new Parent();
int value1 = parent.GetNumber(5);
Console.WriteLine($"Value1:{value1}");

Child child = new Child();
int value2 = child.GetNumber(5);
int value3 = child.GetNumber(5, 7);
Console.WriteLine($"Value2:{value2}");
Console.WriteLine($"Value3:{value3}");

class Parent
{
    public virtual int GetNumber(int i) => i;
}

class Child : Parent
{
    public override int GetNumber(int i) => i + 2;
    public int GetNumber(int i, int j) => i + j;

}
```

Answer:

This code can compile and run successfully. You'll get the following output:

```
Value1:5
Value2:7
Value3:12
```

Explanation:

This code segment shows you an example where you see the concept of method overloading and overriding together. You can see that `GetNumber(int i)` and `GetNumber(int i, int j)` are overloaded inside the `Child` class. In addition, you can see that the method `GetNumber(int i)` is overridden inside the `Child` class.

5.P20 Can you compile the following code?

```
Console.WriteLine("---5.P20---");
class Parent
{
    public virtual int GetNumber(int i)=> i;

}
class Child : Parent
{
    protected override int GetNumber(int i)=>  i + 2;

}
```

Answer:

No. You'll receive the following compile-time error:

```
CS0507   'Child.GetNumber(int)': cannot change access modifiers when
overriding 'public' inherited member 'Parent.GetNumber(int)'
```

5.P21 Can you compile the following code?

```
Console.WriteLine("Case study-(5.P21)");

class Parent
{
    internal virtual int GetNumber(int i) => i;

}
```

```
class Child : Parent
{
    internal override double GetNumber(int i)=> i * 2;
}
```

Answer:

No. You'll receive the following compile-time error:

```
CS0508  'Child.GetNumber(int)': return type must be 'int' to match
overridden member 'Parent.GetNumber(int)'
```

POINT TO REMEMBER

The previous program segments show you that the return types (see 5.P21), method parameters (see 5.P18), and access specifiers (see 5.P20) of virtual and overridden methods must be the same; otherwise, you'll see the compile-time errors.

Method Hiding

5.P22 Can you predict the output?

```
Console.WriteLine("Understanding the new Keyword in C#.");
Parent parent = new Parent();
Console.WriteLine(parent.GetNumber(5));
Console.WriteLine(parent.GetNumber(5, 7));

Console.WriteLine("-----.");
Child child = new Child();
Console.WriteLine(child.GetNumber(5));
Console.WriteLine(child.GetNumber(5, 7));

class Parent
{
    internal virtual int GetNumber(int i) => i;
    public virtual int GetNumber(int i, int j) => i + j;
}
```

```
class Child : Parent
{
    internal override int GetNumber(int i) => i + 2;
    internal new int GetNumber(int i, int j) => i + j + 15;
}
```

Answer:

This code segment will produce the following output:

```
Understanding the new Keyword in C#.
5
12
-----.
7
27
```

Explanation:

This program shows you the use of the `virtual`, `override`, and `new` keywords. Notice that you can also choose a different access modifier for a method inside the `Child` class when you use the new keyword. We'll discuss this program again (see 6.P1) in the next chapter when you see me using polymorphic code.

Note In the next chapter, we'll discuss the polymorphic code and investigate the use of the `virtual`, `override`, and `new` keywords in that context.

Covariance and Contravariance

5.P23 Can you compile the following code?

```
Console.WriteLine("Experimenting covariance.");
Parent parent = new Parent();
Console.WriteLine($"The flag value in the parent class
                is: {parent.GetFlag(5).Flag}");
parent = new Child();
Console.WriteLine($"The flag value in the child class
                   is: {parent.GetFlag(5).Flag}");
```

```
public class Parent
{
    public int Flag;

    public virtual Parent GetFlag(int flag)
    {
        this.Flag = flag;
        return this;
    }
}

public class Child : Parent
{
    public override Child GetFlag(int flag)
    {
        this.Flag = flag * 2;
        return this;
    }
}
```

Answer:

Yes. Though the return type is different, this time you can compile and run this code to produce the following output:

```
Experimenting covariance.
The flag value in the parent class is: 5
The flag value in the child class is: 10
```

Explanation:

In an older version of C#, you can see the following error in a similar context:

```
CS8830   'Child.GetFlag(int)': Target runtime doesn't support covariant
return types in overrides. Return type must be 'Parent' to match overridden
member 'Parent.GetFlag(int)'
```

Did you notice that in 5.P21 you got a compile-time error, because you used different return types (`int` and `double`)? But this program does not show any compile-time error. Why? Because from C# 9 onward, the covariant return type is supported. To learn more about this, you can refer to `https://docs.microsoft.com/en-us/dotnet/csharp/language-reference/proposals/csharp-9.0/covariant-returns`.

In short, covariance enables you to use a more derived type (i.e., more specific) than the originally specified type, while contravariance reverses the scenario, which means that it enables you to use a less derived type (i.e., less specific).

In C#, covariance and contravariance enable implicit reference conversion for array types, delegate types, and generic type arguments. (You'll see a discussion of them in Chapter 10 when I discuss delegates in detail.) You can find Microsoft's documentation for it at `https://docs.microsoft.com/en-us/dotnet/csharp/programming-guide/concepts/covariance-contravariance/`.

5.P24 Can you compile the following code?

```
public class Parent
{
    public int Flag;

    public Parent()
    {
        Flag = 5;
    }

    public virtual void ShowFlag(Child child)
    {
        Console.WriteLine($"The flag value is:{this.Flag}");
    }
}

public class Child : Parent
{
    public Child()
    {
        this.Flag = base.Flag * 10;
    }

    public override void ShowFlag(Parent parent)
    {
        Console.WriteLine($"The flag value is:{this.Flag}");
    }
}
```

Answer:

No. You'll receive the following compile-time error:

```
CS0115   'Child.ShowFlag(Parent)': no suitable method found to override
```

Explanation:

In this context, the contravariant parameter type is not supported yet. The reason for this is discussed at `https://github.com/dotnet/csharplang/discussions/3562`. But you may note that a generic interface or generic delegate type can have both covariant and contravariant type parameters. You'll learn more about them in Chapter 10.

CHAPTER 6

Polymorphism

Ask a developer, "What are the fundamental characteristics of object-oriented programming (OOP)?" You will hear an immediate reply saying that classes (and objects), inheritance, abstraction, encapsulation, and polymorphism are the most important characteristics of OOP. This chapter focuses on polymorphism.

Typically object-oriented programmers pass through three important stages. In the first stage, they become familiar with non-object-oriented constructs/structures. In this stage, they use decision statements, looping constructs, etc. In the second stage, they start creating classes and objects and use the inheritance mechanism. Finally, in the third stage, they use polymorphism to achieve a late binding and make their programs flexible. This is why enterprise code often uses lots of polymorphic code. But the truth is that a novice programmer rarely uses the power of polymorphism.

This chapter helps you to review some simple and interesting code examples using this principle. Here we'll cover the following topics:

- Polymorphism and its benefits
- Abstract classes and their uses
- Interfaces and their uses
- Different types of interfaces
- Writing polymorphic codes using the following:
    - Abstract classes
    - Interfaces

Each of these topics is big. Over the years we have seen new features in this area in C#. Let's look at an example. In the early days, an interface could not contain a default implementation. From C# 8.0 onward, it is allowed. But you have to remember the restrictions (see 6.P22 and 6.P23). Earlier an interface could have methods, properties, indexers, and events. Now an interface can have constants, operators, nested types,

V. Sarcar, *Test Your Skills in C# Programming*, https://doi.org/10.1007/978-1-4842-8655-5_6

static fields, and static constructors too. In this chapter, we'll cover these topics using the constructs that you have already seen in previous chapters. Let us review and test your understanding of these topics now.

Theoretical Concepts

This section includes the theoretical questions and answers about polymorphism.

Polymorphism

6.T1 What do you mean by polymorphism?

Answer:

Polymorphism is a Greek word. We use it to mean *one name with many forms.* Consider the behavior of a pet dog. When it sees an unknown person, it is angry and starts barking a lot. But when it sees its owner, it makes different noises and behaves differently. In both cases, this dog sees with his eyes, but based on the observation, he behaves differently.

Polymorphic code can work in the same way. To illustrate this, let us assume that you hear me saying there is a method that can add some operands. What will your immediate interpretation be? The answer is simple: if the operands are integers, you expect to get a sum of the integers. But if you deal with string operands, you expect to get a concatenated string.

You can also consider popular search engines such as Google, Microsoft Bing, or Yahoo in this context. You know that they all do the same basic task (i.e., search) in their own way.

Polymorphism can be of two types.

- *Compile-time polymorphism*: The compiler knows which method to invoke in which situation once the program is compiled. It is also known as *static binding* or *early binding.*
- *Runtime polymorphism:* The actual method calls are resolved at runtime, but at compile time, you cannot predict which method will be invoked when the program runs. Consider a simple use case: suppose you generate a random number at the very first line when you execute a program. Let's assume that if the generated number is

an even number, you will call a method, `Method1( )`, which prints "Hello"; otherwise, you'll call a method whose name is the same but it prints "Hi." Now, you'll agree that if you execute the program, then only you can see which method is invoked (i.e., the compiler cannot resolve the call at compile time). You do not have any clue as to whether you will see "Hello" or "Hi" prior to the program's execution. This is why sometimes it is also termed as dynamic binding or late binding.

6.T2 Can you give an example of polymorphic code?

Answer:

Before I show you a code example, you need to remember the following points:

- Polymorphic code allows you to use derived classes that implement the same method in different ways. This means that these classes can do the same task in a custom way.
- You mark a base class method with the `virtual` keyword. You know that a `virtual` method can be overridden in a derived class. So, using the `virtual` keyword, you indicate that a derived class can provide an alternative implementation of the parent class method as per its needs. When a derived class does this, it also marks the method with the `override` keyword.
- The `Tiger` and `Dog` are two derived classes of the `Animal` class in the upcoming program. Inside the `Animal` class, there is a virtual method called `Sound()`. The subclasses of the `Animal` class override this method as per their needs.
- Understand that when you use `Dog dog = new Dog();`, we say that you are programming to an implementation. Notice that in this case the reference (variable) type and object both are of the same type.
- Now comes the interesting part: instead of writing something like `Dog dog =new Dog()`, you can write `Animal animal=new Dog();` and the C# compiler is OK with this. Why? It is because the `Dog` class is inherited from the `Animal` class. So, it allows you to use them anywhere an `Animal` object is required. (You can understand the reason behind this kind of design: both tigers and dogs are animals, but the reverse is not necessarily true.)

- So, when the Common Language Runtime (CLR) sees the following code:

  ```
  Animal animal = new Tiger();
  animal.Sound();
  animal = new Dog();
  animal.Sound();
  ```

  it understands which method to invoke at runtime. This type of coding is referred to as *programming to a supertype*, which gives you more flexibility. It allows you to use a reference variable polymorphically.

- Polymorphism means "many forms," and in this situation, you can see that calling the same method results in different behaviors. This type of coding is the heart of polymorphism.

Note You can write polymorphic codes using different language constructs such as abstract classes, interfaces, properties, indexers, etc. Since we have not discussed these constructs yet, I'll start writing the polymorphic code without using them.

Consider the following program and take a look at the output:

```
Console.WriteLine("Polymorphic code example.");
Animal animal = new Tiger();
animal.Sound();
animal = new Dog();
animal.Sound();
class Animal
{
    public virtual void Sound()
    {
        Console.WriteLine("An animal can make sounds.");
    }

}
```

```
class Tiger: Animal
{
    public override void Sound()
    {
        Console.WriteLine("Tigers roar.");
    }
}
class Dog : Animal
{
    public override void Sound()
    {
        Console.WriteLine("Dogs bark.");
    }
}
```

This code produces the following output:

```
Polymorphic code example.
Tigers roar.
Dogs bark.
```

6.T3 I can see that a parent class variable (reference) can point to a child class object, but I get a compile-time error for the reverse scenario. Here is a sample code segment with comments:

```
Animal animal = new Tiger();//Ok
Tiger tiger = new Animal();//Error
```

Can you explain the reason behind this design?

Answer:

You can say that all tigers are animals, but the reverse is not necessarily true because there are other animals like lions, monkeys, etc. In the same manner, in programming terminology, all derived classes are base classes, but the reverse is not necessarily true.

So, you can do an "is-a" test for an inheritance hierarchy, because the direction of "is-a" is always straightforward.

Abstract Class

6.T4 What do you mean by an abstract class?

Answer:

In C#, a method without a body is called an *abstract method*. The `abstract` modifier is used to indicate there is some incomplete information. So, a class that contains at least an abstract method is also incomplete and needs to be marked with the `abstract` keyword. This class is called an *abstract class*.

Since these are incomplete classes, you cannot instantiate objects from them. A child class of an abstract class must complete it by providing the method bodies of the abstract methods that are defined in the abstract class (i.e., its parent class). Otherwise, it is also incomplete, and it becomes another abstract class.

Here is a code example where `Home` is the abstract class and its subclass `CompleteHome` is a concrete class:

```
abstract class Home
{
    public abstract void ShowStatus();
}
class CompleteHome: Home
{
    public override void ShowStatus()
    {
        Console.WriteLine("The home construction is
                                finished.");
    }
}
```

Note As per the C# language reference, you can apply the abstract modifier to classes, methods, properties, indexers, and events.

6.T5 Can you tag a method with both the `abstract` and `sealed` keywords?

Answer:

No. This is like if you say that you want to explore C# but you will not learn through any material. Similarly, by declaring `abstract`, you want to share some common information across the derived classes, and you indicate that overriding is necessary for them (that is, the inheritance chain needs to grow), but at the same time, by declaring `sealed`, you want to put an end on the derivational process so that the inheritance chain cannot grow. Here you are trying to implement two opposite constraints simultaneously.

Interface

6.T6 What is an interface?

Answer:

An interface defines a specific set of functionalities without specifying how to implement them. In simple words, an interface defines a contract. Let us consider a real-world example: smartphones in today's world. You know that a smartphone has a touch screen. It is an interface that a user uses to dial a number or connect to the Internet (using the mobile hotspot). Now, think carefully about the following points in this example:

- A smartphone user knows how to dial a number but may not know "how" it works.
- When the user purchases an upgraded model of this smartphone, the user expects to see a similar interface to get a better service (such as a high-speed connection and faster Internet service).

Similarly, in C# programming, you have a construct called an *interface* that plays the same role as mentioned in the previous example. The Microsoft documentation (`https://docs.microsoft.com/en-us/dotnet/csharp/fundamentals/types/interfaces`) says the following:

> *Interfaces can contain instance methods, properties, events, indexers, or any combination of those four member types. Interfaces may contain static constructors, fields, constants, or operators. An interface can't contain instance fields, instance constructors, or finalizers. Interface members are public by default, and you can explicitly specify accessibility modifiers, such as `public`, `protected`, `internal`, `private`, `protected internal`, or `private protected`. A `private` member must have a default implementation.*

By convention, interface names in C# begin with a capital I. Here is an example that uses an interface:

```
interface IAnimal
{
  void Sound();
}
class Tiger : IAnimal
{
    public void Sound()
    {
        Console.WriteLine("Tigers roar.");
    }
}
```

POINT TO NOTE

You may note an important change: you can mention accessibility modifiers for interface members. So, the following code will compile in .NET 6 (which supports C# 10):

```
interface ISomeInterface
{
protected void Show(); // Error in C# 7.3
}
```

But you'll get the following errors in C# 7.3:

CS8703 The modifier 'protected internal' is not valid for this item in C# 7.3. Please use language version '8.0' or greater.

CS8707 Target runtime doesn't support 'protected', 'protected internal', or 'private protected' accessibility for a member of an interface.

6.T7 Can you tell me the difference between an abstract class and an interface?

Answer:

Here are some differences:

- In C#, instance fields are not allowed in an interface, but they can be present in an abstract class.

- An interface can inherit from another interface. But it cannot inherit from an abstract class. On the contrary, an abstract class can inherit from another abstract class or another interface. For your immediate reference, I provide you with the following code segment with supporting comments:

```
interface IParent1 { }
abstract class Parent2 { }
interface IChild1 : IParent1 { } // OK
abstract class Child2 : Parent2, IParent1 { } // OK
interface IChild3 : Parent2 { } // Error CS0527
```

The last line of the previous code segment raises the following compile-time error:

```
CS0527   Type 'Parent2' in interface list is not an interface
```

You also remember that an interface normally contains the contracts of conduct. Before C# 8.0, an interface cannot have concrete methods. But an abstract class can be fully implemented or partially implemented; that is, in an abstract class, you can see concrete methods. However, from C# 8.0 onward, you can have default interface methods.

6.T8 How do you decide between an abstract class and an interface?
Answer:

I believe that if you want to have centralized or default behaviors, the abstract class is a better choice for closely related objects. In addition, if you want to define some fields in a type, you use an abstract class.

On the other hand, normally an interface implementation starts from scratch. An interface indicates some kind of rules/contracts on what is to be done, but it will not enforce the "how" part of it. It is best suited for providing common functionality to unrelated classes. So, the functionality defined in an interface can be adopted by any type, regardless of where the type appears in the inheritance hierarchy.

Also, interfaces are preferred when you try to implement the concept of multiple inheritance.

6.T9 How do you implement the concept of multiple inheritance using interfaces?
Answer:

In 6.P17, you will see such an example. To make the chapter concise, I have not repeated the code here.

6.T10 What are the benefits of using an interface?

Answer:

Here are some benefits:

- You can write polymorphic code.
- You can implement the concept of multiple inheritance.
- You can develop loosely coupled systems.
- You get support for parallel development.

6.T11 Why do you need an explicit interface implementation?

Answer:

Suppose a class implements two interfaces that have a method with the same signature. So, when you provide an implementation for this method in this class, the same implementation will be used (for example, when you write polymorphic code). But you may not want this. Instead, you want to have separate implementations to be invoked depending on which interface is in use. In such a case, you can use the explicit interface technique. I have discussed this feature with various examples in this chapter. (See 6.P18 and 6.P20.)

6.T12 What is a marker interface?

Answer:

An empty interface is known as a tag/tagging/marker interface. Here is an example for you:

```
interface IMarkerInterface
{

}
```

In this case, the implementing class does not need to define any method because the interface itself does not have any such method. Developers may opt for a marker interface for the following reasons:

- To create a common parent.
- If a class (or a structure) implements an interface, then the instance of it implicitly converts to the interface type.

But Microsoft suggests you avoid using it and use attributes instead. The documentation at `https://docs.microsoft.com/en-us/dotnet/fundamentals/code-analysis/quality-rules/ca1040` says the following:

> *"If your design includes empty interfaces that types are expected to implement, you are probably using an interface as a marker or a way to identify a group of types. If this identification will occur at run time, the correct way to accomplish this is to use a custom attribute."*

Programming Skills

By using the following questions, you can test your programming skills in C#. Note that if I do not mention the namespace, you can assume that all parts of the program belong to the same namespace.

Basic Concepts

6.P1 Can you predict the output?

```
Console.WriteLine("Understanding the new Keyword in C#.");
Parent parent = new Parent();
Console.WriteLine(parent.GetNumber(5));
Console.WriteLine(parent.GetNumber(5, 7));

Console.WriteLine("-----.");
parent = new Child();
Console.WriteLine(parent.GetNumber(5));
Console.WriteLine(parent.GetNumber(5, 7));

class Parent
{
   internal virtual int GetNumber(int i)=> i;

   public virtual int GetNumber(int i, int j)=> i + j;
}
class Child : Parent
{
   internal override int GetNumber(int i)=> i + 2;
```

```
    internal new int GetNumber(int i, int j)=> i + j + 15;
}
```

Answer:

This code segment will produce the following output:

```
Understanding the new Keyword in C#.
5
12
-----.
7
12
```

Explanation:

If you compare this code with 5.P22 in Chapter 5, you'll see that these are very similar, but this time you can see a change in the output (notice the last line). The first two lines of output are straightforward. But wait! This time you have used the concept of polymorphism too. This is why the parent class reference is used to point to a subclass object. So, take a look at the following code:

```
parent = new Child();
```

Now carefully notice the following lines:

```
Console.WriteLine(parent.GetNumber(5));
Console.WriteLine(parent.GetNumber(5, 7));
```

When the `Parent` class reference points to the `Child` class object and then uses the following code:

```
parent.GetNumber(5);
```

it calls the overridden method from the `Child` class. But if you use the following code:

```
parent.GetNumber(5, 7);
```

it does not call the newly defined method from the `Child` class. If you want to invoke the method `GetNumber(int i, int j)` from the `Child` class, you can use the following lines (similar to P5.22 in Chapter 5):

```
Child child = new Child();
```

```
Console.WriteLine(child.GetNumber(5, 7));// Invokes the child
                                         // class method
```

Here is the summarized code segment with comments for your easy reference:

```
parent = new Child();
// GetNumber(int i) was tagged with the override keyword
Console.WriteLine(parent.GetNumber(5));// Calls the derived
                                       // class method.
// GetNumber(int i, int j) was tagged with the new keyword
Console.WriteLine(parent.GetNumber(5, 7));// Calls the parent
                                          // class method.
```

POINTS TO REMEMBER

- In C#, all methods are nonvirtual by default. But, in Java, they are `virtual` by default. So, you need to tag the keyword `override` to avoid any unconscious overriding.
- C# also uses the new keyword to mark a method as nonoverriding.
- I remind you that with C# 9.0+ onward, for an apparent type, you can simplify the new expression. For example, instead of using `Parent parent = new Parent()`, you can use `Parent parent = new();`, and you can refer to the following link in this context: `https://docs.microsoft.com/en-gb/dotnet/fundamentals/code-analysis/style-rules/ide0090`.

6.P2 Can you compile the following code?

```
Vehicle vehicle = new Vehicle();
vehicle.ShowCommonFeature();
vehicle.ShowSpecialFeature();

class Vehicle
{
    public virtual void ShowCommonFeature()
    {
```

```
        Console.WriteLine("Inside Vehicle.ShowCommonFeature");
    }
}
class Bus : Vehicle
{
    public override void ShowCommonFeature()
    {
        Console.WriteLine("Inside Bus.ShowCommonFeature");
    }
    public void ShowSpecialFeature()
    {
        Console.WriteLine("Inside Bus.ShowSpecialFeature");
    }
}
```

Answer:

No. You'll receive the following compile-time error:

```
Error   CS1061   'Vehicle' does not contain a definition
for 'ShowSpecialFeature' and no accessible extension method
'ShowSpecialFeature' accepting a first argument of type 'Vehicle' could be
found (are you missing a using directive or an assembly reference?)
```

Explanation:

The inheritance mechanism allows a child class to add new methods inside its class definition. There is no issue with this, but a problem occurs when you use a parent class reference to invoke a child-specific method. This is because a parent class is created before its child classes. So, a parent class does not have any idea about its child classes. This is why a parent class reference has a restrictive view. So, you need to be careful in similar contexts.

6.P3 Predict the output of the following code segment:

```
Vehicle vehicle = new Bus();
vehicle.ShowCommonFeature();
class Vehicle
{
    public virtual void ShowCommonFeature()
```

```
    {
        Console.WriteLine("The basic features are added.");
    }
}
class Bus : Vehicle
{
    public override void ShowCommonFeature()
    {
        base.ShowCommonFeature();
        Console.WriteLine("The bus-specific features are
                                added.");
    }
}
```

Answer:

You'll get the following output:

```
The basic features are added.
The bus-specific features are added.
```

Explanation:

You have seen another common usage of the base keyword. Using this approach, you override a method by doing everything the old method did, and then you add something more to it.

Abstract Class Case Studies

6.P4 Predict the output of the following code segment:

```
Home home =new CompleteHome();
home.ShowStatus();
abstract class Home
{
    public abstract void ShowStatus();
}
class CompleteHome: Home
{
   public override void ShowStatus()=>
```

```
    Console.WriteLine("The home construction is finished.");
}
```

Answer:

This code will compile, and it'll produce the following output:

```
The home construction is finished.
```

Explanation:

You have seen a common usage of an abstract class. Notice that the derived class-CompletedHome provides the complete implementation of the ShowStatus() method.

6.P5 Can you compile the following code?

```
class Shape
{
    public void About()
    {
        // Some code
    }
    public void ShowArea()
    {
        // Some code
    }
    public abstract void SpecialFeature();

}
```

Answer:

No. In this case, you'll see the following error:

```
CS0513   'Shape.SpecialFeature()' is abstract but it is contained in non-
abstract type 'Shape'
```

Explanation:

If a class contains an abstract method, the class itself is incomplete. So, you need to mark the Shape class with the abstract keyword.

6.P6 Can you compile the following code?

```
abstract class Shape
```

```
{
    public void About()
    {
        // Some code
    }
    public void ShowArea()
    {
        // Some code
    }

}
```

Answer:

Yes. There is no compile-time error for this code. But it is important to note that you cannot make an instance of this class, because you made it abstract. You can do this to force a user to instantiate from a derived class of Shape.

6.P7 Can you compile the following code?

```
Shape shape=new Shape();
abstract class Shape
{
    public void About()
    {
        // Some code
    }
    public void ShowArea()
    {
        // Some code
    }
    public abstract void SpecialFeature();

}
```

Answer:

No. In this case, you'll see the following error:

```
CS0144  Cannot create an instance of the abstract type or
interface 'Shape'
```

6.P8 Predict the output of the following code segment:

```
Animal monkey = new Monkey("black");
monkey.Run();
monkey.Jump();
abstract class Animal
{
    string? color;
    public Animal(string color)
    {
        Console.WriteLine($"Instantiating an animal with
                          {color} color.");
    }

    public void Run() =>
        Console.WriteLine("It can run.");

    public abstract void Jump();

}
class Monkey : Animal
{
    public Monkey(string color) : base(color) =>
        Console.WriteLine("It becomes a monkey.");

    public override void Jump() =>
        Console.WriteLine("It can jump.");
}
```

Answer:

This code will compile and produce the following output:

```
Instantiating an animal with black color.
```

```
It becomes a monkey.
It can run.
It can jump.
```

Explanation:

This code shows the following points:

- An abstract class can contain fields. (Notice the `color` parameter.)
- A derived class must provide the complete implementation for the abstract method that was defined in the abstract class. (Notice the `Jump()` method.)
- A derived class can use a concrete method that is defined in the abstract class. (Notice the `Run()` method.)
- Following the construction initialization order, the base class is instantiated before the derived class.

6.P9 Can you compile the following code?

```
abstract class Shape
{
    public abstract void AboutMe();

    public abstract void ShowArea();

}
class Polygon : Shape
{
    public override void AboutMe()=>
        Console.WriteLine("Polygon");
}
```

Answer:

No. You'll see the following error:

```
CS0534   'Polygon' does not implement inherited abstract member 'Shape.
ShowArea()'
```

Explanation:

The simple formula is as follows: if you want to create objects of a class, the class needs to be complete; that is, it should not contain any abstract methods. So, if the child class cannot provide implementation (i.e., body) of all the abstract methods, it should mark itself again with the keyword `abstract`, like in the following:

```
abstract class Shape
{
    public abstract void AboutMe();

    public abstract void ShowArea();

}
abstract class Polygon : Shape
{
    public override void AboutMe()=>
            Console.WriteLine("Polygon");
}
```

6.P10 Can you compile the following code?

```
abstract sealed class Shape
{
    public abstract void AboutMe();

    public void ShowArea()
    {
        // Some code

    }
}
```

Answer:

No. You'll see the following error:

```
CS0418   'Shape': an abstract type cannot be sealed or static
```

6.P11 Can you compile the following code?

```
abstract class Shape
{
    public abstract Shape()
    {
        // Some code

    }
    public void AboutMe()
    {
        // Some code
    }
}
```

Answer:

You cannot mark a constructor with the `abstract` or `sealed` keyword in C# programming. You'll see the following error in this case:

```
CS0106   The modifier 'abstract' is not valid for this item
```

Interface Case Studies

6.P12 Can you predict the output?

```
Console.WriteLine("Interface case studies.");
IAnimal animal = new Tiger();
animal.Sound();
animal = new Dog();
animal.Sound();
interface IAnimal
{
    void Sound();
}
class Tiger : IAnimal
{
    public void Sound()
    {
```

```
        Console.WriteLine("Tigers roar.");
    }
}
class Dog : IAnimal
{
    public void Sound()
    {
        Console.WriteLine("Dogs bark.");
    }
}
```

Answer:

This code will compile and produce the following output:

```
Interface case studies.
Tigers roar.
Dogs bark.
```

Explanation:

You have seen how to use an interface and polymorphic code.

6.P13 Can you compile the following code?

```
Console.WriteLine("Case study-6.P13");
interface IAnimal
{
    void Sound();
    void Run();
}
class Tiger : IAnimal
{
   public void Sound()=> Console.WriteLine("Tigers roar.");
}
```

Answer:

No. So, in this case, you'll see the following error:

```
CS0535   'Tiger' does not implement interface member 'IAnimal.Run()'
```

Explanation:

A class needs to implement all the methods of an interface; otherwise, it needs to mark itself with the abstract keyword. If you do not want to provide the implementation of the Run() method in the Tiger class, here is a possible fix:

```
// The remaining code skipped
abstract class Tiger : IAnimal
{
    public abstract void Run();

    public void Sound()=>
        Console.WriteLine("Tigers roar.");
}
```

6.P14 Can you compile the following code?

```
IAnimal tiger = new BengalTiger();
tiger.Sound();
tiger.Run();
interface IAnimal
{
    void Sound();
    void Run();
}
abstract class Tiger : IAnimal
{
    public abstract void Run();

    public void Sound() => Console.WriteLine("Tigers roar.");


}
class BengalTiger : Tiger
{
    public override void Run() =>
        Console.WriteLine("Bengal tigers run fast.");
}
```

Answer:

Yes. This code can compile and run to produce the following output:

```
Tigers roar.
Bengal tigers run fast.
```

6.P15 Can you compile the following code?

```
IElectronicDevice laptop = new IdeaPad330S();
laptop.ShowConfiguration();
laptop.DisplayStorage();

interface IElectronicDevice
{
    void DisplayStorage();
    void ShowConfiguration();
}
class Laptop
{
    public virtual void ShowConfiguration()
    {
        Console.WriteLine("A laptop must have an operating
                           system and ram.");
    }
}
class IdeaPad330S : Laptop, IElectronicDevice
{
    public override void ShowConfiguration()
    {
        base.ShowConfiguration();
        Console.WriteLine("An Ideapad330S supports Windows
                           OS,4GB ram, and 1TB HDD storage.");
    }
    public void DisplayStorage()=>
        Console.WriteLine("An Ideapad330S has 1TB HDD
                           storage.");
}
```

Answer:

Yes. This code can compile and run to produce the following output:

```
A laptop must have an operating system and ram.
An Ideapad330S supports Windows OS,4GB ram, and 1TB HDD
 storage.
An Ideapad330S has 1TB HDD storage.
```

6.P16 Suppose, in the previous code segment, you define the `Ideapad330s` class as follows:

```
class IdeaPad330S : IElectronicDevice, Laptop
{
  // The remaining code skipped
}
```

Can you compile the code now?

Answer:

No. You'll see the following error:

```
CS1722    Base class 'Laptop' must come before any interfaces.
```

Explanation:

The previous error description is self-explanatory. When a class extends from another class (provided it is not sealed or there are no other similar constraints) and an interface, you need to remember the *positional notations*. The parent class is positioned first, followed by a comma, followed by the interface name(s), such as in the following:

```
class ChildClass: BaseClass,IInterface1,IInterface2
{
 // Some code
}
```

6.P17 Can you compile the following code?

```
SuperCar car = new ();
Console.WriteLine("Car details:");
Console.WriteLine($"Has an air
                    conditioner?{car.AirConditioner()}");
Console.WriteLine($"Number of
                    wheels:{car.ShowNumberOfWheels()}");
```

```
interface IWheels
{
    int ShowNumberOfWheels();
}
interface IACFacility
{
    bool AirConditioner();
}
class SuperCar : IACFacility, IWheels
{
    public bool AirConditioner() => true;

    public int ShowNumberOfWheels() => 4;

}
```

Answer:

Yes. This code can compile and run to produce the following output:

```
Car details:
Has an air conditioner? True
Number of wheels: 4
```

Explanation:

This example shows that you can implement the concept of multiple inheritance using interfaces in C#. Probably you have also noticed that I have used a simplified `new()` statement. So, the following line of code `SuperCar car = new ();` also compiled.

6.P18 Can you compile the following code?

```
IVehicle car = new Car();
car.Describe();

interface IVehicle
{
    void Describe();
}
```

```
class Car : IVehicle
{
    void IVehicle.Describe()
    {
        Console.WriteLine("This is a car.");
    }
}
```

Answer:

Yes. This code can compile and run to produce the following output:

```
This is a car.
```

Explanation:

Here I have written some polymorphic code. In addition, you have seen an *explicit interface implementation*. Note that in an explicit interface implementation, the method name is preceded by the interface name, such as `<interfacename>.methodname(){...}`.

6.P19 Can you compile the following code?

```
XyzCar car = new ();
car.Describe();

interface IVehicle
{
    void Describe();
}
interface ICompany
{
    void Describe();
}

class XyzCar : IVehicle,ICompany
{
    public void Describe()=>
        Console.WriteLine("This is a car from XYZ company.");
}
```

Answer:

Yes. This code can compile and run to produce the following output:

```
This is a car from XYZ company.
```

Explanation:

The Microsoft documentation at `https://docs.microsoft.com/en-us/dotnet/csharp/programming-guide/interfaces/explicit-interface-implementation` says the following:

> *If a class implements two interfaces that contain a member with the same signature, then implementing that member on the class will cause both interfaces to use that member as their implementation.*

6.P20 Can you compile the following code?

```
Console.WriteLine("Experimenting with implicit and explicit
 interface implementations.");
XyzCar car = new();
car.Describe();

((IVehicle)car).Describe();
((ICompany)car).Describe();

// Case study-6.P20
interface IVehicle
{
    void Describe();
}
interface ICompany
{
    void Describe();
}

class XyzCar : IVehicle, ICompany
{
    public void Describe() =>
        Console.WriteLine("This is a car from XYZ company.");
```

```
    void IVehicle.Describe() =>
        Console.WriteLine("Implementing
                        IVehicle.Describe().");

    void ICompany.Describe() =>
        Console.WriteLine("Implementing
                            ICompany.Describe().");
}
```

Answer:

Yes. This code can compile and run to produce the following output:

```
Experimenting with implicit and explicit interface
 implementations.
This is a car from XYZ company.
Implementing IVehicle.Describe().
Implementing ICompany.Describe().
```

Explanation:

You saw the power of explicit interface implementations when the interfaces have methods with the same signature. In such a case, you may not want to invoke the same implementation for both interfaces.

To achieve this, you call a class member through the specified interface. We name the class member by prefixing it with the name of the interface and a period.

6.P21 Can you compile the following code?

```
Console.WriteLine("Experimenting with a default interface
                   method.");
IVehicle vehicle = new Car();
vehicle.Describe();
interface IVehicle
{
    internal void Describe()=>
       Console.WriteLine("The XYZ company makes this car.");
}
```

```
class Car : IVehicle
{

}
```

Answer:

Yes. This code can compile and run to produce the following output:

```
Experimenting with a default interface method.
The XYZ company makes this car.
```

Explanation:

You have seen a way to invoke a default interface method (in C# 8.0 onward, this is allowed).

6.P22 Can you compile the following code?

```
Console.WriteLine("Experimenting a default interface
  method.");
Car car = new();
car.Describe();

interface IVehicle
{
    internal void Describe()=>
       Console.WriteLine("The XYZ company makes this car.");
}
class Car : IVehicle
{

}
```

Answer:

No. This time you'll see the following error:

```
CS1061   'Car' does not contain a definition for 'Describe' and no
accessible extension method 'Describe' accepting a first argument of type
'Car' could be found (are you missing a using directive or an assembly
reference?)
```

Explanation:

The Microsoft documentation (see `https://docs.microsoft.com/en-us/dotnet/csharp/programming-guide/interfaces/explicit-interface-implementation`) says the following about this kind of error:

> *If a class inherits a method implementation from an interface, that method is only accessible through a reference of the interface type. The inherited member doesn't appear as part of the public interface.*

In a similar situation, you can override the default interface method. Either you can apply the explicit interface implementation or you can override it as a public method. Here is some sample code:

```
Car car = new();
car.Describe();//Ok now

// Calling the explicit interface implementation
((IVehicle)car).Describe();

interface IVehicle
{
    internal void Describe() =>
        Console.WriteLine("The XYZ company makes this car.");

}
class Car : IVehicle
{
    internal void Describe()
    {
        Console.WriteLine("Overriding the default interface
                            method.");
        // Some other code-if any
    }
    void IVehicle.Describe()
    {
        Console.WriteLine("Explicitly overriding the default
                            interface method.");
        // Some other code-if any
    }

}
```

6.P23 Can you compile the following code?

```
Console.WriteLine("Can an interface inherit from a class?");
class SomeClass
{
    // Some code
}
interface ISomeInterface : SomeClass { }
```

Answer:

No. You'll see the following error:

```
CS0527   Type 'SomeClass' in interface list is not an interface
```

Explanation:

You must remember that an interface can inherit from one or more base interfaces, but not from a class. A class or structure can have some implementations. So, if you allow an interface to inherit from them, the interface may contain the implementations, which is against the core aim of an interface.

6.P24 Can you compile the following code?

```
Console.WriteLine("Can an interface contain fields?");

interface ISomeInterface
{
    int _flag;

}
```

Answer:

No. You'll see the following error:

```
CS0525   Interfaces cannot contain instance fields.
```

Explanation:

The Microsoft documentation confirms this by saying the following (you can refer `https://docs.microsoft.com/en-us/dotnet/csharp/fundamentals/types/interfaces`):

> *An interface may not declare instance data such as fields, auto-implemented properties, or property-like events.*

6.P25 Can you compile the following code?

```
Console.WriteLine("Can an tag an interface method with the
                   abstract keyword?");

interface ISomeInterface
{
    abstract void Show();

}
```

Answer:

Starting with C#8.0, this code can compile and run. But in the earlier editions, you'll see errors. For example, if you use this interface definition in .NET Framework 4.5, you'll see the following compile-time error:

```
CS8703   The modifier 'abstract' is not valid for this item in C# 7.3.
Please use language version '8.0' or greater.
```

6.P26 Can you compile the following code?

```
Console.WriteLine("Can an interface contain a class?.");


public interface ISample
{
    public class SomeClass
    {
    }
}
```

Answer:

If you run this code prior to C# 8, you'll see the compile-time error. But now it is a correct behavior. If interested, you can refer to `https://github.com/dotnet/docs/issues/28427`.

One C# 11 Feature

6.P27 Can you compile the following code?

```
Console.WriteLine("Testing a C#11 feature");
public interface ISample
{
    static abstract void ShowInterfaceName();
}
```

Answer:

If you run this code prior to C# 10, you'll see the compile-time error. Here is a sample:

```
CS8703   The modifier 'abstract' is not valid for this item in C# 10.0.
Please use language version 'preview' or greater.
```

This message is self-explanatory. So, you understand that this feature is added in C# 11. But you need to remember that only interface members that aren't fields can be static abstract. So, if you write something like the following:

```
public interface ISample
{
    static abstract int SomeFlag; // ERROR CS0681
}
```

you'll see the following error:

`CS0681 The modifier 'abstract' is not valid on fields. Try using a property instead.`

In short, you can remember the following code segment with the supporting comments:

```
public interface ISample
{
    //static abstract int SomeFlag1; // ERROR CS0681
    // CA 2211: Non-constant fields should not be visible
    static int SomeFlag2=1; // OK, but warning message
                            // (CA2211)
    //int _someFlag3; // ERROR CS0525
```

```
    const int SomeFlag3 = 3;
    static abstract void ShowInterfaceName1(); // OK
    void ShowInterfaceName(); // OK
}
```

Note In Chapter 15, you'll see how to test preview features. There you'll see some of the new features too.

CHAPTER 7

Encapsulation Using Properties and Indexers

In object-oriented programming, we do not allow free data flow inside the system. Instead, we like to wrap the data and functions (i.e., methods) into a single unit (similar to forming a capsule). Why is this important? The answer is that if you want to promote security, your data should not be visible from the outside world. So, in general, you allow access to this data only through the methods defined inside the class. Therefore, you can think of these methods as the interface between the object's data and the outside world. This is why data encapsulation is one of the key features of a class. You can say that the purpose of encapsulation is at least one of the following:

- Creating restrictions so that the data of an object cannot be accessed directly
- Binding the data with methods that will act on that data

In C#, you can implement encapsulation in various ways. For example, you can use the access specifiers (i.e., modifiers) and getter/setter methods in this context. The use of the getters and setters are common in Java, but in C#, we like to use a simplified version of them, called *properties*. Indexers are similar to properties, but they allow instances of a class or struct to be indexed just like arrays. This chapter focuses on them and covers the following topics:

- Introduction to encapsulation and how it is different from abstraction
- Properties and their usage
- Different ways to create a property
- The usage of the get and set accessors
- Virtual and abstract properties

V. Sarcar, *Test Your Skills in C# Programming*, https://doi.org/10.1007/978-1-4842-8655-5_7

- The `init` accessor
- Indexers and their usage
- How the indexers and properties can work with an interface
- Different aspects of properties and indexers

Let us review and test your understanding of these topics now.

Theoretical Concepts

This section includes the theoretical questions and answers on data encapsulation and related topics in C#.

7.T1 How is abstraction different from encapsulation?
Answer:

Abstraction focuses on the noticeable behavior of an object, and encapsulation focuses on the implementation part of that behavior. Encapsulation helps you to bundle your data, and at the same time, it can hide some information that you do not want to disclose to the outside world.

So, the key purpose of abstraction is to show only the essential details and hide the background details of implementation. Abstraction is also very much related to encapsulation, but the difference may be easily understood with a simple day-to-day scenario: when you press a button on our remote control to switch on the television (TV), you may not know about the internal circuits of the TV or how the remote control enables a TV. You simply know that different buttons on the remote control have different functionalities, and as long as they work properly, you are happy. So, a user is isolated from the complex implementation details that are *encapsulated* within the remote control (or TV). At the same time, the common operations that can be performed through a remote control can be thought of as an *abstraction* of the remote control.

7.T2 What do you mean by a property in C#? How is it useful?
Answer:

A property is a member that provides a flexible mechanism to read, write, or compute the value of a private field. Initially, properties may appear similar to fields, but they have either a get block or a set block, or both blocks. These special blocks represent some methods that are called *accessors*. But this construct helps us to replace any `GetX` or SetX method using a simpler syntax, without needing to publicly expose the data. In simple terms, get blocks are used for reading purposes, and set blocks are used for assigning purposes.

Note When a property has only the get accessor, you call it a *read-only property*. If the property contains only the set accessor, you call it a *write-only property*. Normally, you see a property with both accessors, and that kind of property is known as a *read-write property*.

In addition to this type of control and flexibility, you can impose some constraints and validations using the properties, and these characteristics make them unique. You can also take actions based on the validation rules such as raising an event or notification. Finally, the properties in C# are important and useful because they help encapsulate an object's state.

7.T3 Why do you impose so much importance on the private data of a class?

Answer:

Following the encapsulation principle, a class should protect the integrity of its data. In general, an "unwritten but well-known rule" for an experienced developer is that a class should keep its internal data private but can allow a public method to read the current state of that data. If needed, the developer can also allow a user to set a new value for that data using another public method. This enables a class to act as a gatekeeper that allows only the acceptable changes to it.

7.T4 I am confused: how a class can act as a gatekeeper when it allows making a change to its data?

Answer:

You are allowed to make reasonable changes only. To avoid an unwanted change, you can provide constraints inside the methods to validate whether a change request is reasonable/valid. If required, you can also perform some additional computations on the data before you store the data or return it. You know that properties allow those kinds of methods using some simple syntax. (You can consider 7.P3 in this context.)

Creating a Property

7.T5 How can you demonstrate the use of properties in C#?

Answer:

This is a sample program. Here you see a Game class that has a read-write property named Score. I have kept some comments for your easier understanding.

```
Console.WriteLine("Properties.Demo-1.");
Game game = new();
// game._score = 10;//Error CS0122: it is inaccessible
// Setting  a new value
game.Score = 70; // Ok.
// Reading the value
Console.WriteLine($"Current score:{game.Score}");

class Game
{
    private int _score; // The "backing" field
    public int Score // The public property
    {
        get
        {
            return _score;
        }
        set
        {
            _score = value;
        }
    }
}
```

When you execute this program, you will see the following output:

```
Properties.Demo-1.
Current score:70
```

POINTS TO REMEMBER

- The contextual keyword `value` is an implicit parameter associated with properties. You typically use it for assignment.
- Sometimes the private field that stores the data exposed by a public property is called a *backing store* or a *backing field*. So, `_score` is the private backing field in the preceding example.
- You can mark a property as `public`, `private`, `internal`, `protected`, `protected internal`, or `private protected`. You can also mark it with other keywords such as `virtual`, `abstract`, new, `override`, `sealed`, or `static`.
- Starting from C# 9, we can use the `init` keyword to define an accessor method in a property (or indexer). The `init`-only setters can assign a value to the property (or the indexer) element only during object construction.

Alternative Code to Create a Property

Starting with C# 7.0, you can use expression-bodied members to simplify the Score property in the Game class as follows:

```
class Game
{
    private int _score; // The "backing" field
    public int Score // The public property
    {
        get => _score;
        set => _score = value;
    }
}
```

I have not used any validation logic inside the get or set accessor. So, using the auto-implemented properties, you can further simplify this code as follows:

```
class Game
{
    public int Score
    {
        get;set;
    }
}
```

The previous code segment creates a backing field behind the scenes. This is a commonly used technique to create simple properties. But in this case, you cannot have direct access to the backing field.

You can also set a default value in the previous code segment. Here is a code snippet:

```
class Game
{
    public int Score
    {
        get; set;
    } = 60;
}
```

Author's Note: When you download the source code from the Apress website, you can see the complete programs in the Demo_7.T5, Demo_7.T5B, and Demo_7.T5C folders.

7.T6 Why should I prefer public properties rather than public fields?

Answer:

You can promote encapsulation, which is one of the key features of OOP.

7.T7 When should you prefer read-only properties?

Answer:

One possible use case is to create immutable types.

7.T8 What are the different ways to create an immutable property?

Answer:

Immutability is a big topic. But the documentation at https://docs.microsoft.com/en-us/dotnet/csharp/programming-guide/classes-and-structs/how-to-implement-a-lightweight-class-with-auto-implemented-properties summarizes it nicely:

- Declare only the get accessor, which makes the property immutable everywhere except in the type's constructor.
- Declare an init accessor instead of a set accessor, which makes the property settable only in the constructor or by using an object initializer.
- Declare the set accessor to be private. The property is settable within the type, but it is immutable to consumers.

Creating an Indexer

7.T9 What is an indexer? Why are they useful?

Answer:

Indexers are similar to properties, except their accessors can take parameters.

Using indexers, you can use instances of a class (or struct) to be indexed like arrays.

These index values can be set or retrieved easily without specifying the type or instance member. Here are some useful notes for you.

The keyword this is used to define the indexer. So, you'll find that the following program (see 7.T10) is similar to properties, but the key difference is that the name of the property is this.

7.T10 How can you create an indexer in C#?

Answer:

Here is a simple program to demonstrate this:

```
Console.WriteLine("***Indexer Demo.***");
Animals animals = new();
Console.WriteLine("Here are the animals:");
Console.WriteLine(animals[0]);
Console.WriteLine(animals[1]);

// Updating the animal type at index 0
animals[0] = "Cat";
Console.WriteLine("The updated list of the animals:");
Console.WriteLine(animals[0]);
Console.WriteLine(animals[1]);
```

```
class Animals
{
    private string[] _names;
    public Animals()
    {
        _names = new string[] { "Tiger", "Lion" };
    }
    public string this[int index]
    {
        get
        {
            string temp = String.Empty;
            if (index >= 0 && index < _names.Length)
            {
                temp = _names[index];
            }
            else
            {
                // You can throw an error
            }

            return temp;
        }
        set
        {
            if (index >= 0 && index < _names.Length)
            {

                _names[index] = value;
            }
            else
            {
                // You can throw an error
            }

        }
    }
}
```

Once you compile and run this program, you will see the following output:

```
***Indexer Demo.***
Here are the animals:
Tiger
Lion
The updated list of the animals:
Cat
Lion
```

POINTS TO REMEMBER

- You can apply different modifiers such as `private`, `public`, `protected`, `internal`, `protected internal`, or `private protected` to an indexer.
- The return type can be a valid C# data type.
- You can create a type with multiple indexers, each with different types of parameters.
- As usual, you can create read-only indexers by eliminating the set accessor. Though it is syntactically correct, some developers like to use a method in those scenarios (e.g., it is always good to use a method to retrieve employee information corresponding to the employee ID). So, I normally avoid this:

```
Class Employee{
  // Using indexers to get employee details
            public string this[int empId]
            {
                get
                {
                    //return Employee details
                }
            }
}
```

7.T11 Can we declare a property or an indexer inside of an interface?

Answer:

Yes. The overall concept is the same: you are allowed to provide an explicit or an implicit interface implementation in those cases. You'll see some code examples in 7.P13, 7.P14, and 7.P15.

Note Starting with C# 8.0, an interface may define a default implementation for properties also. But this type of implementation is rare because interfaces may not define instance data fields.

7.T12 How a property is different from an indexer?

Answer:

- The most significant difference is that a property is accessed through a name, whereas an indexer is accessed through an index.
- In addition, a property can allow some methods to be called as if they were public data members. But an indexer allows elements of an internal collection of an object to be accessed by using array notation on the object itself.
- An indexer must be an instance member, but a property can be a static member or an instance member.

Many of the remaining differences will be prominent to you when you go through the program segments in this chapter. Also, I have not covered some of them in a previous chapter. So, I prefer not to mention all the differences here. But you can refer to the following link to see the differences between these two:

`https://docs.microsoft.com/en-us/dotnet/csharp/programming-guide/indexers/comparison-between-properties-and-indexers`

Programming Skills

By answering the following questions, you can test your programming skills in C#. Note that if I do not mention the namespace, you can assume that all parts of the program belong to the same namespace.

Basic Concepts

7.P1 Predict the output of the following code segment:

```
Console.WriteLine("Experimenting properties in C#.");
Game game = new();
Console.WriteLine($"Current level: {game.Level}");
game.Level = 2;
Console.WriteLine($"Current level: {game.Level}");
class Game
{
    private int _level;
    public Game() { _level = 1; }
    public int Level
    {
        get => _level;

        set => _level = value;

    }
}
```

Answer:

This code can compile and run successfully. You'll get the following output:

```
Experimenting properties in C#.
Current level: 1
Current level: 2
```

Explanation:

You have seen a simple example of a read-write property named Level inside the Game class. This example also demonstrates the usage of the expression-bodied members and a simplified new() expression.

7.P2 Can you compile the following code?

```
Console.WriteLine("Experimenting properties in C#.");
Game game = new();
game.Level = 2;
```

```
class Game
{
    private int level;
    public int Level
    {
        get => level;

        private set => level = value;

    }
}
```

Answer:

No. You'll receive the following compile-time error:

```
CS0272  The property or indexer 'Game.Level' cannot be used in this
context because the set accessor is inaccessible.
```

Explanation:

Remember the following guidelines from the Microsoft documentation (see `https://docs.microsoft.com/en-us/dotnet/csharp/programming-guide/classes-and-structs/how-to-implement-a-lightweight-class-with-auto-implemented-properties`) that states the following:

> *When you declare a private* `set` *accessor, you cannot use an object initializer to initialize the property. You must use a constructor or a factory method.*

7.P3 Predict the output of the following code segment:

```
Game game = new();
Console.WriteLine($"Current level: {game.Level}");
game.Level = 2;
Console.WriteLine($"Current level: {game.Level}");
game.Level = 3;
Console.WriteLine($"Current level: {game.Level}");

class Game
{
    private int level=1;
    public int Level
```

```
    {
        get => level;

        set
        {
            if (value < 0 || value> 2)
            { level = 0; }
            else { level = value; }
        }

    }
}
```

Answer:

This code can compile and run successfully. You'll get the following output:

```
Current level: 1
Current level: 2
Current level: 0
```

Explanation:

This is an example where constraints are applied to a property. You can see that when I tried to set the level of the game to greater than 2, the program logic considers setting the new level as 0.

7.P4 Can you compile the following code?

```
Game game = new();
Console.WriteLine($"The current level: {game.Level}");
game.Level = 3;
Console.WriteLine($"The current level: {game.Level}");

class Game
{
    public int Level
    {
        get; set;

    } = 2;
}
```

Answer:

Yes, this code can compile and run successfully. You'll get the following output:

```
The current level: 2
The current level: 3
```

Explanation:

The Level here is an auto-implemented property. I set an initial value of 2.

Virtual and Abstract Properties

7.P5 Can you predict the output of the following code segment?

```
Console.WriteLine("Experimenting with a virtual property in
                  C#.");
Shape shape = new();
Console.WriteLine($"The area of the {shape} is {shape.Area}
                  square units.");
shape = new Circle(10);
Console.WriteLine($"The area of the {shape} is {shape.Area}
                  square units.");

class Shape
{
    public virtual double Area
    {
        get => 0;
    }
    public override string ToString()
    {
        return "unknown shape";
    }
}
class Circle : Shape
{
    readonly int _radius;
```

```
    public Circle(int radius)
    {
        this._radius = radius;
    }
    public int Radius
    {
        get => _radius;
    }
    public override double Area
    {
        get => 3.14 * _radius * _radius;
    }
    public override string ToString()
    {
        return "circle";
    }
}
```

Answer:

Here is the output:

```
Experimenting with a virtual property in C#.
The area of the unknown shape is 0 square units.
The area of the circle is 314 square units.
```

Explanation:

This program shows the usage of a virtual property. In addition, the shape variable is used polymorphically.

Inside the Circle class, I have overridden the Area property using the override keyword. What will happen if I use the new keyword instead of using the override keyword in this program? As you might guess, in this case, you'll get the following output (the change is shown in bold):

```
Experimenting with a virtual property in C#.
The area of the unknown shape is 0 square units.
The area of the circle is 0 square units.
```

The reason is obvious: the shape variable is used polymorphically in this program, but we have not overridden the virtual property Area. So, the parent class variable shape considers using the parent class property, but not the child class property.

But in this case, if you use a child class variable, the program will consider using the child class property again. So, the following code segment:

```
Circle circle = new Circle(10);
Console.WriteLine($"The area of the {shape} is {circle.Area}
  square units.");
```

can produce the following output:

```
The area of the circle is 314 square units.
```

7.P6 Predict the output of the following code segment:

```
Console.WriteLine("Experimenting with an abstract property in
                  C#.");
Shape shape = new Rectangle();
Console.WriteLine($"The area of the {shape} is {shape.Area}
                  square units.");

abstract class Shape
{
    public abstract double Area { get; }

    public override string ToString()
    {
        return "unknown shape";
    }
}
class Rectangle : Shape
{
    public override double Area
    {
        get => 100;
    }
    public override string ToString()
    {
```

```
        return "rectangle";
    }
}
```

Answer:

Here is the output:

```
Experimenting with an abstract property in C#.
The area of the rectangle is 100 square units.
```

Explanation:

This program shows how to use an abstract property. In addition, the shape variable is used polymorphically.

Author's Note: I said earlier that you can create a property with different types of modifiers. In this section, we have experimented with two of them: virtual properties and abstract properties.

The Usage of the init Keyword

7.P7 Can you compile the following code?

```
Console.WriteLine("Experiment with the 'init' keyword.");
Game game = new();
Console.WriteLine($"Game name: {game.Name}");

class Game
{
    private string _name;
    public Game() { _name = "SuperGame"; }
    public string Name
    {
        get => _name;

        init => _name = value;

    }
}
```

Answer:

This code can compile and run successfully. You'll get the following output:

```
Experiment with the 'init' keyword.
Game name: SuperGame
```

Explanation:

You have seen a simple usage of the `init` accessor for the property called `Name`. Here I use a single statement to assign a value; so, I was able to implement the `init` accessor as an expression-bodied member.

7.P8 Can you compile the following code?

```
Console.WriteLine("Experiment with the 'init' keyword.");
Game game = new();
game.Name = "SuperGame2";
class Game
{
    private string _name;
    public Game() { _name = "SuperGame"; }
    public string Name
    {
        get => _name;

        init => _name = value;

    }
}
```

Answer:

No. You'll receive the following compile-time error that is self-explanatory:

```
CS8852  Init-only property or indexer 'Game.Name' can only be assigned in
an object initializer, or on 'this' or 'base' in an instance constructor or
an 'init' accessor.
```

7.P9 Can you predict the output of the following code segment?

```
Game game = new();
Console.WriteLine($"The game name: {game.Name}");
game = new() { Name="Airplane Simulator"};
Console.WriteLine($"The new game name: {game.Name}");

class Game
{
    private string _name;
    public Game() { _name = "Car Simulator"; }
    public string Name
    {
        get => _name;

        init => _name = value;

    }
}
```

Answer:

This code can compile and run successfully. You'll get the following output:

```
The game name: Car Simulator
The new game name: Airplane Simulator
```

Author's Note: This program demonstrates the usage of object initializer syntax with the `init` accessor.

7.P10 Can you compile the following code?

```
Console.WriteLine("A usage of auto-implemented property with
                   the 'init' keyword.");
Game game = new();
Console.WriteLine($"Game name: {game.Name}");
class Game
{
  public string Name { get; init; } = "SuperGame";
}
```

Answer:

Yes, this code can compile and run successfully. You'll get the following output:

```
A usage of auto-implemented property with the 'init' keyword.
Game name: SuperGame
```

Using Indexers

7.P11 Can you compile the following code?

```
Console.WriteLine("***Indexer Demo.***");
Animals animals = new();
Console.WriteLine("Here are the animals:");
Console.WriteLine(animals[0]);
Console.WriteLine(animals[1]);

class Animals
{
    private string[] _names;
    public Animals()
    {
        _names = new string[] { "Tiger", "Lion" };
    }
    public string this[int index]
    {
        get => _names[index];

        set => _names[index] = value;

    }
}
```

Answer:

This code can compile and run successfully. You'll get the following output:

```
***Indexer Demo.***
Here are the animals:
Tiger
Lion
```

Explanation:

This program shows that both the get and set accessors can be implemented as expression-bodied members. This has been allowed since C# 7.0.

7.P12 Suppose, in the previous program, I replaced the following line:

```
Console.WriteLine(animals[1]);
```

with the following line:

```
Console.WriteLine(animals[2]);
```

What is the expected output?

Answer:

In this case, you'll receive the following runtime error:

```
System.IndexOutOfRangeException: 'Index was outside the bounds of
the array.'
```

Author's Note: You need to be careful when you deal with indexed values in programs like this. For example, without proper validation, the following line will also cause a similar error:

```
animals[2] = "Cat";//Error again
```

So, proper validation can make your code safer.

Properties and Indexers in Interfaces

7.P13 Predict the output of the following code segment:

```
Console.WriteLine("Case studies with the interfaces.");
IEmployee emp = new Employee("Sam", 1);
Console.WriteLine($"Name: {emp.Name}, ID:{emp.Id}");
interface IEmployee
{
    public string Name { get; set; }
    public int Id { get; set; }
}
```

```
class Employee : IEmployee
{
    string _name;
    int _id;
    public Employee(string name, int Id)
    {
        this._name = name;
        this._id = Id;
    }
    public string Name
    {
        get => _name;
        set => _name = value;
    }
    public int Id
    {
        get => _id;
        set => _id = value;
    }
}
```

Answer:

This code can compile and run successfully. You'll get the following output:

```
Case studies with the interfaces.
Name: Sam, ID:1
```

Author's Note: You have seen an example of an interface property.

7.P14 Predict the output of the following code segment:

```
Console.WriteLine("Case studies with the interfaces.");
IEmployee emp = new Employee("Kate", 2);
Console.WriteLine($"Name: {emp.Name}, ID:{emp.Id}");
interface IEmployee
{
```

```
    public string Name { get; set; }
    public int Id { get; set; }
}
class Employee : IEmployee
{
    string _name;
    int _id;
    public Employee(string name, int Id)
    {
        this._name = name;
        this._id = Id;
    }

    string IEmployee.Name
    {
        get => _name;
        set => _name = value;
    }
    int IEmployee.Id
    {
        get => _id;
        set => _id = value;
    }
}
```

Answer:

This code can compile and run successfully. You'll get the following output:

```
Case studies with the interfaces.
Name: Kate, ID:2
```

Author's Note: This program demonstrates the usage of an explicit interface implementation of the properties.

7.P15 Let us analyze a longer program. There are some supporting comments to help you understand the code. Will this code compile? If so, can you predict the output?

```
Console.WriteLine("Case studies with the interfaces.");
IEmployee emp = new EmployeeStore();

// Picking the employee name from the ID
Console.WriteLine($"The name of emp[0] is {emp[0]}");
Console.WriteLine($"The name of emp[1] is {emp[1]}");
Console.WriteLine($"The name of emp[2] is {emp[2]}");

Console.WriteLine("**************");

// Picking the employee ID from the name
Console.WriteLine($"The ID of Sam is {emp["Sam"]}");
Console.WriteLine($"The ID of Kate is {emp["Kate"]}");
Console.WriteLine($"The ID of Jack is {emp["Jack"]}");

class Employee
{
    string _name;
    int _id;
    public Employee(string name, int Id)
    {
        this._name = name;
        this._id = Id;
    }

    public int EmployeeId
    {
        get => _id;
    }
    public string Name
    {
        get => _name;
    }

}
interface IEmployee
```

```
{
    public string this[int id] { get; }
    public int this[string name] { get; }
}
class EmployeeStore : IEmployee
{
    Employee[] employees;
    public EmployeeStore()
    {
        employees = new Employee[] {

            new Employee("Sam", 1),
            new Employee("Kate", 2),
            new Employee("Jack", 3),

        };
    }
    public string this[int id]
    {
        get => employees[id].Name;

    }
    public int this[string name]
    {
        get
        {
            int temp = 0;
            if (name.Equals("Sam")) temp =
                    employees[0].EmployeeId;
            if (name.Equals("Kate")) temp =
                    employees[1].EmployeeId;
            if (name.Equals("Jack")) temp =
                    employees[2].EmployeeId;
            return temp;
        }
    }
}
```

Answer:

Yes, this code can compile and run successfully. You'll get the following output:

```
Case studies with the interfaces.
The name of emp[0] is Sam
The name of emp[1] is Kate
The name of emp[2] is Jack
**************
The ID of Sam is 1
The ID of Kate is 2
The ID of Jack is 3
```

Explanation:

If you understand this program, you are doing very well. Here are some key points about this program:

- We do not have to use ints as an index. We can use other types (such as strings) as well. This is why when using `emp["Sam"]`, I could pick his ID. So, you can decide how to define the specific lookup mechanism.
- This program also shows that indexers can be overloaded.
- This program also shows that in a particular code segment the set accessors are not mandatory. Notice that `EmployeeId` and `Name` are read-only properties.
- Though the previous code compiles and runs, it is not high-quality code, because I have not used proper validation for these indexes. So, you may encounter the runtime exception `System.IndexOutOfRangeException` if you try to proceed with something like `emp[3]`. You can understand the reason: in this program, the valid employees' IDs are `1`, `2`, and `3`.

Bonus Q&A

7.P16 Can you compile the following code? If so, can you predict the output?

```
Console.WriteLine("***Indexers with multiple parameters.***");
IEmployee emp = new EmployeeStore();
```

```
// Picking the employee ID from the name
Console.WriteLine($"Does the employee Sam with ID 1 exist?
                    {emp["Sam", 1]}");
Console.WriteLine($"Does the employee Kate with ID 3 exist?
                    {emp["Kate", 3]}");
Console.WriteLine($"Does the employee Jack with ID 3 exist?
                    {emp["Jack", 3]}");

class Employee
{
    string _name;
    int _id;
    public Employee(string name, int Id)
    {
        this._name = name;
        this._id = Id;
    }

}
interface IEmployee
{
    public bool this[string name, int id] { get; }
}
class EmployeeStore : IEmployee
{
    Employee[] employees;
    public EmployeeStore()
    {
        employees = new Employee[] {

            new Employee("Sam", 1),
            new Employee("Kate", 2),
            new Employee("Jack", 3),

        };
    }
```

```
    public bool this[string name, int id]
    {
        get
        {
            bool temp = false;
            if (name.Equals("Sam") && id == 1) temp = true;
            if (name.Equals("Kate") && id == 2) temp = true;
            if (name.Equals("Jack") && id == 3) temp = true;
            return temp;
        }
    }
}
```

Answer:

Yes, this code can compile and run successfully. You'll get the following output:

```
***Indexers with multiple parameters.***
Does the employee Sam with ID 1 exist? True
Does the employee Kate with ID 3 exist? False
Does the employee Jack with ID 3 exist? True
```

Author's Note: This program demonstrates that an indexer can take more than one parameter, and these can be of different types.

7.P17 Can you compile the following code?

```
Rectangle rect = new(5.5,10);
Console.WriteLine($"The area of the rectangle is {rect.Area}
                    square units.");

class Rectangle
{
    double length, breadth;
    public Rectangle(double length, double breadth)
    {
        this.length = length;
        this.breadth = breadth;
    }
```

```
    public double Area
    {
        get => length * breadth;
    }
}
```

Answer:

Yes, this code can compile and run successfully. You'll get the following output:

```
The area of the rectangle is 55 square units.
```

Explanation:

This code demonstrates that a property can be computed from other data. So, in this case, the area of the rectangle is computed from the `length` and `breadth` of the rectangle.

CHAPTER 8

Handling Exceptions

When you write code for an application, you expect that it will execute as per your plan, but you will often encounter sudden surprises. These surprises may occur through some careless mistakes. For example, you have implemented the wrong logic, or you have ignored some loopholes in the code paths of the program. However, many of the failures are beyond the control of a programmer. Developers call these unwanted situations *exceptions*. Handling these exceptions is essential when you write an application. This chapter focuses on exception handling and covers the following topics:

- Exceptions and their uses in C# programming
- Use of the `try`, `catch`, and `finally` blocks
- Use of multiple `catch` blocks in a program
- Use of a general `catch` block
- Throwing and rethrowing exceptions
- Use of exception filters
- Custom exception class and its usage

Let us review and test your understanding of these topics now.

Theoretical Concepts

This section includes the theoretical questions and answers on the exception handling mechanism in C# programming.

V. Sarcar, *Test Your Skills in C# Programming*, https://doi.org/10.1007/978-1-4842-8655-5_8

Basic Concepts

8.T1 What do you mean by exceptions in C#?

Answer:

These are C#'s built-in error handling mechanisms. Exceptions help you deal with any unexpected or exceptional situations that occur when a program is running. In simple terms, you can think of an exception as an event that breaks the normal execution flow of a program.

When exceptional situations arise, an exception object is created and thrown into the method that created the exception. That method may or may not handle the exception. If it cannot handle the exception, it will pass the responsibility to another method. (Similar to our daily life, when a situation goes beyond our control, we seek advice from others.) If there is no method to take responsibility for handling a particular exception, an error dialog box appears (indicating an unhandled exception), and the execution of the program stops.

8.T2 Why is exception handling important?

Answer:

When you write a program, you can classify the possible errors into the following broad categories:

- Compile-time errors
- Runtime errors

Compile-time errors are comparatively easy to fix because you know about them much earlier (i.e., at compile time). These may occur mainly due to syntax errors or typing mistakes. The compiler can easily point to them so that you can take corrective measures immediately.

On the contrary, runtime errors are dangerous because you encounter them only when a program was being executed. Since the program is compiled early, you expect it to be run successfully, but the problem may arise due to some typical cases such as you are trying to divide a number by 0, open a file, or connect to a database using a wrong password or incorrect implementation of logic. As a result, this type of error is tough to fix and is costly. C#'s exception handling mechanism is important because it helps you deal with these typical runtime errors in advance.

8.T3 What are the common keywords in C#'s exception handling mechanism? How are they used?

Answer:

You can use the following keywords to deal with C# exceptions: `try`, `catch`, `throw`, and `finally`. In addition, starting with C# 6.0, you can see the use of the contextual keyword `when` in a `catch` statement to filter an exception. Here I summarize their usage:

- You can guard an exception using a `try-catch` block. The code that may throw an exception is placed inside a `try` block, and this exceptional situation is handled inside a `catch` block.
- The code in the `finally` block must execute. In general, this block is placed after a `try` block or a `try-catch` block.
- When an exception is raised inside a `try` block, the control jumps to the respective `catch` or `finally` block. The remaining part of the `try` block will not be executed.
- You can associate multiple `catch` blocks with a `try` block. In this case, you must place them from the most specific to the least specific types.

To illustrate the previous bullet point, I show you a sample code segment that uses three `catch` blocks. These are used to handle different types of exceptions. Here you'll notice the following points:

- The `catch(ArithmeticException ex)` block is placed after `catch(DivideByZeroException ex){...}`.
- Also, `catch(Exception ex){...}` is placed after all other `catch` blocks.
- The `DivideByZeroException` class inherits from the `ArithmeticException` class, which inherits from the `SystemException` class, which again inherits from the `Exception` class.

Now go through the following code segment to review your understanding:

```
Console.WriteLine("***Case study with multiple catch
                   blocks.***");
```

```
try
{
    // Some code
}
catch (DivideByZeroException ex)
{
    // Some code
}
catch (ArithmeticException ex)
{
    // Some code
}

catch (Exception ex)
{
    // Some code
}
finally
{
    // Some code
}
```

In addition, anyone can raise an exception with the `throw` keyword. Here is some sample code for you:

```
try
{
    // Some code before
    throw new IndexOutOfRangeException("Index is out of
                                        range.");

}
// Remaining code skipped
```

Finally, as mentioned, you can use exception filters that allow you to catch an exception when a certain condition is met. 8.P10 in this chapter shows you a complete example of this. For now, let me pick a particular code segment to demonstrate this:

```
catch (Exception ex) when (ex.Message.Contains("Timeout"))
{
    Console.WriteLine($"Caught: " + ex.Message);
}
```

Author's Note: All C# exceptions are runtime exceptions. So, there is no concept of compile-time checked exceptions. This is why the `throws` keyword is absent in C#, but it is present in Java.

8.T4 What is the base class for all exceptions in C#?
Answer:

`System.Exception` is the base class for all exceptions in C#.

8.T5 Why is analyzing a stack trace important in exception handling?
Answer:

In many cases, when you invoke a method, that method may call another method that may cause an exception. In that situation, the CLR will look for a `catch` block that can handle the exception, and it will execute the first such `catch` block that it finds. So, analyzing the stack trace of an exception is important to understand the real cause of the problem, and you will often use the `StackTrace` property of `System.Exception` in this context.

8.T6 How is the `finally` block used?
Answer:

The `finally` block will always execute. It does not matter whether an exception is thrown. These blocks are typically used to write the cleanup code such as closing a file or releasing resources. A `finally` block can execute in any of the following situations:

- After a `try` block ends
- After a `catch` block ends
- After the control leaves, the `try` block (due to a typical reason such as there is a `return` statement or an exception raised in this block)

A few things can still defeat the purpose of the `finally` block such as if the program encounters an infinite loop or you have written a bad code segment something like the following:

```
// The previous code skipped
finally
{
 Console.WriteLine("You cannot skip me!");
 //return; // It will raise the error CS0157
 throw new Exception("Exceptions in finally");
 // Unreachable code
 Console.WriteLine("End of the finally block.");
}
```

8.T7 Can you name some built-in exception classes in C#?

Answer:

There are many such exceptions. In this chapter, I have used the base class `System.Exception` in many places. In addition, I've used the following in this chapter:

```
System.DivideByZeroException
System.FormatException
System.ArithmeticException
```

In addition, you may find the following exceptions used widely:

```
System.InvalidCastException
System.NullReferenceException
System.OutOfMemoryException
System.IndexOutOfRangeException
System.NotImplementedException
```

8.T8 I understand that I can suppress an error using the exception handling mechanism. Also, if I encounter an exception, I can rethrow a different exception. Is this correct?

Answer:

Yes, but it is never recommended. However, when you learn to create a custom exception, you can combine this original exception with the custom exception message and then rethrow it for better readability.

Exception Filters

8.T9 Why do you use exception filters?

Answer:

An exception type may not be fine-grained enough. For example, consider a case when you encounter a WebException. You understand that this error can be a result of various reasons, such as if there is a protocol error, a timeout error, or a different error. Based on these possible reasons, you may take different actions to handle a situation. The exception filters help you in such a context. For example, in this case, you can introduce different catch blocks with different filters to provide the best action as follows:

```
try
{
     //  Some code that can raise a WebException
}
catch (WebException ex) when (ex.Status ==
                              WebExceptionStatus.Timeout)
{
   //some code
}

catch (WebException ex) when (ex.Status ==
                             WebExceptionStatus.ProtocolError)
{
//some code
}
// The remaining code skipped
```

Author's Note: In 8.P10, you can see a complete demonstration that uses the concept of exception filters.

Custom Exception

8.T10 Write a program to create a custom exception and show its usage.

Answer:

The following program demonstrates the use of a custom exception. Before I show you the complete example, I'd like you to note the following guidelines from Microsoft (refer to `https://docs.microsoft.com/en-us/dotnet/standard/exceptions/how-to-create-user-defined-exceptions`):

- You can create a custom exception class by deriving it from the `Exception` class.
- When we create a custom exception, the class name should end with the word `Exception`.
- Supply the three overloaded versions of constructors (as described in the upcoming example).

There is an additional guideline in this context (see `https://docs.microsoft.com/en-us/dotnet/api/system.applicationexception?redirectedfrom=MSDN&view=net-6.0`):

> *"You should derive custom exceptions from the Exception class rather than the ApplicationException class. You should not throw an ApplicationException exception in your code, and you should not catch an ApplicationException exception unless you intend to rethrow the original exception."*

Let's get back to the example. In this program, I assume that if a divisor is 1 or less, we'll throw an exception. Here is the complete program where `SmallDivisorException` is a custom exception class that has three common constructors:

```
Console.WriteLine("***Custom Exception Example***");
int a = 10, b = 2, result;
try
{
    b--;
    if (b == 1)
```

```
    {
        throw new SmallDivisorException($"The divisor
                                              becomes {b}");
       // throw new SmallDivisorException();
    }
    result = a / b;
}
catch (SmallDivisorException ex)
{
    Console.WriteLine($"Caught the custom exception:
                      {ex.Message}");
}
finally
{
    Console.WriteLine("\nThank you!");
}

class SmallDivisorException : Exception
{
    public SmallDivisorException() {}
    public SmallDivisorException(string msg) : base(msg) { }
    public SmallDivisorException(string msg, Exception inner)
                                         : base(msg, inner)
    { }
}
```

Output:

When you compile and run this program, you'll see the following output:

```
***Custom Exception Example***
Caught the custom exception: The divisor becomes 1

Thank you!
```

Explanation:

You can see that I have used the second overloaded version of the constructor. If you want to use the default constructor (which was commented on earlier), there is a different message (which I've shown in bold):

```
***Custom Exception Example***
Caught the custom exception: Exception of type 'SmallDivisorException'
was thrown.

Thank you!
```

Programming Skills

By using the following questions, you can test your programming skills in C#. Note that if I do not mention the namespace, you can assume that all parts of the program belong to the same namespace.

Fundamentals

8.P1 Predict the output of the following code segment:

```
Console.WriteLine("***Case study on exception handling.***");
int a = 10, b = 0;
try
{
    int c = a / b;
    Console.WriteLine($"The a=10,b=0.So,a/b is :{c}");
}
catch (Exception ex)
{
    Console.WriteLine($"Encountered: {ex.Message}");
}
finally
{
    Console.WriteLine("Inside the finally block: you cannot
                        skip me!");
}
```

Answer:

You'll get the following output:

```
***Case study on exception handling.***
Encountered: Attempted to divide by zero.
Inside the finally block: you cannot skip me!
```

Explanation:

You can verify the following points from this program:

- When an exception is raised inside a `try` block, the control jumps to the respective `catch` block. The remaining part of the `try` block does not execute.
- The code in the `finally` block always executes even though we encounter an exception.

Using Multiple Catch Blocks

8.P2 Predict the output of the following code segment when a user supplies the following inputs:

- 234
- 23.456
- 9876543219
- abc

```
Console.WriteLine("***Case study with multiple catch blocks.***");
try
{
    Console.WriteLine("Enter an integer:");
    string input = Console.ReadLine();
    int number = Convert.ToInt32(input);
    Console.WriteLine($"You have entered the number:
                        {number}");
}
```

```
catch (FormatException ex)
{
    Console.WriteLine("You need to enter an integer.");
    Console.WriteLine($"The exception detail:
                        {ex.StackTrace}");
}
catch (OverflowException ex)
{
    Console.WriteLine(" You need to provide smaller number.");
    Console.WriteLine($"The exception detail:
                        {ex.StackTrace}");
}

catch (Exception ex)
{
    Console.WriteLine($"Encountered an unknown error.");
    Console.WriteLine($"The exception detail:
                        {ex.StackTrace}");
}
finally
{
    Console.WriteLine("Thank you for testing this scenario.");
}
```

Answer:

Here are the outputs as per the user inputs. I have made certain lines bold to highlight the difference in the output messages.

Case-Study-1: User enters 234

```
***Case study with multiple catch blocks.***
Enter an integer:
234
You have entered the number: 234
Thank you for testing this scenario.
```

Case-Study-2: User enters 23.456

```
***Case study with multiple catch blocks.***
Enter an integer:
23.456
You need to enter an integer.
The exception detail:    at System.Number.ThrowOverflowOrFormatException(Pa
rsingStatus status, TypeCode type)
   at System.Convert.ToInt32(String value)
   at Program.<Main>$(String[] args) in E:\MyPrograms\TestC#Skills\
Exceptions\Program2\Program.cs:line 6
Thank you for testing this scenario.
```

Case-Study-3: User enters 9876543219

```
***Case study with multiple catch blocks.***
Enter an integer:
9876543219
 You need to provide smaller number.
The exception detail:    at System.Number.ThrowOverflowOrFormatException(Pa
rsingStatus status, TypeCode type)
   at System.Convert.ToInt32(String value)
   at Program.<Main>$(String[] args) in E:\MyPrograms\TestC#Skills\
   Exceptions\Program2\Program.cs:line 6
Thank you for testing this scenario.
```

Case-Study-4: User enters abc

```
***Case study with multiple catch blocks.***
Enter an integer:
abc
You need to enter an integer.
The exception detail:    at System.Number.ThrowOverflowOrFormatException(Pa
rsingStatus status, TypeCode type)
   at System.Convert.ToInt32(String value)
   at Program.<Main>$(String[] args) in E:\MyPrograms\TestC#Skills\
   Exceptions\Program2\Program.cs:line 6
Thank you for testing this scenario.
```

Explanation:

The output messages are self-explanatory. From this output, once again you have verified the following points from this program:

- When an exception is raised inside a `try` block, the control jumps to the respective `catch` block. The remaining part of the `try` block does not execute.
- Only one `catch` block is used to handle an exception.
- The code in the `finally` block executes in every possible case.

8.P3 Predict the output of the following code segment:

```
Console.WriteLine("***Case study with multiple catch blocks.***");
int a = 100, b = 0;
try
{
    Console.WriteLine($"The result of a/b is :{a/b}");
}
catch (ArithmeticException ex)
{
    Console.WriteLine("Encountered the ArithmeticException");
}
catch (DivideByZeroException ex)
{
    Console.WriteLine("Encountered the DivideByZeoException");
}
```

Answer:

You'll receive the following compile-time error:

```
CS0160   A previous catch clause already catches all exceptions of this or
of a super type ('ArithmeticException')
```

Explanation:

Exceptions follow the inheritance hierarchy, and you need to place catch blocks accordingly. Let us examine the Microsoft documentation at https://docs.microsoft.com/en-us/dotnet/api/system.exception?view=net-6.0#TryCatch. Here you find the following:

> *A catch block handles an exception of type T if the type filter of the catch block specifies T or any type that T derives from. The system stops searching after it finds the first catch block that handles the exception. For this reason, in application code, a catch block that handles a type must be specified before a catch block that handles its base types...*

It continues:

> *A catch block that handles* ***System.Exception*** *is specified last.*

Now examine the program. Note that DivideByZeroException is a subclass of ArithmeticException. So, you need to place catch (DivideByZeroException ex){} prior to catch (ArithmeticException ex){}. When you are in doubt, you can check the inheritance hierarchy from Visual Studio. Figure 8-1, Figure 8-2, and Figure 8-3 show three such snapshots for your reference:

```
namespace System
{
    [...]public class DivideByZeroException : ArithmeticException
    {
        [...]public DivideByZeroException()[...]
        [...]protected DivideByZeroException(SerializationInfo info, StreamingContext context)[...]
        [...]public DivideByZeroException(string? message)[...]
        [...]public DivideByZeroException(string? message, Exception? innerException)[...]
    }
}
```

Figure 8-1. *The DivideByZeroException class inherits from the ArithmeticException class.*

```
namespace System
{
    [...]public class ArithmeticException : SystemException
    {
        [...]public ArithmeticException()[...]
        [...]protected ArithmeticException(SerializationInfo info, StreamingContext context)[...]
        [...]public ArithmeticException(string? message)[...]
        [...]public ArithmeticException(string? message, Exception? innerException)[...]
    }
}
```

Figure 8-2. *The ArithmeticException class inherits from the SystemException class.*

```
namespace System
{
    [...]public class SystemException : Exception
    {
        [...]public SystemException()[...]
        [...]protected SystemException(SerializationInfo info, StreamingContext context)[...]
        [...]public SystemException(string? message)[...]
        [...]public SystemException(string? message, Exception? innerException)[...]
    }
}
```

***Figure 8-3.** The SystemException class inherits from the Exception class.*

Now you understand that to avoid this compile-time error, you need to place these `catch` blocks as follows:

```
// The previous code skipped
try
{
    Console.WriteLine($"The result of a/b is :{a/b}");
}
catch (DivideByZeroException ex)
{
    Console.WriteLine("Encountered the DivideByZeoException");
}
catch (ArithmeticException ex)
{
    Console.WriteLine("Encountered the ArithmeticException");
}
```

Additional Note:

In this example, I have not used the variable ex, which was declared inside the `catch` blocks. So, the C# compiler will show you two warning messages (both are the same).

```
CS0168   The variable 'ex' is declared but never used
```

In general, you use these variables to get some useful information such as printing the exception message or tracking a stack trace. When you do not use them, you can avoid declaring them inside the `catch` blocks. *However, I do not recommend this* practice, because the exception messages or stack traces are very useful to understand the exceptions. But I show this demonstration to remind you that the following block (or a similar block where you do not mention the exception variable) does not raise any compile-time error:

```
// Also OK
catch (DivideByZeroException)
{
   // Some code
}
```

Using a General Catch Block

8.P4 Can you compile the following code?

```
int a = 100, b = 0;
try
{
    Console.WriteLine($"The result of a/b is :{a / b}");
}
catch (Exception ex)
{
    Console.WriteLine($"The exception caught: {ex.Message}");
}
catch
{
    Console.WriteLine("Caught a non-CLS exceptions.");
}
```

Answer:

Yes, this code can compile and run successfully. You'll get the following output:

```
The exception caught: Attempted to divide by zero.
```

Explanation:

The output of the previous program is straightforward. But I use this example to demonstrate a variety of catch blocks. Notice the final catch block. It is often called a general catch block.

Why is this important? As per the language specification, a `catch` clause that does not name an exception class can handle any exception. Also, some exceptions do not derive from `System.Exception`. These are called non-CLS exceptions. Some .NET languages, including C++/CLI, support these exceptions. In C#, you cannot throw non-CLS exceptions, but you can catch them in the following ways:

- Option 1: Use a `catch (RuntimeWrappedException e)` block.
- Option 2: Use the `catch{}` block and place it after all the other `catch` blocks.

Option 1 is useful when you need to access the original exception, but option 2 is useful when you do not need to access the exception details (consider the case when you want to log the details without worrying about anything else).

By default, a Visual C# assembly catches non-CLS exceptions as wrapped exceptions. You can use the `RuntimeWrappedException.WrappedException` property to process the exception. This is why even though this program compiles and executes, you will see the following warning message:

```
CS1058   A previous catch clause already catches all exceptions. All non-
exceptions thrown will be wrapped in a System.Runtime.CompilerServices.
RuntimeWrappedException.
```

Author's Note: For more information on this topic, you can refer to `https://docs.microsoft.com/en-us/dotnet/csharp/how-to/how-to-catch-a-non-cls-exception`.

8.P5 Will the following code segment compile?

```
int a = 100, b = 0;
try
{
    Console.WriteLine($"The result of a/b is :{a / b}");
}
catch
{
    Console.WriteLine("Caught a non-CLS exceptions.");
}
```

```
catch (Exception ex)
{
    Console.WriteLine($"The exception caught: {ex.Message}");
}
```

Answer:

No. You'll receive the following compile-time error:

```
CS1017   Catch clauses cannot follow the general catch clause of a try
statement.
```

Explanation:

In 8.P4 I mentioned the Microsoft documentation, which states that you need to place the general catch block after all other catch blocks.

Throwing and Rethrowing an Exception

8.P6 Predict the output of the following code segment:

```
Console.WriteLine("***The case study on the throw statement.***");
try
{
    // Some code before
    throw new IndexOutOfRangeException("Index is out of range.");

}
catch (Exception ex)
{
    Console.WriteLine($"The exception caught: {ex.Message}");

}
```

Answer:

You'll get the following output:

```
***The case study on the throw statement.***
The exception caught: Index is out of range.
```

Explanation:

This program shows that you can explicitly throw an exception using C#'s throw statement.

8.P7 Predict the output of the following code segment:

```
Console.WriteLine("***The case study on the throw statement.***");
NumberMaker numberMaker = new();
try
{
    Console.WriteLine($"numbers[0]={numberMaker.GetNumber(0)}");
    Console.WriteLine($"numbers[3]={numberMaker.GetNumber(3)}");
}
catch (Exception ex)
{
    Console.WriteLine($"\nThe Main() caught: {ex.Message}");
    Console.WriteLine($"\tStacktrace:{ex.StackTrace}");

}
class NumberMaker
{
    int[] _numbers = { 1, 2, 3 };

    internal int GetNumber(int index)
    {
        try
        {
            if (index < 0 || index >= _numbers.Length)
            {
                throw new IndexOutOfRangeException("Index is
                                                   out of range.");
            }
        }
        catch (Exception ex)
        {
            Console.WriteLine($"\nThe GetNumber(...) caught:{ex.Message}");
```

```
            Console.WriteLine($"\tStacktrace: {ex.StackTrace}");
            throw;
            // throw ex; // Not used in this program
        }
        return _numbers[index];

    }
}
```

Answer:

You'll get the following output:

```
***The case study on the throw keyword.***
numbers[0]=1

The GetNumber(...) caught: Index is out of range.
        Stacktrace:   at NumberMaker.GetNumber(Int32 index) in E:\
        MyPrograms\TestC#Skills\Exceptions\Program7\Program.cs:line 26

The Main() caught: Index is out of range.
        Stacktrace:   at NumberMaker.GetNumber(Int32 index) in E:\
        MyPrograms\TestC#Skills\Exceptions\Program7\Program.cs:line 26
   at Program.<Main>$(String[] args) in E:\MyPrograms\TestC#Skills\
   Exceptions\Program7\Program.cs:line 7
```

Explanation:

Notice that there is the `throw` statement inside the `GetNumber(…)` method. This program uses this statement inside the `catch` block to rethrow the exception. You can see that it does not use any exception variable (something like `throw ex;`) before it throws the exception. It is most useful when a method passes an argument from a caller to some "other" method, and this "other" method throws an exception that is needed to be passed on to the caller.

Notice that in this program, I also invoked the `GetNumber(…)` method from `Main()` (since I have used the top-level statements, you are not seeing the `Main()` method).

8.P8 Instead of `throw`, now you use `throw ex;` in the previous program. I show you the change in bold for your reference:

```
//The previous code skipped
catch (Exception ex)
```

```
{
  Console.WriteLine($"\nThe GetNumber(...) caught: {ex.Message}");
  Console.WriteLine($"\tStacktrace:{ex.StackTrace}");
  // throw; // Not used in this program
  throw ex;
 }
//The remaining code skipped
```

Can you predict the output?

Answer:

This code can compile and run successfully. But you'll see the following warning message:

```
CA2200   Re-throwing caught exception changes stack information
```

Confused? Let's run the program and see the output. I have made the important change in bold.

```
***The case study on the throw keyword.***
numbers[0]=1

The GetNumber(...) caught: Index is out of range.
        Stacktrace:   at NumberMaker.GetNumber(Int32 index) in E:\
        MyPrograms\TestC#Skills\Exceptions\Program7\Program.cs:line 26

The Main() caught: Index is out of range.
        Stacktrace:   at NumberMaker.GetNumber(Int32 index) in E:\
        MyPrograms\TestC#Skills\Exceptions\Program7\Program.cs:line 33
   at Program.<Main>$(String[] args) in E:\MyPrograms\TestC#Skills\
   Exceptions\Program7\Program.cs:line 7
```

Notice that when the exception was caught inside the `GetNumber` method, it pointed to line 26, and when the exception is caught inside the `Main` method, it pointed to a different line, specifically, line 33. But in 8.P7, both lines pointed to the same line: 26.

To understand this output better, Figure 8-4 shows a snapshot of the program so that you see the line numbers that the call stack points to.

```
Console.WriteLine("---8.P8---");
Console.WriteLine("***The case study on the throw keyword.***");
NumberMaker numberMaker = new();
try
{
    Console.WriteLine($"numbers[0]={numberMaker.GetNumber(0)}");
    Console.WriteLine($"numbers[3]={numberMaker.GetNumber(3)}");
}
catch (Exception ex)
{
    Console.WriteLine($"\nThe Main() caught: {ex.Message}");
    Console.WriteLine($"\tStacktrace:{ex.StackTrace}");
}



2 references
class NumberMaker
{
    int[] _numbers = { 1, 2, 3 };
    2 references
    internal int GetNumber(int index)
    {
        try
        {
            if (index < 0 || index >= _numbers.Length)
            {
                throw new IndexOutOfRangeException("Index is out of range.");
            }
        }
        catch (Exception ex)
        {
            Console.WriteLine($"\nThe GetNumber(...) caught: {ex.Message}");
            Console.WriteLine($"\tStacktrace:{ex.StackTrace}");
            throw ex;
        }
```

Figure 8-4. *A partial snapshot of the program in 8.P8*

Explanation:

The Microsoft documentation (`https://docs.microsoft.com/en-us/dotnet/csharp/language-reference/keywords/throw`) confirms the difference between the statements: `throw;` and `throw ex;`. It says the following:

> *You can use the `throw e` syntax in a catch block to instantiate a new exception that you want to pass on to the caller. In this case, the stack trace of the original exception, which is available from the StackTrace property, is not preserved.*

8.P9 Can you compile the following code?

```
Console.WriteLine("***The case study on the throw expression.***");
try
{
    int a = 10;
    // Returns a random number between 0(inclusive)
    // and 2(exclusive)
    int b = new Random().Next(0, 2);
    Console.WriteLine($"b={b}");
    int c = b > 0 ? (a / b) :
                throw new DivideByZeroException("b becomes 0");
    Console.WriteLine("Thank you.");
}
catch (Exception ex)
{
    Console.WriteLine($"Caught: "+ex.Message);
}
```

Answer:

Yes. Here is some possible output (when b is 0):

```
***The case study on the throw expression.***
b=0
Caught: b becomes 0
```

Here is some other possible output (when b is 1):

```
***The case study on the throw expression.***
b=1
Thank you.
```

Explanation:

The Microsoft documentation says that starting with C# 7.0, this code can compile and run successfully. This is why I can use the following statement without a compile-time error:

```
int c = b > 0 ? (a / b) :
                throw new DivideByZeroException("b becomes 0");
```

Author's Note: You saw the use of the throw expression with the conditional operator in 8.P9. You can use it with other C# constructs as well such as an expression-bodied method or a null-coalescing operator.

Filtering Exceptions

8.P10 Does the following code segment compile?

```
using System.Net;

Console.WriteLine("***A case study on exception filters.***");
try
{
    int a = 10;
    // Returns a random number between 0(inclusive)
    // and 2(exclusive)
    int b = new Random().Next(0, 2);
    Console.WriteLine($"b={b}");
    int c = b > 0 ? throw new WebException("Timeout error") :
                    throw new WebException("Protocol error");
    Console.WriteLine("Thank you.");
}
catch (Exception ex) when (ex.Message.Contains("Timeout"))
{
    Console.WriteLine($"Caught: " + ex.Message);
}

catch (Exception ex) when (ex.Message.Contains("Protocol"))
{
    Console.WriteLine($"Caught: " + ex.Message);
}
```

Answer:

Yes, this code can compile and run successfully. Here is a possible output (when b is 0):

```
***A case study on exception filters.***
b=0
Caught: Protocol error
```

Here is another possible output(when b is 1):

```
***A case study on exception filters.***
b=1
Caught: Timeout error
```

Explanation:

In this scenario, the when clause acts as a filter: if a WebException is thrown and the Boolean condition (which is followed by when) is true, then only a corresponding catch block will handle that exception. Using this kind of filter, we can catch the same exception but handle it in a different catch block.

Author's Note: You'll want to use this technique when a particular exception object can point to multiple errors. In a real-world application, each error can be associated with an error code. Following this demonstration, you can use this error code to handle a particular error inside a catch clause.

CHAPTER 9

Useful Concepts

Before you move to Part III of this book, let's review some other useful concepts in C#. This will help you remove many common doubts and enhance your programming skills. This chapter covers the following topics:

- Type conversions including boxing and unboxing
- Static data
- Extension methods
- Value types and reference types in C#
- The difference between passing value-type by value and passing value-type by reference
- A quick overview of pointers in C#
- Use of the `const` and `readonly` keywords in a program

Let us review these topics and test your understanding now.

Theoretical Concepts

This section includes the theoretical questions and answers on various topics in C#.

Type Conversions

9.T1 Why do you use casting? How can you differentiate different types of casting?
Answer:

Casting helps you convert one data type to another. Often it is called *type conversion*. Basically, there are two types of casting: implicit and explicit.

V. Sarcar, *Test Your Skills in C# Programming*, https://doi.org/10.1007/978-1-4842-8655-5_9

As the name suggests, implicit casting is automatic, and you do not need to worry about it. But, you need cast operators for explicit casting.

In implicit casting, the conversion path follows small to large integral types, or derived types to base types. For example, the following segment of code will compile and run perfectly:

```
int a = 1;
// Implicit casting
double b = a; // OK
```

Explicit casting considers the reverse case. If you write something like this:

```
double d = 12.5;
int c = d;// ERROR CS0266
```

you'll see the compile-time error:

```
CS0266  Cannot implicitly convert type 'double' to 'int'. An explicit
conversion exists (are you missing a cast?)
```

To avoid this error, you can apply an explicit casting like the following:

```
// Explicit casting
int c = (int)d; // OK
```

In this context, you must remember the following points:

- Casting is possible only when one type is convertible to another type. For example, you cannot assign a string to an integer. You will always encounter errors with those kinds of attempts. For example, using the following code:

  ```
  int c1 = (int) "hello"; // ERROR CS0030
  ```

  you can observe the compile-time error `CS0030    Cannot convert type 'string' to 'int'.`

- Implicit casting is type-safe (there is no loss of data because you travel from a small container to a large container so that you have sufficient space). Explicit conversion is not type-safe (because in this case, the data moves from a large container to a small container).

9.T2 Can you differentiate between boxing and unboxing?

Answer:

When you convert a value type to an `object` type (or to any interface type implemented by this value type), the procedure is called *boxing*, and the reverse procedure is known as *unboxing*.

Note Notice that I used the word *object* type. You may remember that in C#, all types(predefined and user-defined), value types and reference types inherit directly or indirectly from `System.Object` and the `object` type is an alias for `System.Object`.

Using boxing, a value type allocates an object instance on the heap and then boxes (stores) the copied value into that object. Here is an example of boxing:

```
int i = 1;
object o = i; // Boxing
```

Now consider the reverse scenario and look at the last line in the following code segment. If you try to write code like this:

```
int i = 1;
object o = i; // Boxing
// int j = o; // ERROR CS0266
```

you will get the compile-time error that says the following:

```
CS0266  Cannot implicitly convert type 'object' to 'int'. An explicit
conversion exists (are you missing a cast?)
```

To avoid this, you need to do unboxing, like the following:

```
object o = i;
int j = (int)o; // Unboxing
```

You may also notice that boxing is implicit. So, you do not need to write code like the following (notice the bold line in the following code segment):

```
int i = 1;
object o = (object)i;
// object o=i; // It is OK, because since boxing is implicit.
```

9.T3 Can you create a top-level static class in C#? Also, can you mention some of the C# constructs where you can apply the `static` keyword?

Answer:

The answer to the first part of the question is yes. The following code will not raise any compile-time error:

```
// static class Rectangle
static class Rectangle
{
    readonly static int _flag = 20;
    public static void CalculateArea()
    {
        Console.WriteLine("The area is shown.");
    }
}
```

To answer the second part of this question, refer the following summary from Microsoft (`https://docs.microsoft.com/en-us/dotnet/csharp/language-reference/keywords/static`):

> *The static modifier can be used to declare static classes. In classes, interfaces, and structs, you may add the static modifier to fields, methods, properties, operators, events, and constructors. The static modifier can't be used with indexers or finalizers.*

9.T4 What are the main characteristics of a static class in C#?

Answer:

At the time of this writing, these are the main characteristics of a static class in C#:

- Only static members are allowed inside a static class.
- You cannot instantiate a static class.
- A static class is sealed by nature.
- A static class cannot contain instance constructors.

9.T5 When should you consider using a static class?

Answer:

A static class is best used when your class contains methods that do not depend on the instance fields. For example, notice the built-in `System.Math` class. This class contains constant fields and static methods. These methods operate on the input parameters only. Here is an example:

```
double flag = -625.0;
Console.WriteLine(Math.Abs(flag)); // Prints 625
Console.WriteLine(Math.Sqrt(-flag)); // Prints 25
```

C# Types

9.T6 What are the different types in C#?

Answer:

C# types can be broadly classified into the following categories:

- Value types
- Reference types
- Pointer types
- Generic types

You can see the use of value types and reference types throughout this book. The generic types are discussed in Chapter 13.

Author's Note: Pointer types are commonly used in unmanaged code (for example, interoperability with C APIs). A detailed discussion of them is beyond the scope of this book.

9.T7 Give some examples of value types in C#.

Answer:

As mentioned in Chapter 3, we often refer to the bool type, char type, integral, and floating-point numeric types as simple types. All the simple types are built-in value types in C#. A value type can be further classified into the following categories: structure types and enumeration types. All simple types are structure types.

Author's Note: Remember that string is a built-in reference type.

9.T8 Can you give some examples of reference types in C#?

Answer:

The built-in object, dynamic, and string types belong to the reference type. You often see the use of the `class`, `interface`, and `delegate` keywords to declare a reference type. Beginning with C# 9, you can use the `record` keyword also to define a reference type.

9.T9 How do the value types differ from the reference types?

Answer:

The fundamental difference between these types is the way they are handled inside the memory. Microsoft (`https://docs.microsoft.com/en-us/dotnet/csharp/language-reference/keywords/reference-types`) summarizes the difference nicely as follows:

> *Variables of reference types store references to their data (objects), while variables of value types directly contain their data. With reference types, two variables can reference the same object; therefore, operations on one variable can affect the object referenced by the other variable. With value types, each variable has its own copy of the data, and it is not possible for operations on one variable to affect the other (except in the case of in, ref and out parameter variables).*

Unsafe Code

9.T10 I often hear about the safe code and unsafe code. What do these terms mean?

Answer:

Up until now, you have seen safe code only. This type of code does not allocate raw memory or directly use pointers to access a memory location. Since .NET tools can verify the safety of code, Microsoft calls them *verifiably safe code.*

But in an "unsafe" context, you can write unverifiable code using pointers. Here you can allocate or deallocate a memory block and use function pointers. Since the .NET tools cannot verify the safety issues of these operations, this code is called *unverifiable code* or *unsafe code.*

Note The key takeaway is that "unsafe" code is risky, but not necessarily dangerous. It often increases the performance of the application. Unsafe code is also useful when your code calls a native function that requires pointers.

9.T11 Can you demonstrate a simple program that uses pointers?

Answer:

Before you see the program, you need to be familiar with the common terms and their usage. So, let me remind you about the common terms:

- An example of a pointer type declaration is `type* identifier` or `void* identifier`.
- The type specified before the asterisk (*) is called the *referent* type.
- Only an unmanaged type can be a referent type.
- The *pointer indirection operator* (*) is used to obtain the variable pointed by a pointer.

Here are some examples of pointer type declarations with meanings for your reference:

- `int* p` means p is a pointer to an integer.
- `int** p` means that p is a pointer to a pointer to an integer.
- `char* p` means that p is a pointer to a char.
- `void* p` means that p is a pointer to an unknown type (although it is allowed, use it with care).

Consider the following code and follow the instructions before you compile this program:

```
int a = 100;
unsafe
{
    int* p;
    p = &a;
    Console.WriteLine("Pointer Type Demo.");
    Console.WriteLine($"*p is {*p}");
}
```

If you see the following error:

```
CS0227 Unsafe code may only appear if compiling with /unsafe
```

you know that you need to follow the Visual Studio IDE's suggestion to compile this program. When you work with the unsafe code, you can apply the setting shown in Figure 9-1 (see the arrow).

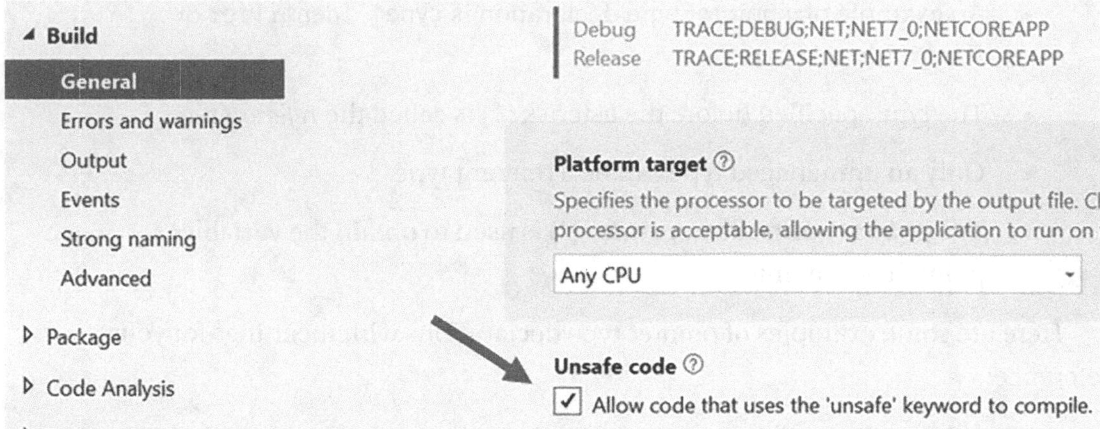

***Figure 9-1.** Unsafe code is allowed in a project.*

Now you can run this program and get the following output:

```
Pointer Type Demo.
*p is 100
```

Additional Notes:

For the declaration `int* p`, the expression `*p` denotes the `int` variable found at the address contained in `p`. **Here is some additional information:**

- You cannot convert between a pointer type and an object.
- Pointers do not inherit from objects.
- Boxing and unboxing are not applicable for pointers.
- To declare multiple pointers at the same place, the * is written with the underlying type, such as

  ```
  int* a, b, c; // OK
  ```

- But if we write something like this, we encounter a compiler error:

  ```
  int *a,*b,*c;// Error in C#
  ```

- You have probably heard about garbage collection (in my book *Interactive C#* I discuss this in detail), which basically operates on references. The garbage collector can collect the object references during the cleanup process, even if some pointer points to them. This is why a pointer cannot point to a reference (or any structure that contains a reference).

- But what do you do if you need movable managed variables? The answer is that you need to be familiar with the fixed statement that "pins" the variable in an unsafe context. As a result, the garbage collector (GC) cannot relocate the variable. So, you can say that a fixed statement "pins" the variable.

Extension Methods

9.T12 What is an extension method in C#?

Answer:

An extension method tells that you can "add" a custom method to an existing type without creating a new derived type, recompiling, or otherwise modifying the original type. These are static methods but called with instance method syntax.

In 9.P5, 9.P6, 9.P7, and 9.P8, you'll see a detailed discussion on this topic with examples.

Constants in C#

9.T13 How do you deal with constants in C#?

Answer:

In this context, C# supports two special keywords, `const` and `readonly`, to prevent the modification of a field. Still, they have some different characteristics.

First, you need to understand that you can have two types of constants: compile-time constants and runtime constants. You use the `const` keyword for compile-time constants. But you need to be aware of the following restrictions before you use the `const` keyword:

- You can apply `const` to the built-in types (except `System.Object`) only. At the time of this writing, you cannot use them for user-defined types, including `class`, `struct`, and `arrays`.
- You cannot apply them to a method, an event, or a property.
- You can initialize a constant field only at the declaration.

On the contrary, for the runtime constants, you should use the `readonly` keyword. You can assign to a `readonly` field multiple times. You must initialize them in the field declaration or inside a constructor. But you cannot assign a new value to the field once the control comes out from the constructor.

9.T14 What are the advantages of using constants in the program?

Answer:

They are easy to read and modify. You can modify the variable in a single place to reflect the changes across the program. Otherwise, you need to find out each occurrence of the variable across the program. You can understand that this alternative approach is not recommended at all, because it is tedious and error-prone.

9.T15 When should you prefer `readonly` over `const`?

Answer:

In 9.T13, I already told you that `readonly` helps you deal with a runtime constant. In addition, you can apply `readonly` to a static as well as a nonstatic variable, whereas compile-time constants are always static. So, using the `readonly` modifier, different instances of a class can have different values for a field. To understand this, let us consider the following program:

```
Console.WriteLine(new Sample()._flag2);
Console.WriteLine(new Sample()._flag2);

class Sample
{
    // The following line causes the error CS0133
    //public const int _flag1 = new Random().Next();
    public readonly int _flag2 = new Random().Next(500);
}
```

Here is the possible output from this program (it may differ in your system because I've generated the random integers):

```
447
199
```

Notice that in this program, one line is commented out. If you uncomment this line, you will see the following error:

```
CS0133   The expression being assigned to 'Sample._flag1' must be constant.
```

Author's Note: A common use of the `readonly` modifier can be found when you set pieces of information about a software license.

Bonus Q&A

9.T16 I often see people using the terms *boxing/unboxing* and *type casting* interchangeably. Is there any difference?

Answer:

Yes, there is a difference; it may appear confusing, but if you focus on the primary rule, you can easily avoid the confusion. Basically, using these terms, you are telling the outside world that you are trying to convert one type into another, and that is the similarity.

Now let's focus on the specialties of boxing and unboxing. Boxing and unboxing are transformations between value types and object types. With boxing, a copy of the value type from the stack is moved to a heap, and unboxing does the reverse operation. So, you can say that by using boxing you cast a value type to a reference type (and obviously, unboxing is the counterpart of this kind of operation).

But in a broader sense, the word *casting* does not force you to assume the movements of elements between stacks and heaps. For example, when you write something like this:

```
int i = 1;
double d = i;
```

there is no problem, and this is not boxing for sure.

9.T17 I often hear that unboxing is risky. Can you explain the reason behind this statement?

Answer:

This is true not only for unboxing, but any type of downcasting is risky. This is because you may encounter exceptions when you run that code. For example, attempting to unbox a null object causes `NullReferenceException`. Also, if the target object is incompatible, you encounter `InvalidCastException`. So, you need to be careful before you downcast or unbox an object.

Programming Skills

By using the following questions, you can test your programming skills in C#. Note that if I do not mention the namespace, you can assume that all parts of the program belong to the same namespace.

Static Data

9.P1 Can you compile the following code?

```
double length = 15.5;
double breadth = 7;
double area = Rectangle.GetArea(length, breadth);
Console.WriteLine($"The rectangle's area is {area} square
                    units.");
class Rectangle
{
    public static double GetArea(double len, double bre)
    {
        return len * bre;
    }
}
```

Answer:

Yes, this code can compile and run successfully. You'll get the following output:

```
The rectangle's area is 108.5 square units.
```

Explanation:

The `GetArea` method is static. So, instead of creating an instance of the `Rectangle` class, you can access this method through the class name directly. Remember that when a method is marked with the `static` keyword, it belongs to the class as a whole, instead of an instance. Microsoft says the following (see `https://docs.microsoft.com/en-us/dotnet/csharp/language-reference/keywords/static`):

> *Use the static modifier to declare a static member, which belongs to the type itself rather than to a specific object.*

Note Throughout this book, you are seeing the use of `Console.WriteLine(...)`. Have you noticed that `WriteLine` is a static method inside the `Console` class?

9.P2 In 9.P1, if you replace the following line:

```
double area = Rectangle.Area(length, breadth);
```

with the following line:

```
double area = new Rectangle().Area(length, breadth);
```

can you compile the code?

Answer:

No. You'll receive the following compile-time error:

```
CS0176  Member 'Rectangle.GetArea(double, double)' cannot be accessed with
an instance reference; qualify it with a type name instead
```

9.P3 Can you compile the following code?

```
// static class Rectangle
static class Rectangle
{
    public static void CalculateArea()
    {
        Console.WriteLine("The area is shown.");
    }
    public void DisplaySomethingElse()
    {
        Console.WriteLine("Display something (except area).");
    }
}
```

Answer:

No. You'll receive the following compile-time error:

```
CS0708   'DisplaySomethingElse': cannot declare instance members in a
static class
```

Additional note:

The following code segment works fine:

```
// Non-static class Rectangle2
class Rectangle2
{
    // NO ERROR
    public static void CalculateArea()
    {
        Console.WriteLine("The area is shown.");
    }

    public void DisplaySomethingElse()
    {
        Console.WriteLine("Display something (except area).");
    }
}
```

From these code segments, you can see that a static class can contain a `static` method, but it won't contain a nonstatic method. On the contrary, a nonstatic class can contain both categories.

Microsoft's documentation is useful in this context (see `https://docs.microsoft.com/en-us/dotnet/csharp/programming-guide/classes-and-structs/static-classes-and-static-class-members`):

> *Creating a static class is therefore basically the same as creating a class that contains only static members and a private constructor. A private constructor prevents the class from being instantiated. The advantage of using a static class is that the compiler can check to make sure that no instance members are accidentally added. The compiler will guarantee that instances of this class cannot be created.*

9.P4 Can you compile the following code?

```
class Rectangle
{
    readonly int _flag = 20;

    public static void DisplayFlag()
    {
```

```
        Console.WriteLine($"Flag1 is{_flag}");
    }
}
```

Answer:

No. You'll receive the following compile-time error:

```
CS0120  An object reference is required for the non-static field, method,
or property 'Rectangle._flag'
```

Additional Note:

The error message is self-explanatory. You can use any of the following options to remove this compile-time error:

- Make the field static; for example, you can use `static readonly int _flag = 20;`.
- Make the `DisplayFlag` method nonstatic by removing the static modifier.

Using Extension Methods

9.P5 Predict the output of the following code segment:

```
using Extensions;

int flag1 = 15;
int flag2 = flag1.IncrementByFive();
Console.WriteLine($"flag2 is {flag2}");

namespace Extensions
{
    public static class IntExtension
    {
        public static int IncrementByFive(this int i)
        {
            return i + 5;
        }
    }
}
```

Answer:

This code can compile and run successfully. You'll get the following output:

```
flag2 is 20
```

Explanation:

You have seen an example of an extension method. It is a static method, but you can call it with the instance method syntax. So, the following code segment does not cause any errors:

```
int flag1 = 15;
int flag2 = flag1.IncrementByFive();
```

Now notice the extension method closely:

```
public static int IncrementByFive(this int i)
{
  // remaining code skipped
}
```

You can see that the `int` parameter is preceded by the `this` modifier. This means that you are working on the `int` type.

POINT TO NOTE

You may have noticed that I have used the `using` directive. Why? An extension method makes it seem like it is defined in the original type, but actually, that is not the case. It is in scope only when you explicitly import the required namespace. So, if you comment out (or exclude) the following line:

using Extensions;

you'll see a compile-time error that says the following:

CS1061 'int' does not contain a definition for 'IncrementByFive' and no accessible extension method 'IncrementByFive' accepting a first argument of type 'int' could be found (are you missing a using directive or an assembly reference?)

9.P6 Predict the output of the following code segment:

```
using Extensions;
Sample sample = new();
sample.DisplayNumber();
sample.DisplayString();

public class Sample
{
    int _flag = 10;
    public void DisplayNumber()
    {
        Console.WriteLine(_flag);
    }
}

namespace Extensions
{
    public static class SampleExtension
    {
        public static void DisplayString(this Sample s)
        {
            Console.WriteLine(s.ToString());
        }
    }
}
```

Answer:

This code can compile and run successfully. You'll get the following output:

```
10
Sample
```

Additional Note:

This time you have seen an example where an extension method works on a custom type (i.e., `Sample`).

9.P7 Suppose, in the previous program (9.P6), you added one more line of code to the extension method as follows:

```
public static void DisplayString(this Sample s)
{
  Console.WriteLine(s.ToString());
  Console.WriteLine(s._flag);
}
```

Can you predict the output?

Answer:

You'll receive the following compile-time error:

```
CS0122   'Sample._flag' is inaccessible due to its protection level
```

Explanation:

An extension method cannot access the private variables in the type it is extending. This is why by using the extension methods, you do not violate the encapsulation principle.

9.P8 Predict the output of the following code segment:

```
using Extensions;
Sample sample = new();
sample.Display();

public class Sample
{
    public void Display()
    {
        Console.WriteLine("The instance method is called.");
    }
}

namespace Extensions
{
    public static class SampleExtension
    {
        public static void Display(this Sample s)
        {
```

```
            Console.WriteLine("The extension method is called.");
        }
    }
}
```

Answer:

This code can compile and run successfully. You'll get the following output:

```
The instance method is called.
```

Explanation:

Using an extension method, you cannot override the original definition. So, if you have an extension method with the same name and signature as an interface or class method, it'll never be called. Microsoft makes this clear by saying the following (`https://docs.microsoft.com/en-us/dotnet/csharp/programming-guide/classes-and-structs/extension-methods`):

> *When the compiler encounters a method invocation, it first looks for a match in the type's instance methods. If no match is found, it will search for any extension methods that are defined for the type, and bind to the first extension method that it finds.*

Passing the Value-Type by Value

9.P9 Predict the output of the following code segment:

```
Console.WriteLine("Passing a value type by value.");
int flag = 50;
Sample.Change(flag);
Console.WriteLine($"The final value is {flag}");
class Sample
{
   internal static void Change(int x)
    {
      x *= 2;
      Console.WriteLine($"Inside Change(), the value is {x}");
    }
}
```

Answer:

This code can compile and run successfully. You'll get the following output:

```
Passing a value type by value.
Inside Change(), the value is 100
The final value is 50
```

Explanation:

A value type variable directly contains its data, and a reference type variable contains a reference to its data.

So passing a value type variable to a method by value means that you pass a copy to the method. So, if the method makes any change to that copied parameter, it does not affect the original data.

Note If you want the change made by the called method to reflect original data, you need to pass it by reference with either a `ref` keyword or an `out` keyword. You'll see them in the upcoming programs.

Passing the Value-Type by Reference

9.P10 Predict the output of the following code segment:

```
int flag = 50;
Sample.Change(ref flag);
Console.WriteLine($"The final value is {flag}");
class Sample
{
    internal static void Change(ref int x)
    {
      x *= 2;
      Console.WriteLine($"Inside Change(), the value is {x}");
    }
}
```

Answer:

This code can compile and run successfully. You'll get the following output:

```
Inside Change(), the value is 100
The final value is 100
```

Explanation:

This time the changed value is reflected outside the Change() method too. Notice that we have used the ref keyword, which has done the trick. Using ref int x, we are not targeting the value of the integer parameter; rather, it is a reference to the integer (which is the flag variable in this case).

POINTS TO NOTE

You need to initialize the flag variable before you pass it to the Change() method; otherwise, you'll see the following compile-time error:

```
CS0165 Use of unassigned local variable 'flag'
```

9.P11 Predict the output of the following code segment:

```
int flag;
Sample.Change(out flag);
Console.WriteLine($"The final value is {flag}");
class Sample
{
    internal static void Change(out int x)
    {
      x = 100;

      Console.WriteLine($"Inside Change(), the value is {x}");
    }
}
```

Answer:

This code can compile and run successfully. You'll get the following output:

```
Inside Change(), the value is 100
The final value is 100
```

Explanation:

This time you see the use of the out keyword. It also causes arguments to be passed by reference. But, in this program, I did not initialize the flag variable before I pass it to the Change method. So, you understand that this kind of initialization is not mandatory when you use the out keyword (but for ref, it is a must). You may also notice that in the Change method I assigned a value (for the passed parameter) before it came out of the function. It was mandatory because Microsoft says this (https://docs.microsoft.com/en-us/dotnet/csharp/language-reference/keywords/out-parameter-modifier):

> *To use an out parameter, both the method definition and the calling method must explicitly use the out keyword.*

So, if you comment out the x=100; in 9.P11, you'll see the following errors:

```
CS0177   The out parameter 'x' must be assigned to before control leaves
  the current method
CS0269   Use of unassigned out parameter 'x'
```

POINTS TO REMEMBER

For the out parameter, this initialization is not mandatory (but for ref, it is a must). On the other hand, you need to assign a value before it comes out of the function.

Using the is Operator

9.P12 Can you compile the following code?

```
Circle circle = new();
Rectangle rectangle = new();
Console.WriteLine($"Is the circle a special type of shape?
                    {circle is Shape}");
Console.WriteLine($"Is the circle a special type of
                    rectangle? {circle is Rectangle}");
class Shape { }
class Circle : Shape { }
class Rectangle : Shape { }
```

Answer:

This code can compile and run successfully. You'll get the following output:

```
Is the circle a special type of shape? True
Is the circle a special type of rectangle? False
```

Explanation:

The `is` keyword checks if the runtime type of an expression is compatible with a given type. It compares with a given type and returns true if the casting is possible; otherwise, it will return false.

9.P13 Can you compile the following code?

```
double i = 60.5;
object iBoxed = i;
double? jNullable = 40.2;
if (iBoxed is double a && jNullable is double b)
{
    Console.WriteLine($"Result is {a + b}");
}
```

Answer:

This code can compile and run successfully. You'll get the following output:

```
Result is 100.7
```

Explanation:

This example shows the use of a *declaration pattern*. It is useful to check whether the runtime type of an expression is compatible with a given type. You can see that using this pattern, you can declare a new local variable. When a declaration pattern matches an expression, you can assign the expression result to the declared variable. This program demonstrates this usage.

Using as Operator

9.P14 Can you compile the following code?

```
Shape shape = new();
Circle circle = new();
Shape? convertedShape = circle as Shape;
```

```
Console.WriteLine($" The conversion 'circle as Shape' produces
                    {convertedShape}");
Circle? convertedCircle = shape as Circle;
if (convertedCircle == null)
{
    Console.WriteLine($" The conversion 'shape as Circle'
                        produces null.");
}
else
{
    Console.WriteLine($" The conversion 'shape as Circle'
                        produces {convertedCircle}");
}
class Shape { }
class Circle : Shape { }
```

Answer:

This code can compile and run successfully. You'll get the following output:

```
The conversion 'circle as Shape' produces Circle
The conversion 'shape as Circle' produces null.
```

Explanation:

You often see the use of the `as` keyword in the expression `E as T` where `E` is an expression that returns a value and `T` is the name of a type or a type parameter. Using the `as` keyword, you can cast a given object to a specified type if it is convertible; otherwise, it will return null. So, using this keyword, you can check the "conversion possibility" as well as the "actual conversion." The `as` keyword is very helpful because it never throws an exception.

This program shows a common pattern: you compare the result of an `as` expression with `null` to check whether the conversion is successful.

You may note an important point here: starting with C# 7.0, you have got additional flexibility with the `is` keyword. In 9.P13, you saw that you can use the `is` operator both to test whether the conversion succeeds and then to assign its result to a new variable.

9.P15 Can you compile the following code?

```
Circle circle = new();
Shape? shape = circle as Rectangle;
class Shape { }
class Circle : Shape { }
class Rectangle : Shape { }
```

Answer:

No. You'll receive the following compile-time error:

```
CS0039   Cannot convert type 'Circle' to 'Rectangle' via a reference
conversion, boxing conversion, unboxing conversion, wrapping conversion, or
null type conversion
```

Explanation:

The error message is self-explanatory. In addition, I want you to note another important point: the Microsoft documentation says the following (see `https://docs.microsoft.com/en-us/dotnet/csharp/language-reference/operators/type-testing-and-cast#as-operator`):

> *The as operator considers only reference, nullable, boxing, and unboxing conversions. You can't use the as operator to perform a user-defined conversion. To do that, use a cast expression.*

A Method That Returns Multiple Values

9.P16 Can you compile the following code?

```
Console.WriteLine("Testing a method that returns multiple
                   values.");
double radius = 10.0;
double area, perimeter;
string description = string.Empty;
Sample.UpdateDetails(radius, out area, out perimeter,
                     out description);
Console.WriteLine($"The area of the circle is  {area} sq.
                   units.");
```

```
Console.WriteLine($"The perimeter of the circle is {perimeter}
                  units.");
Console.WriteLine($"Description: it is a {description}
                  circle.");
class Sample
{
    public static void UpdateDetails(double x,
                                     out double area,
                                     out double peri,
                                     out string desc)
    {
        area = 3.14 * x * x;
        peri = 2 * 3.14 * x;
        desc = "filled";
    }
}
```

Answer:

This code can compile and run successfully. You'll get the following output:

```
Testing a method that returns multiple values.
The area of the circle is  314 sq. units.
The perimeter of the circle is 62.800000000000004 units.
Description: it is a filled circle.
```

Additional Note:

You have seen a technique that helps you set multiple values using a single method.

Comparing the const and readonly Keywords

9.P17 Can you compile the following code?

```
new Sample().Display();

class Sample
{
    private static readonly int s_flag = 1;
    static Sample()
```

```
    {
        s_flag = 25;
    }
    public void Display()
    {
        Console.WriteLine($"Flag is {s_flag}");
    }
}
```

Answer:

This code can compile and run successfully. You'll get the following output:

```
Flag is 25
```

Explanation:

You are allowed to modify the `readonly` field inside the constructor. Refer to the online documentation (`https://docs.microsoft.com/en-us/dotnet/csharp/language-reference/keywords/readonly`) that states the following:

> *A readonly field can be assigned multiple times in the field declaration and in any constructor. Therefore, readonly fields can have different values depending on the constructor used.*

9.P18 Can you compile the following code?

```
new Sample().Display();
class Sample
{
    private static readonly int s_flag = 1;
    public Sample()
    {
        s_flag = 25;
    }
    public void Display()
    {
        Console.WriteLine($"Flag is {s_flag}");
    }
}
```

Answer:

No. Notice that this time the constructor is not static. You'll receive the following compile-time error:

```
CS0198   A static readonly field cannot be assigned to (except in a static constructor or a variable initializer)
```

9.P19 Can you compile the following code?

```
new Sample().Display();
class Sample
{
    private const int _flag = 1;
    public Sample()
    {
        _flag = 25;
    }
    public void Display()
    {
        Console.WriteLine($"Flag is {_flag}");
    }
}
```

Answer:

No. You'll receive the following compile-time error:

```
CS0131   The left-hand side of an assignment must be a variable, property or indexer
```

Explanation:

Microsoft clearly states the following (`https://docs.microsoft.com/en-us/dotnet/csharp/language-reference/keywords/readonly`):

A const field can only be initialized at the declaration of the field.

9.P20 Can you compile the following code?

```
Console.WriteLine(new Sample()._flag);
class Sample
{
    internal const int _flag = 1;

}
```

Answer:

No. You'll receive the following compile-time error:

```
CS0176	Member 'Sample._flag' cannot be accessed with an instance
reference; qualify it with a type name instead
```

Explanation:

The `_flag` variable is implicitly `static`. So, you cannot access it through an instance reference. Microsoft's online documentation (`https://docs.microsoft.com/en-us/dotnet/csharp/programming-guide/classes-and-structs/constants`) says the following about it:

> *Constants are accessed as if they were static fields because the value of the constant is the same for all instances of the type. You do not use the static keyword to declare them.*

Additional Note:

Note that the following code:

```
internal static const int _flag = 1; // ERROR CS0504
```

will also raise a compile-time error:

```
CS0504	The constant '_flag' cannot be marked static
```

The documentation at `https://docs.microsoft.com/en-us/dotnet/csharp/language-reference/compiler-messages/cs0504?f1url=%3FappId%3Droslyn%26k%3Dk` (`CS0504`) explicitly describes this situation.

> *The constant 'variable' cannot be marked static. If a variable is const, it is also static. If you want a const and static variable, just declare that variable as const; if all you want is a static variable, just mark it static.*

9.P21 Can you predict the output?

```
new Sample().Display();
class Sample
{
    private static readonly int s_flag = 1;
    public void Display()
    {
        s_flag = 25; // ERROR CS0198
```

```
        Console.WriteLine($"Flag is {s_flag}");
    }
}
```

Answer:

You'll receive the following compile-time error:

```
CS0198  A static readonly field cannot be assigned to (except in a static
constructor or a variable initializer)
```

Explanation:

I told you (see 9.T13) that you can assign to a `readonly` field multiple times. But you must initialize them in the field declaration or inside a constructor. You cannot assign a new value to the field once the control comes out from the constructor.

One C# 10 Feature

9.P22 Can you compile the following code?

```
const string Language = "C#";
const string Version = "10.0";
const string Info = "supports constant interpolated strings";
const string Description = $"{Language} {Version} {Info}.";

Console.WriteLine(Description);
```

Answer:

Starting with C# 10, this code can compile and run successfully. You'll get the following output:

```
C# 10.0 supports constant interpolated strings.
```

Additional Note:

If you try to run this code in C#9, there are two types of errors:

```
CS8773  Feature 'constant interpolated strings' is not available in C#
9.0. Please use language version 10.0 or greater.

CS8773  Feature 'global using directive' is not available in C# 9.0.
Please use language version 10.0 or greater.
```

PART III

Advanced C#

Years ago, I attended a course on advanced C#. The instructor started the discussion with delegates. A few years later, I attended a seminar, and it began in the same way. So, we know that delegates are the foundation for advanced C#. But the discussion of delegates is incomplete without events and lambda expressions. These are the integral parts of advanced programming in C#. Part III of this book covers all these topics.

In addition, you'll see big chapters on generics (Chapter 13) and multithreading (Chapter 14). These help you write better and more efficient C# programs. Finally, in Chapter 15), you will learn about some preview features. Reading these chapters will make you confident in C# programming.

I have excluded other advanced topics such as asynchronous programming and LINQ queries from this book to keep the target readers in my mind. Still, Part III is essential to understand advanced features in C#.

PART III

Advanced C#

CHAPTER 10

Delegates

Welcome to Part III of the book. Here you will start reviewing the concept of delegates, which are the foundation for advanced programming in C#. Before we jump into it, let's review some basic stuff.

To create an object, say `obA` from class `A`, you can write something like the following: `A obA=new A();`. Here, `obA` is a reference (often called a *variable*) that points to an object named `A`. Similarly, a delegate is also a reference type, but it points to methods.

Let's understand its significance from another point of view. You know what a variable is and how it behaves. You have seen that you can put different Boolean values (`true`/`false`), strings (or, words), and numbers (integer, double, etc.) in the respective type of variables. But when you use delegates, you can assign a method to a variable and pass it around.

In short, using delegates, you can treat your methods like objects. So, you can store a delegate in a variable, pass it as a method parameter, and return it from a method. This chapter focuses on delegates and covers the following topics:

- Delegates and their uses
- Multicast delegates
- Some commonly used built-in delegates
- Covariance and contravariance using delegates

Let us review and test your understanding of these topics now.

Theoretical Concepts

This section includes the theoretical questions and answers on delegates in C#.

V. Sarcar, *Test Your Skills in C# Programming*, https://doi.org/10.1007/978-1-4842-8655-5_10

Delegates in C#

10.T1 Explain delegates in C# with an example.

Answer:

A delegate is a reference type derived from `System.Delegate`, and its instances are used to call methods with matching signatures. The dictionary meaning of the word *delegate* is "a representative." Therefore, you can say that these delegates represent methods with matching signatures.

POINTS TO NOTE

Delegates are one of the most important concepts in C# programming. I want you to understand them clearly. So, I begin this chapter with a simple demonstration that indicates the core purpose of using a delegate. Before proceeding, keep the following points in your mind:

- If you analyze the IL code, you'll find that once you create a delegate, the C# compiler turns it into a class that is derived from `Delegate`. More specifically, it derives from `MulticastDelegate`, which is derived from `Delegate`. But the delegate types are `sealed`. So, your custom classes cannot derive from `Delegate`.
- The online documentation at `https://docs.microsoft.com/en-us/dotnet/csharp/fundamentals/coding-style/coding-conventions` suggests you use `Func<>` and `Action<>` instead of defining delegate types. You'll experiment with these built-in delegates soon.
- Ideally you should put the delegates and classes inside the namespaces. If you do not follow this convention, you'll see a message from Visual Studio IDE saying: `CA1050 Declare types in namespaces`. What does this mean? It suggests you define types within namespaces to organize your code better. This activity also helps you avoid name collisions. When you declare a type without a namespace, it belongs to the global namespace that cannot be referenced in code.
- Initially, I'll use full syntax for using a delegate. Shortly, you'll see the concise syntax for it.

In the following example, we examine two cases:

- In case 1, you invoke a method without using a delegate.
- In case 2, you invoke the same method using a delegate.

Let's see the program now (I have added some extra comments to show you the alternative syntaxes for using delegates):

```
int a = 25, b = 75;
static int Sum(int a, int b) {
    return a + b;
}

// Case-1
Console.WriteLine("Called the Sum method without using a
                   delegate.");
Console.WriteLine($" a+b={Sum(a, b)}");

// Case-2
Program_10_T1.Calculate del = new
                             Program_10_T1.Calculate(Sum);
// Program_10_T1.Calculate del = new (Sum);// OK
// Also OK. I'll use the following next time onwards.
// Program_10_T1.Calculate del = Sum;

Console.WriteLine("Called the Sum method using a delegate.");
Console.WriteLine($"a+b={del(a, b)}");

//  del(a,b) is shorthand for del.Invoke(a,b)
Console.WriteLine("Called the Sum method using a delegate.
                   Used the Invoke method directly.");
Console.WriteLine($"a+b={del.Invoke(a, b)}");

namespace Program_10_T1
{
    public delegate int Calculate(int x, int y);
}
```

Once you compile and run this program, you'll see the following output:

```
Called the Sum method without using a delegate.
a+b=100
Called the Sum method using a delegate.
a+b=100
Called the Sum method using a delegate. Used the Invoke method directly.
a+b=100
```

You have seen me use the full syntax of a delegate. You can also write an equivalent line of code using the simplified `new` expression syntax. In addition, you can use a condensed syntax that I'll show you next time. Let's look at the equivalent lines of code with supporting comments for your easy reference (excluding the namespace name):

```
Calculate del = new Calculate(Sum); // Using full syntax
Calculate del = new (Sum);// Using simplified new expression
Calculate del = Sum; // Condensed Syntax. I'll use this next time.
```

POINTS TO NOTE

This program shows that `del(a,b)` is the syntactic shortcut for `del.Invoke(a,b)`.

10.T2 Explain the use of a multicast delegate with an example.

Answer:

When you use a delegate to encapsulate multiple methods with matching signatures, you call it a *multicast delegate*. These delegates are subtypes of `System.MulticastDelegate`, which is a subclass of `System.Delegate`. The following program uses a multicast delegate to invoke the methods `DisplaySum` and `DisplayDifference` from a `Sample` class instance:

```
Program_10_T2.MultiDel del = Program_10_T2.Sample.DisplaySum;
del += Program_10_T2.Sample.DisplayDifference;
del += Program_10_T2.Sample.DisplayProduct;
del(90, 10);
```

```
namespace Program_10_T2
{
    public delegate void MultiDel(int x, int y);
    class Sample
    {
        public static void DisplaySum(int a, int b) =>
           Console.WriteLine($"Sum={a + b}");

        public static void DisplayDifference(int a, int b) =>
           Console.WriteLine($"Difference={a - b}");

        public static void DisplayProduct(int a, int b) =>
           Console.WriteLine($"Product={a * b}");
    }
}
```

Once you compile and run this program, you'll see the following output:

```
Sum=100
Difference=80
Product=900
```

POINTS TO NOTE

You can see that I have added methods to the delegate using the += operator. The Visual Studio IDE also suggests that you use this combined assignment. But, you can surely guess that instead of using the combined assignment, you could write something like the following:

del = del+ Program_10_T2.Sample.DisplayDifference;

You can remove a method from this delegate using the -= operator as follows:

del -= Program_10_T2.Sample.DisplayDifference;

Additional Note:

It is useful to know that when you use the +, +=, -, or -= operators in similar cases for a delegate, you actually use the built-in static methods `Combine` and `Remove` from the `Delegate` class. To test this, you can play with the following code segment:

```
Console.WriteLine("\nTesting Combine method.");
Program_10_T2.MultiDel delSum =
                 Program_10_T2.Sample.DisplaySum;
Program_10_T2.MultiDel delDiff =
                 Program_10_T2.Sample.DisplayDifference;
Program_10_T2.MultiDel delProd =
                 Program_10_T2.Sample.DisplayProduct;

Program_10_T2.MultiDel del2 = Delegate.Combine(delSum,
                 delDiff) as Program_10_T2.MultiDel;

Console.WriteLine("\nInvoking del2.");
del2(90, 10);

Program_10_T2.MultiDel del3= Delegate.Combine(del2, delProd)
                  as Program_10_T2.MultiDel;
Console.WriteLine("\nInvoking del3 now.");
del3(90, 10);

Console.WriteLine("\nRemoving one method from the
                   delegate(using Remove method).");
del3 = Delegate.Remove(del3, delProd) as Program_10_T2.MultiDel;
del3(90, 10);
```

This code segment will produce the following output:

```
Testing Combine method.

Invoking del2.
Sum=100
Difference=80

Invoking del3 now.
Sum=100
Difference=80
Product=900

Removing one method from the delegate(using Remove method).
Sum=100
Difference=80
```

10.T3 In the preceding example, the return type of the multicast delegate is void. What is the intention behind this?

Answer:

Normally, you use a multicast delegate to invoke multiple methods together. In C# programming, if you experiment with methods that have a nonvoid return type, you will receive the return value from the last method only. All of the other results are completely ignored. You'll see such a program (10.P7) in the "Programming Skills" section. This is the reason you rarely want to use multicast delegates to invoke methods with nonvoid return types.

10.T4 Does this mean that if you use a nonvoid return type with a multicast delegate, you will not see any compilation error. Is this understanding correct?

Answer:

Yes. As mentioned, in this case, you'll receive the return value from the last method only. If it makes sense to you, you need to write your code accordingly.

10.T5 Can we use delegates to define callback methods?

Answer:

Yes. It is one of the key purposes of using delegates.

10.T6 What is the invocation list of a delegate?

Answer:

A delegate instance encapsulates and maintains a set of methods. This is called the *invocation list,* which may consist of one or more elements. When you call a multicast delegate, the delegates in the invocation list are called synchronously in the order in which they appear. If any error occurs during the execution, it throws an exception.

10.T7 This means if an exception is raised due to a multicast delegate invocation, it is a challenging situation to handle. Is this correct?

Answer:

Absolutely. This is why you need to pay special attention to guarding those situations.

Author's Note: In my book *Getting Started with Advanced C#,* I demonstrated this case with a simple program. Here I leave this exercise to you.

Generic Delegates

Let's review some of the generic delegates. In this section, I'll cover three important built-in generic delegates called Func, Action, and Predicate, which are very common in generic programming. Let's start.

10.T8 Can you name some of the generic delegates in C#? Why are they useful?

Answer:

At the beginning of this chapter, I showed you that Microsoft wants you to use Func<> and Action<> instead of defining delegate types. These are built-in generic delegates. This gives you the clue that though you can create custom delegates, you can avoid this activity because you have built-in support for generic delegates that are very flexible and cover most situations.

10.T9 How does a Func delegate differ from an Action delegate?

Answer:

The Action delegates have a void return type, but the Func delegates have a generic return type.

At the time of this writing, there are 17 overloaded versions of the Func delegate. They can take 0 to 16 input parameters but always have one return type. Here's an example:

```
Func<out TResult>
Func<in T, out TResult>
Func<in T1, in T2,out TResult>
Func<in T1, in T2, in T3, out TResult>
......
Func<in T1, in T2, in T3,in T4, in T5, in T6,in T7,in T8,in T9,in T10,in
  T11,in T12,in T13,in T14,in T15,in T16, out TResult>
```

To understand the usage, let's consider the following method inside the sample class:

```
class Sample
{
  public static int ApproximateTotal(double a, double b)
    {
        // Some other code, if any
        double temp = a + b;
```

```
        return (int)temp;
    }
}
```

In this case, you can use a Func delegate as follows:

```
Func<double, double, int> del = Sample.ApproximateTotal;
Console.WriteLine($"Approximately, the sum of {10.5} and
                  {20.7} is: {del(10.5, 20.7)}");
```

So, in this case, the Func delegate considers all the input arguments (both are double in this example) and returns an int. Now you may be confused and ask which parameter denotes the return type. If you move your cursor over this in the Visual Studio IDE, you can see that the last parameter (TResult) is considered the return type of the function, and the others are considered input types. For example, here are the definitions from Visual Studio:

```
//
// Summary:
//     Encapsulates a method that has two parameters and returns a value of
//     the type specified by the TResult parameter.
//
// Parameters:
//   arg1:
//     The first parameter of the method that this delegate encapsulates.
//
//   arg2:
//     The second parameter of the method that this delegate encapsulates.
//
// Type parameters:
//   T1:
//     The type of the first parameter of the method that this delegate
       encapsulates.
//
//   T2:
//     The type of the second parameter of the method that this delegate
       encapsulates.
```

```
//
//   TResult:
//      The type of the return value of the method that this delegate
        encapsulates.
//
// Returns:
//      The return value of the method that this delegate encapsulates.
public delegate TResult Func<in T1, in T2, out TResult>(T1 arg1, T2 arg2);
```

`Action` delegates can take 1 to 16 input parameters but do not have a return type. The overloaded versions are as follows:

```
Action<in T>
Action<in T1,in T2>
Action<in T1,in T2, in T3>
....
Action<in T1, in T2, in T3,in T4, in T5, in T6,in T7,in T8,in T9,in T10,in
T11,in T12,in T13,in T14,in T15,in T16>
```

For example, if you have a method called `DisplaySum` inside the `Sample` class, this method takes two ints as input parameters whose return types are `void`, as follows:

```
class Sample
{
    public static void DisplaySum(int a, int b)
    {
        Console.WriteLine($"The sum of {a} and {b} is: {a+b}");
        // Some other code, if any
    }

}
```

Now you can use an `Action` delegate to get the sum of two integers, as follows:

```
Action<int, int> actionDel = Sample.DisplaySum;
actionDel(10,20);
```

10.T10 Can you use a Func delegate to point to a method that has a void return type?

Answer:

If you have a method with a void return type, it is recommended that you use an Action delegate to point it. Let's consider the previous code segment:

```
class Sample
{
    public static void DisplaySum(int a, int b)
    {
        Console.WriteLine($"The sum of {a} and {b} is: {a+b}");
        // Some other code, if any
    }
}
```

Now, if, by mistake, you use the following line of code:

```
Func<int, int, void> funcDel2 = Sample.DisplaySum; // Error
```

you'll receive the compile-time error saying the following:

```
CS1547   Keyword 'void' cannot be used in this context
```

10.T11 I have learned that in the case of method overloading, the return type of the methods doesn't matter, but in the context of delegates, it looks like it matters. Is this understanding correct?

Answer:

Yes. It's an important point to remember. Microsoft (https://docs.microsoft.com/en-us/dotnet/csharp/programming-guide/delegates/) says the following about it:

> *In the context of method overloading, the signature of a method does not include the return value. But in the context of delegates, the signature does include the return value. In other words, a method must have the same return type as the delegate.*

10.T12 Methods need to match the delegate types exactly. Is this correct?

Answer:

No. Once you learn about covariance and contravariance, you'll learn that Microsoft provides you flexibility for matching a delegate type.

10.T13 What do you mean by method group variance?

Answer:

Go through the following points:

- *Covariance*: This allows you to pass a derived type where a parent type was expected, and in the case of delegates, you apply this concept to the return types.
- *Contravariance*: This allows you to use a more generic (less derived) type than originally specified. In the case of delegates, you can assign a method with base class parameters to a delegate that expects to get the derived class parameters.
- *Invariance*: This allows you to use only the type originally specified. It's neither covariant nor contravariant.

In C# programing, you often refer to covariance and contravariance collectively as the variance. In the context of delegates, the documentation at `https://docs.microsoft.com/en-us/dotnet/csharp/programming-guide/concepts/covariance-contravariance/variance-in-delegates` briefly says the following:

> *.NET Framework 3.5 introduced variance support for matching method signatures with delegate types in all delegates in C#. This means that you can assign to delegates not only methods that have matching signatures but also methods that return more derived types (covariance) or that accept parameters that have less derived types (contravariance) than that specified by the delegate type. This includes both generic and non-generic delegates.*

You'll experiment with these concepts in the "Programming Skills" section soon.

10.T14 What is a `Predicate` delegate?

Answer:

A `Predicate` delegate is used to evaluate something. For example, let's assume that you have a method that defines some criteria and you need to check whether an object can meet the criteria.

Suppose inside the `Sample` class you have a method to evaluate whether an input is greater than 50:

```
class Sample
{
    public static bool TestGreaterThan50(int input)
    {
        return input > 50;
    }
}
```

You can use the Predicate delegate to perform the test, as follows:

```
Predicate<int> isGreater = Sample.TestGreaterThan50;
Console.WriteLine($"51 is greater than 50? {isGreater(51)}");
Console.WriteLine($"49 is greater than 50? {isGreater(49)}");
```

This code can produce the following output:

```
51 is greater than 50? True
49 is greater than 50? False
```

Programming Skills

By using the following questions, you can test your programming skills in C#. Note that if I do not mention the namespace, you can assume that all parts of the program belong to the same namespace.

Custom Delegates

10.P1 Predict the output of the following code segment:

```
int a = 25, b = 35;
Sample sample = new();

CustomDelegates.MyDel1 del1 = Sample.AddFive;
Console.WriteLine($"{a}+5= {del1(a)}");

CustomDelegates.MyDel2 del2 = sample.AddFive;
Console.WriteLine($"{a}+{b}+5= {del2(a,b)}");
```

```
namespace CustomDelegates
{
    public delegate int MyDel1(int x);
    public delegate int MyDel2(int x, int y);
}

class Sample
{
    public static int AddFive(int a) { return a + 5; }
    public int AddFive(int a, int b) { return a + b + 5; }
}
```

Answer:

This code can compile and run successfully. You'll get the following output:

```
25+5= 30
25+35+5= 65
```

Additional Note:

I have shown you this program to demonstrate these two important points:

- The C# compiler can bind the correct overloaded method.
- Notice that `AddFive(int a){...}` is a static method and `AddFive(int a, int b){...}` is an instance method. So, using delegates, you can point to a static method as well as a nonstatic method.

10.P2 Can you compile the following code?

```
CustomDelegate.MyDel del = Sample.Sum;
Console.WriteLine($"The sum of {10} and {20} is: {del(10)}");

namespace CustomDelegate
{
    public delegate int MyDel(int x, int y);
}
```

```
class Sample
{
    public static int Sum(int a, int b)
    {
        Console.WriteLine("The Sum method of the Sample class
                                is invoked.");
        return a + b;
    }
}
```

Answer:

No. You'll receive the following compile-time error:

```
CS7036   There is no argument given that corresponds to the required formal
parameter 'y' of 'MyDel'
```

Explanation:

The error is easy to understand: to invoke the `Sum` method, you need to pass the second argument too. For example, the following code can invoke the intended method properly:

```
Console.WriteLine($"The sum of {10} and {20} is: {del(10,20)}");
```

So, you understand that when you want to pass any method to a delegate, the delegate signature and the method signature need to match. For this reason, they are often called *type-safe function pointers*.

10.P3 Predict the output of the following code segment:

```
class Sample: System.Delegate
{
    // Some code
}
```

Answer:

No. You'll receive the following compile-time error:

```
CS0644   'Sample' cannot derive from special class 'Delegate'
```

Explanation:

Microsoft's online documentation at https://docs.microsoft.com/en-us/dotnet/csharp/misc/cs0644?f1url=%3FappId%3Droslyn%26k%3Dk(CS0644) says the following:

> *Classes cannot explicitly inherit from any of the following base classes: System.Enum, System.ValueType, System.Delegate, and System.Array. These are used as implicit base classes by the compiler.*

Multicast Delegates

10.P4 Can you compile the following code?

```
Program_10_P4.MultiDel multiDel = Program_10_P4.Sample.Show1;
multiDel += Program_10_P4.Sample.Show2;
multiDel += Program_10_P4.Sample.Show3;
multiDel();
namespace Program_10_P4
{
    public delegate void MultiDel();

    class Sample
    {
        public static void Show1()
        {
            Console.WriteLine("Show1() is called.");
        }
        public static void Show2()
        {
            Console.WriteLine("Show2() is called.");
        }
        public static void Show3()
        {
            Console.WriteLine("Show3() is called.");
        }

    }
}
```

Answer:

Yes, this code can compile and run successfully. You'll get the following output:

```
Show1() is called.
Show2() is called.
Show3() is called.
```

Explanation:

You have seen an example of a multicast delegate. When a delegate is used to encapsulate more than one method of a matching signature, you call it a *multicast delegate.*

Author's Note: You may remember that `System.MulticastDelegate` inherits from `System.Delegate`.

10.P5 Predict the output of the following code segment:

```
Action multiDel = Program_10_P5.Sample.Show1;
multiDel += Program_10_P5.Sample.Show2;
multiDel += Program_10_P5.Sample.Show3;
multiDel();
namespace Program_10_P5
{
    public delegate void MultiDel();

    class Sample
    {
        public static void Show1()
        {
            Console.WriteLine("Show1() is called.");
        }
        public static void Show2()
        {
            Console.WriteLine("Show2() is called.");
        }
        public static void Show3()
        {
            Console.WriteLine("Show3() is called.");
        }

    }
}
```

Answer:

The program segments of 10.P4 and 10.P5 are the same (the name of the namespace is changed only to match the question number); the only difference is that you have used the built-in Action delegate instead of the custom delegate that was used in 10.P4. As a result, you will see the same output as in 10.P4.

```
Show1() is called.
Show2() is called.
Show3() is called.
```

Generic Delegates

10.P6 Can you compile the following code?

```
Func<double,double,int> del = Sample.Sum;
Console.WriteLine($"Approximately, the sum of {10.5} and
                    {20.7} is: {del(10.5, 20.7)}");
class Sample
{
    public static int Sum(double a, double b)
    {
        Console.WriteLine("The Sum method of the Sample class
                           is invoked.");
        double temp = a + b;
        return (int)temp;
    }
}
```

Answer:

Yes, this code can compile and run successfully. You'll get the following output:

```
The Sum method of the Sample class is invoked.
Approximately, the sum of 10.5 and 20.7 is: 31
```

Explanation:

This time you have seen an example of a built-in Func delegate. Notice that the Sum method accepts two double types as the arguments and returns the result as an int. So, I have used Func<double, double, int> (the last type indicates the return type). I know what you are thinking: yes, this is not great code. I intentionally typecast the double to an int to match the return type. It is because I wanted to use a different return type to help you not to be confused with other parameters in the Func delegate.

10.P7 Can you compile the following code?

```
Func<int, int, int> del = Program_10_P7.Sample.Sum;
del += Program_10_P7.Sample.Difference;
int finalValue = del(10, 5);
Console.WriteLine($"The final value is {finalValue}");

namespace Program_10_P7
{
    class Sample
    {
        public static int Sum(int a, int b)
        {
            return a + b;
        }
        public static int Difference(int a, int b)
        {
            return a - b;
        }
    }
}
```

Answer:

This code can compile and run successfully. You'll get the following output:

```
The final value is 5
```

Explanation:

You have seen that to compile and run a program that uses a multicast delegate, you don't need to use the methods that have the void return type only. But the problem is that if you code like this, then you get the value from the last invoked method in the invocation/calling chain. All other return values are discarded in between, but there will be no alert for you. Therefore, it is suggested that you experiment with a multicast delegate for the methods that have `void` return types.

Variance in Delegates

10.P8 Can you compile the following code?

```
Prog_10_P8.Vehicle vehicleOb = new();
Prog_10_P8.Bus busOb = new ();
Func<Prog_10_P8.Vehicle> del = vehicleOb.CreateVehicle;
del();
del = busOb.CreateBus;
del();

namespace Prog_10_P8
{
    class Vehicle
    {
        Vehicle? vehicle;
        public Vehicle CreateVehicle()
        {
            vehicle = new Vehicle();
            Console.WriteLine("One vehicle is created.");
            return vehicle;
        }
    }
    class Bus : Vehicle
    {
        Bus? bus;
        public Bus CreateBus()
        {
            bus = new Bus();
            Console.WriteLine("One bus is created.");
            return bus;
        }
    }
}
```

Answer:

Yes, this code can compile and run successfully. You'll get the following output:

```
One vehicle object is created.
One bus object is created.
```

Explanation:

The first line of the output is easy to understand. There is no magic. But the second line of output is interesting. So, look at this line of code again:

```
del = busOb.CreateBus;
```

You can see that the compiler did not complain about this line because of the covariance support for delegates.

10.P9 Can you compile the following code?

```
Prog_10_P9.Vehicle myVehicle = new();
Prog_10_P9.Bus myBus = new();
// Normal case
Action<Prog_10_P9.Bus> del = Prog_10_P9.Bus.ShowBus;
del(myBus);
// Testing contravariance
del = Prog_10_P9.Vehicle.ShowVehicle;
del(myBus);

namespace Prog_10_P9
{
    class Vehicle
    {
        public static void ShowVehicle(Vehicle myVehicle)
        {
            Console.WriteLine("ShowVehicle is called.");
            Console.WriteLine("This is a generic vehicle.\n");
        }
    }
    class Bus : Vehicle
    {
```

```
        public static void ShowBus(Bus myBus)
        {
            Console.WriteLine("ShowBus is called.");
            Console.WriteLine("This is a bus.\n");
        }
    }
}
```

Answer:

Yes, this code can compile and run successfully. You'll get the following output:

```
ShowBus is called.
This is a bus.

ShowVehicle is called.
This is a generic vehicle.
```

Explanation:

The first two lines of the output are easy to understand. There is no magic. But the next two lines are interesting. So, notice the line of code again:

```
del = Prog_10_P9.Vehicle.ShowVehicle;
```

The `ShowVehicle` method accepts a `Vehicle` object, but not a `Bus` object as a parameter; still, the delegate can point to it. The compiler did not complain about this line due to the contravariance support for delegates.

Delegate Compatibility

10.P10 Can you compile the following code?

```
Prog_10_P10.MyDel1 del1 = Prog_10_P10.Sample.Sum;
Prog_10_P10.MyDel2 del2 = del1;

namespace Prog_10_P10
{
    public delegate int MyDel1(int x, int y);
    public delegate int MyDel2(int x, int y);
```

```
    class Sample
    {
        public static int Sum(int a, int b)
        {
            Console.WriteLine("The Sum method is invoked.");
            return a + b;
        }
    }
}
```

Answer:

No. You'll receive the following compile-time error:

```
CS0029   Cannot implicitly convert type 'Prog_10_P10.MyDel1' to 'Prog_10_
P10.MyDel2'
```

Explanation:

The delegate types are all incompatible with one another, even if their signatures are the same. It is interesting to note that if you write the following:

```
// The following is OK
Prog_10_P10.MyDel2 del2 = new Prog_10_P10.MyDel2(del1);
```

this time C# compiler will not raise any compile-time error.

CHAPTER 11

Events

The support for events is considered one of the most exciting features in C#. It is useful because you can send notifications from one code segment to another code segment by using events. These are common in GUI applications such as when you fill in an online form or click the submit button and then notice some interesting change in the UI (for example, you may see a pop-up message saying that the data was submitted properly). The Visual Studio IDE provides a lot of support when your code deals with events. Since these concepts are at the core of C#, it's good to learn them well. So, before we jump into the Q&A sessions, I suggest you read the following points:

- Delegates are the backbones of events. See Microsoft's online documentation at `https://docs.microsoft.com/en-us/dotnet/csharp/programming-guide/events/how-to-implement-custom-event-accessors` where it says: "*An event is a special kind of multicast delegate that can only be invoked from within the class that it is declared in.*" So, it will be helpful for you to learn about delegates before you play with events.

- In an event-driven program, you notice a publisher-subscriber model where one object raises a notification (event) and one or multiple objects listen to those events. The object that raises the event is called the *sender* (or publisher or broadcaster), and the object that receives the event is called the *receiver* (or, a subscriber).

- A sender does not care about how the receivers interpret the events. The sender also does not care about who is registering or unregistering to get their events or notifications.

- You can relate this model to Facebook or Twitter. If you follow someone, you can get notifications when that person updates something in their profile. If you do not want to get notifications,

V. Sarcar, *Test Your Skills in C# Programming*, https://doi.org/10.1007/978-1-4842-8655-5_11

you can always unsubscribe. In short, a subscriber can decide when to start listening to events and when to stop listening to events. (In programming terms, you can specify when to register for events and when to unregister the events.)

- The publisher is the type that contains the delegate. Subscribers register themselves by using += on the publisher's delegate and unregister themselves by using -= on that delegate. So, when we apply += or -= to an event, it has a special meaning (in other words, in those contexts, these are not shortcuts for assignments).
- Subscribers do not communicate with each other. As a result, you can make a loosely coupled system. It is often the key goal in an event-driven architecture.
- You will often see the use of a built-in `EventHandler` delegate (or its generic version). It is a predefined delegate made for simple events. This delegate has a return type of `void` and has two parameters, a nullable object, which is the "sender" of the event, and an `EventArgs` object. The `EventArgs` object stores some basic information about the event itself. I am showing its definition from Visual Studio for your immediate reference:

  ```
  public delegate void EventHandler(object? sender,
  EventArgs e);
  ```
- It is also interesting to know that to support backward compatibility, many events in the .NET Framework follow the nongeneric custom delegate pattern.
- Here is an example of an event declaration:

  ```
  public event EventHandler FlagChanged;
  ```
- This simply indicates that `FlagChanged` is the name of the event and `EventHandler` is the corresponding delegate.

You can note that the modifier need not be public always. You may choose other nonpublic modifiers such as `private`, `protected`, and `internal` for your event. You can also use keywords such as `static`, `virtual`, `override`, `abstract`, `sealed`, and `new` in this context.

This chapter helps you to review your understanding of events and discusses the following:

- Events creation and their uses
- How to pass data when an event is raised
- Use of event accessors
- Use of interface events (both implicit and explicit)
- Simplified coding with events

Let us test your understanding of these topics now.

Theoretical Concepts

This section includes the theoretical questions and answers on C# events.

Understanding Events

11.T1 Explain a simple program to demonstrate the use of an event.

Answer:

Before you see the complete program, I want you to review the following discussions and code explanations.

Before you declare the event, you need a delegate. But you won't see the delegate declaration in this program. This is because I have used the predefined delegate `EventHandler`. Here is the code for the event declaration:

```
public event EventHandler? FlagChanged;
```

Now let's focus on our implementation. Here you'll see two classes, `Sender` and `Receiver`, and two objects called `sender` and `receiver`. You can easily guess that the `sender` is a `Sender` class object and the `receiver` is a `Receiver` class object. As per the names, `Sender` plays the role of the broadcaster and raises the event `FlagChanged` when you change the instance value `_flag` using the public property `Flag` as follows:

```
sender.Flag = 1;
```

The `Receiver` class plays the role of the consumer. It has a method called `GetNotification`. To get a notification from the sender, you'll notice the use of the following code with supporting comments:

```
// Receiver registers for a notification from the sender
sender.FlagChanged += receiver.GetNotification;
```

After some time, the receiver does not show any interest to get further notifications from the sender. So, it unsubscribes the event using the following code:

```
// Unregistering now
sender.FlagChanged -= receiver.GetNotification;
```

Now the question is: how do you raise this event? In legacy code, you might see the following format to raise an event:

```
if (FlagChanged != null)
{
   FlagChanged(this, EventArgs.Empty);
}
```

Let us analyze this code. It checks whether the event is null. If so, there is no event handler attached to this event. This check is important because raising an event with no event handlers results in a `NullReferenceException` (you can check this by commenting out `if (FlagChanged != null)` in the upcoming program).

Once you know an event has event handlers attached to it, you can raise it by calling this event with the parameters required by the delegate. For example, in this case, you need to pass a reference to the sender (`this`) and an `EventArgs` object (though you have used the static `EventArgs.Empty` object in this case).

Here is the complete program (use the comments for your reference):

```
Console.WriteLine("---10.T1---");
Sender sender = new();
Receiver receiver = new();
// Receiver registers for a notification from sender
sender.FlagChanged += receiver.GetNotification;

Console.WriteLine("Setting the flag to 1.");
sender.Flag = 1;
```

```
Console.WriteLine("Setting the flag to 2.");
sender.Flag = 2;
// Unregistering now
sender.FlagChanged -= receiver.GetNotification;
Console.WriteLine("Setting the flag to 3.");
// No notifications sent for the receiver now.
sender.Flag = 3;
Console.WriteLine("Setting the flag to 4.");
sender.Flag = 4;
class Sender
{
    private int _flag;
    public int Flag
    {
        get
        {
            return _flag;
        }
        set
        {
            _flag = value;
            OnFlagChanged();
        }
    }
    public event EventHandler? FlagChanged;
    public void OnFlagChanged()
    {
        if (FlagChanged != null)
        {
            FlagChanged(this, EventArgs.Empty);
        }
        // Simplified form:
        // FlagChanged?.Invoke(this, EventArgs.Empty);
    }
}
```

```
class Receiver
{
    public void GetNotification(object? sender,
                                System.EventArgs e)
    {
        Console.WriteLine($"ALERT: The flag value is changed
                            in the Sender.");
    }
}
```

Once you compile and run this program, you'll see the following output:

```
Setting the flag to 1.
ALERT: The flag value is changed in the Sender.
Setting the flag to 2.
ALERT: The flag value is changed in the Sender.
Setting the flag to 3.
Setting the flag to 4.
```

POINT TO NOTE

Starting now, to avoid Visual Studio's message of `IDE1005 Delegate invocation can be simplified`, you'll see a simplified version of this code segment, as shown here:

```
// Simplified form.
FlagChanged?.Invoke(this, EventArgs.Empty);
```

11.T2 Can I use any arbitrary method for a specific event?

Answer:

No. It should match the delegate's signature. For example, let's assume that the `Receiver` class has another method, called `UnRelatedMethod`, as follows:

```
public void UnRelatedMethod()
{
   Console.WriteLine(" An unrelated method. ");
}
```

Now, in the previous demonstration, if you want to attach this method to `FlagChanged` using the following statement:

```
sender.FlagChanged += receiver.UnRelatedMethod; //Error
```

you'll receive the following compile-time error:

CS0123 No overload for 'UnRelatedMethod' matches delegate 'EventHandler'

Different Aspects of Using Events

11.T3 What are the key benefits of using user-defined event accessors?

Answer:

You'll see an example of event accessors in 11.P3. There I wrote the following:

> *These event accessors are similar to property accessors except they are named* `add` *and* `remove`*. In normal cases, you do not need to supply custom event accessors. But when you define them, you are instructing the C# compiler not to generate the default field and accessors for you.*

When you look closely at these accessors, you'll understand that *by* using these constructs you *create* a property-like wrapper around your delegate. As a result, you have better control over your code. These are also useful when you explicitly implement an interface that contains an event. The program that is discussed in 11.P5 shows you an example of this.

11.T4 How can my class implement multiple interfaces when the interface events have the same name?

Answer:

Yes, this situation is interesting, and you can follow the explicit interface implementation technique. But there is one important restriction for you. It says that you need to supply the `add` and `remove` event accessors in such a case. Normally, the compiler supplies these accessors for you, but, in this case, it cannot.

11.T5 I understand that delegates are the backbone for events, and in general, you follow an Observer design pattern when you write code for events and register and unregister those events. Is this understanding correct?

Answer:

Design patterns are advanced concepts, and you can refer to the book *Design Patterns in C#* (2nd edition) to learn more about them. But if you know them already, the answer to this question is yes.

11.T6 In some event-driven programs, I see the `new` keyword. What is this for?

Answer:

The first thing to understand is that throughout this chapter, I have used the short form for registering an event. For example, in 11.T1, you saw the following line of code when I registered the event:

```
sender.FlagChanged += receiver.GetNotification;
```

Now if you recall the short form used in the context of delegates from Chapter 10, you can understand that you can write equivalent code as follows:

```
sender.FlagChanged += new EventHandler(receiver.GetNotification);
```

Consider another case in which your sender class contains a sealed event. In this case, you cannot modify the event in a derived class. Instead, the derived class can use the `new` keyword to indicate that it is not overriding the base class event.

11.T7 I understand that `EventHandler` is a predefined delegate. But in many places, I've seen people use the term *event handler* in a broad sense. Is there any special meaning associated with it?

Answer:

Simply, an event handler is a procedure, and you decide what to do when a specific event is raised (for example, when the user clicks a button in a GUI application). It is important to note that your event can have multiple handlers, and at the same time, the method that handles the event can also change dynamically. In this chapter, you'll see program segments that give you the idea; they show how the events work and, particularly, how a receiver class handles them. But if you use a readymade construct like Windows Forms Designer in Visual Studio, you can code events easily.

Programming Skills

Using the following questions, you can test your programming skills in C#. Note that if I do not mention the namespace, you can assume that all parts of the program belong to the same namespace.

Using a Built-in Event

11.P1 Can you compile the following code?

```
Sender sender = new();
// Sender will receive its own notification now onwards.
sender.FlagChanged += sender.SelfNotification;
Console.WriteLine("Setting the flag to 1.");
sender.Flag = 1;
Console.WriteLine("Setting the flag to 2.");
sender.Flag = 2;

class Sender
{
    private int _flag;
    public int Flag
    {
        get
        {
            return _flag;
        }
        set
        {
            _flag = value;
            OnFlagChanged();
        }
    }

    public event EventHandler? FlagChanged;
    public void OnFlagChanged()
    {
        FlagChanged?.Invoke(this, EventArgs.Empty);
    }

    public void SelfNotification(object? sender, System.EventArgs e)
    {
```

```
        Console.WriteLine($"Personal ALERT: The flag becomes {_flag}.");
    }
}
```

Answer:

Yes, this code can compile and run successfully. You'll get the following output:

```
Setting the flag to 1.
Personal ALERT: The flag becomes 1.
Setting the flag to 2.
Personal ALERT: The flag becomes 2.
```

Explanation:

This program demonstrates that a sender can send a self-notification too.

Passing Data with Events

11.P2 Predict the output of the following code segment:

```
Sender sender = new();
Receiver receiver = new();
// Receiver registers for a notification from sender
sender.FlagChanged += receiver.GetNotification;

Console.WriteLine("Setting the flag to 1.");
sender.Flag = 1;
Console.WriteLine("Setting the flag to 2.");
sender.Flag = 2;

// Using this class to pass an event argument.
class FlagEventArgs
{
    int _currentFlag;
    public int CurrentFlag
    {
        get { return _currentFlag; }
        set { _currentFlag = value; }
    }
}
```

```
class Sender
{
    public delegate void FlagChangedEventHandler(object?
                            sender, FlagEventArgs eventArgs);
    public event FlagChangedEventHandler? FlagChanged;

    private int _flag;
    public int Flag
    {
        get
        {
            return _flag;
        }
        set
        {
            _flag = value;
            OnFlagChanged();
        }
    }
    public void OnFlagChanged()
    {
        FlagEventArgs flagEventArgs = new ();
        flagEventArgs.CurrentFlag = _flag;
        FlagChanged?.Invoke(this, flagEventArgs);
    }
}

class Receiver
{
  public void GetNotification(object? sender, FlagEventArgs e)
   {
     Console.WriteLine($"ALERT: The flag value is changed
                          to {e.CurrentFlag}.");
    }
}
```

Answer:

This code can compile and run successfully. You'll get the following output:

```
Setting the flag to 1.
ALERT: The flag value is changed to 1.
Setting the flag to 2.
ALERT: The flag value is changed to 2.
```

Explanation:

This program uses a custom delegate and shows you how to pass data to an event. It is also important to note that often you subclass from the EventArgs class to do this.

Additional Note:

If you'd like to use built-in delegates in your program, you can replace the following two lines of code:

```
public delegate void FlagChangedEventHandler(object? sender,
                                   FlagEventArgs eventArgs);
public event FlagChangedEventHandler? FlagChanged;
```

with this single line of code:

```
public event Action<object?,FlagEventArgs>? FlagChanged;
```

to get the same output. In this case, the built-in Action delegate makes your programming easy.

But my favorite approach is to use the generic version of an Event delegate. This delegate has the following definition:

```
public delegate void EventHandler<TEventArgs>(object? sender,
                                              TEventArgs e);
```

Why is this useful? It is useful because the use of this generic version can also help me to get the same output, and this single line of code can replace the two lines of code (shown in the comments) as follows:

```
//public delegate void FlagChangedEventHandler(object? sender,
                                   FlagEventArgs eventArgs);
//public event FlagChangedEventHandler? FlagChanged;
public event EventHandler<FlagEventArgs>? FlagChanged;
```

Event Accessors

11.P3 Predict the output of the following code segment:

```
Sender sender = new();
Receiver receiver = new();
// Receiver registers for a notification from sender
Console.WriteLine("Registering the notification event.");
sender.FlagChanged += receiver.GetNotification;

Console.WriteLine("Setting the flag to 1.");
sender.Flag = 1;
Console.WriteLine("Unregistering the event.");
sender.FlagChanged -= receiver.GetNotification;

class FlagEventArgs
{
    int _currentFlag;
    public int CurrentFlag
    {
        get { return _currentFlag; }
        set { _currentFlag = value; }
    }
}

class Sender
{
    public delegate void FlagChangedEventHandler(object?
                            sender, FlagEventArgs eventArgs);
    private event FlagChangedEventHandler? InnerFlagChanged;
    public event FlagChangedEventHandler? FlagChanged
    {
        add
        {
            Console.WriteLine("The entry point of the add
                                 accessor.");
            InnerFlagChanged += value;
        }
```

```
        remove
        {
            InnerFlagChanged -= value;
            Console.WriteLine("The exit point of the remove accessor.");
        }
    }

    private int _flag;
    public int Flag
    {
        get
        {
            return _flag;
        }
        set
        {
            _flag = value;
            OnFlagChanged();
        }
    }
    public void OnFlagChanged()
    {
        FlagEventArgs flagEventArgs = new();
        flagEventArgs.CurrentFlag = _flag;
        InnerFlagChanged?.Invoke(this, flagEventArgs);
    }
}

class Receiver
{
  public void GetNotification(object? sender, FlagEventArgs e)
  {
     Console.WriteLine($"\nALERT: The flag value is changed to
                                                {e.CurrentFlag}.");
  }
}
```

Answer:

This code can compile and run successfully. You'll get the following output:

```
Registering the notification event.
The entry point of the add accessor.
Setting the flag to 1.

ALERT: The flag value is changed to 1.
 Unregistering the event.
 The exit point of the remove accessor.
```

Additional Note:

This program shows you the use of event accessors in a program. I want you to note some other typical points about this program. First, notice the name of the private event in the following line:

```
private event FlagChangedEventHandler? InnerFlagChanged;
```

Visual Studio IDE suggests you use Pascal casing to name the private events too. So, I have named it accordingly.

Generic programming lovers can use the built-in `Action` delegate (instead of using a custom delegate that is shown in this program) to produce the same output. You can refer to the following code segment as a sample:

```
// public delegate void FlagChangedEventHandler(object?
                                sender, FlagEventArgs eventArgs);
// private event FlagChangedEventHandler? InnerFlagChanged;
// public event FlagChangedEventHandler? FlagChanged
private event Action<object?, FlagEventArgs>? InnerFlagChanged;
public event Action<object?, FlagEventArgs>? FlagChanged
 {
   add
    {
     // The remaining code is skipped
```

These event accessors are similar to property accessors except they are named add and remove. Earlier I told you that in normal cases, you do not need to supply custom event accessors. But you define them to instruct the C# compiler not to generate the default field and accessors for your program.

To verify this, consider the program 11.P1 where you did not specify these accessors. But, in the IL code, you can see the presence of add_<EventName> and remove_<EventName>. Figure 11-1 shows a partial snapshot.

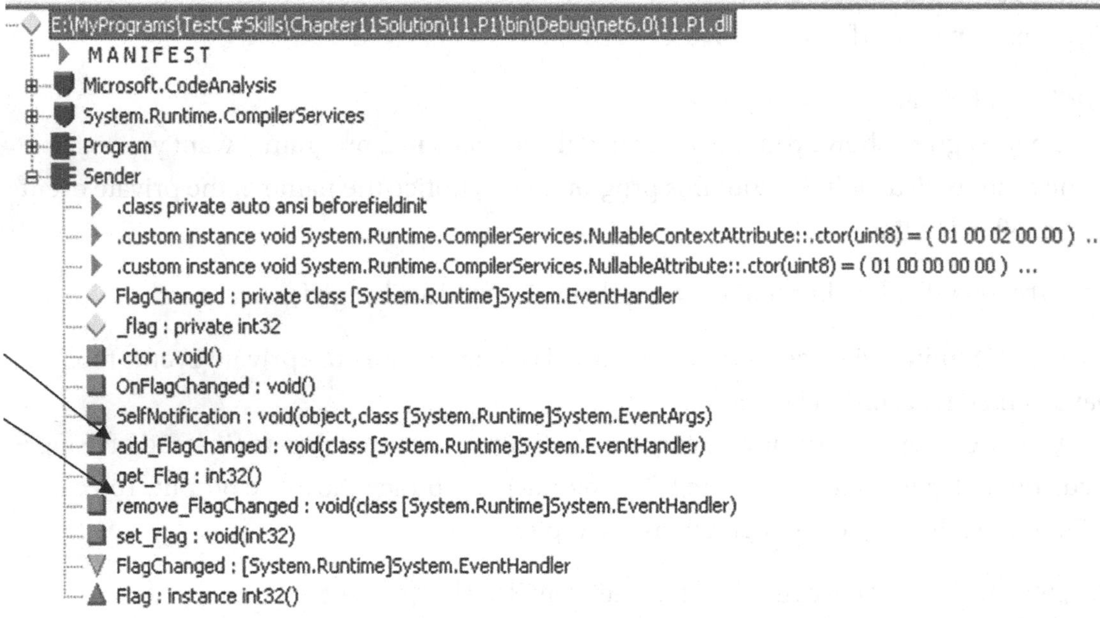

Figure 11-1. *Partial snapshot of IL code for program 11.P1*

POINT TO REMEMBER

The documentation at https://docs.microsoft.com/en-us/dotnet/csharp/programming-guide/events/how-to-implement-custom-event-accessors says the following:

> *Although you can substitute any code inside the accessors, we recommend that you lock the event before you add or remove a new event handler method.*

In general, locking operations are expensive. To make these examples simple, I have ignored this suggestion in this chapter.

Interface Events

11.P4 Predict the output of the following code segment:

```
Sender sender = new ();
Receiver receiver = new();
// Receiver registers for a notification from the sender
sender.FlagChanged += receiver.GetNotification;
Console.WriteLine("Setting the flag to 1.");
sender.Flag = 1;
Console.WriteLine("Setting the flag to 2.");
sender.Flag = 2;
// Unregistering now
sender.FlagChanged -= receiver.GetNotification;
interface ISender
{
    event EventHandler? FlagChanged;
}
class Sender:ISender
{
    private int _flag;
    public int Flag
    {
        get
        {
            return _flag;
        }
        set
        {
            _flag = value;
            OnFlagChanged();
        }
    }

    public event EventHandler? FlagChanged;
```

```
    public void OnFlagChanged()
    {
        FlagChanged?.Invoke(this, EventArgs.Empty);
    }
}
class Receiver
{
    public void GetNotification(object? sender, System.EventArgs e)
    {
        Console.WriteLine($"ALERT: The flag value is changed
                                in the Sender.");
    }
}
```

Answer:

This code can compile and run successfully. You'll get the following output:

```
Setting the flag to 1.
ALERT: The flag value is changed in the Sender.
Setting the flag to 2.
ALERT: The flag value is changed in the Sender.
```

Explanation:

Similar to implementing an interface method or property, this program implements an interface event.

11.P5 Predict the output of the following code segment:

```
Sender sender = new();
Receiver receiver = new();
// Receiver registers for a notification from the sender
((ISender)sender).FlagChanged += receiver.GetNotification;
Console.WriteLine("Setting the flag to 1.");
sender.Flag = 1;
Console.WriteLine("Setting the flag to 2.");
sender.Flag = 2;
```

```
// Unregistering now
((ISender)sender).FlagChanged -= receiver.GetNotification;
interface ISender
{
    event EventHandler? FlagChanged;
}
class Sender : ISender
{
    private int _flag;
    public int Flag
    {
        get
        {
            return _flag;
        }
        set
        {
            _flag = value;
            OnFlagChanged();
        }
    }
    private event EventHandler? FlagChanged;
    event EventHandler? ISender.FlagChanged
    {
        add
        {
            Console.WriteLine(" The entry point of the add
                                accessor.");
            FlagChanged += value;
        }

        remove
        {
            FlagChanged -= value;
```

```
            Console.WriteLine(" The exit point of the remove
                                   accessor.");
        }
    }
    public void OnFlagChanged()
    {
        FlagChanged?.Invoke(this, EventArgs.Empty);
    }
}
class Receiver
{
    public void GetNotification(object? sender,
                                    System.EventArgs e)
    {
        Console.WriteLine($"ALERT: The flag value is changed
                                in the Sender.");
    }
}
```

Answer:

This code can compile and run successfully. You'll get the following output:

```
The entry point of the add accessor.
Setting the flag to 1.
ALERT: The flag value is changed in the Sender.
Setting the flag to 2.
ALERT: The flag value is changed in the Sender.
The exit point of the remove accessor.
```

Explanation:

This time you have implemented the interface explicitly.

Bonus Questions

11.P6 Can you compile the following code?

```
Sender sender = new();
Receiver receiver = new();
// Receiver registers for a notification from the sender
sender.FlagChanged += receiver.GetNotification;

Console.WriteLine("Setting the flag to 5.");
sender.Flag = 5;
Console.WriteLine("Setting the flag to 7.");
sender.Flag = 7;

// Using this class to pass an event argument.
class FlagEventArgs:System.EventArgs
{
    int _currentFlag;
    public int CurrentFlag
    {
        get { return _currentFlag; }
        set { _currentFlag = value; }
    }
}

class Sender
{
    public event EventHandler<FlagEventArgs>? FlagChanged;

    private int _flag;
    public int Flag
    {
        get
        {
            return _flag;
        }
```

```
        set
        {
            _flag = value;
            OnFlagChanged();
        }
    }
    public void OnFlagChanged()
    {
        FlagEventArgs flagEventArgs = new();
        flagEventArgs.CurrentFlag = _flag;
        FlagChanged?.Invoke(this, flagEventArgs);
    }
}

class Receiver
{
  public void GetNotification(object? sender,FlagEventArgs e)
  {
    Console.WriteLine($"ALERT: The flag value is changed to
                                                {e.CurrentFlag}.");
  }
}
```

Answer:

Yes, this code can compile and run successfully. You'll get the following output:

```
Setting the flag to 5.
ALERT: The flag value is changed to 5.
Setting the flag to 7.
ALERT: The flag value is changed to 7.
```

Additional Note:

This program shows you a common pattern for an event-driven program. Notice that `FlagEventArgs` derives from `System.EventArgs`, and I have used the generic version of the `EventHandler` delegate to pass the event data.

11.P7 Can you compile the following code?

```
class FlagEventArgs
{
    int _currentFlag;
    public int CurrentFlag
    {
        get { return _currentFlag; }
        set { _currentFlag = value; }
    }
}

abstract class ParentSender
{
    public abstract event EventHandler<FlagEventArgs>?
                                              FlagChanged;

}

class Sender:ParentSender
{
    public override event EventHandler<FlagEventArgs>?
                                               FlagChanged;
    // The remaining code skipped
}

// The receiver class and other code skipped
```

Answer:

Yes. I told you that you can mark an event with different keywords such as `static`, `virtual`, `override`, `abstract`, `sealed`, and `new`.

11.P8 Predict the output of the following code segment:

```
class FlagEventArgs:EventArgs
{
    int _currentFlag;
    public int CurrentFlag
    {
```

```
        get { return _currentFlag; }
        set { _currentFlag = value; }
    }
}

class ParentSender2
{
 public virtual event EventHandler<FlagEventArgs>? FlagChanged;
}

class ParentSender3:ParentSender2
{
 public sealed event EventHandler<FlagEventArgs>? FlagChanged;
}

// The receiver class and other code skipped
```

Answer:

No. You'll receive the following compile-time error:

```
CS0238   'ParentSender3.FlagChanged' cannot be sealed because it is not an
override
```

Explanation:

The error is self-explanatory. The following line can remove this compile-time error:

```
public override sealed event EventHandler<FlagEventArgs>? FlagChanged;
```

CHAPTER 12

Lambda Expressions

Lambda expressions and anonymous methods are two important concepts in advanced programming. Collectively, these are often referred to as anonymous functions. The concept of anonymous delegates (or methods) was introduced in C# 2.0, and lambda expressions were introduced in C# 3.0. Over time, lambda expressions became more popular than anonymous methods. If you target the .NET Framework 3.5 or later, it is recommended that you use lambda expressions. As a result, in most cases, today lambda expressions are used instead of anonymous methods. This chapter focuses on lambda expressions and covers the following topics:

- Lambda expressions and their use
- Expression-bodied members
- Use of local variables inside lambda expressions
- Event handling using lambda expressions
- Use of a static lambda
- Understanding natural types

Let us review and test your understanding of these topics now.

Theoretical Concepts

This section includes the theoretical questions and answers on lambda expressions in C#.

V. Sarcar, *Test Your Skills in C# Programming*, https://doi.org/10.1007/978-1-4842-8655-5_12

Understanding Lambdas

12.T1 What are the lambda expressions in C#?

Answer:

In simple words, a lambda expression is an anonymous method that is written in a different form and is easily readable. But what is an anonymous method, and why is it useful? As the name suggests, an anonymous method is a method that does not have a name. In certain situations, they are very helpful. For example, consider a case when you point to a method using a delegate but the method is present in a different location of the source file (or, in an extreme case, it is in a different source file). This segregated code is difficult to understand, debug, and maintain. In such situations, anonymous methods are helpful because in those cases, you can define an "inline" method without a name to serve your purpose.

The name *lambda* came from lambda calculus, which can be used to simulate a Turing machine. You spell it with the Greek letter lambda (λ), which your keyboard does not have. So, to denote the lambda operator, you use the symbol `=>`. The left side of the operator specifies the input parameters (if any), and the right side of the operator specifies either an expression or a statement block. The `=>` part is right-associative, and its precedence is the same as `=`. While reading the code that contains the lambda operator, you replace the lambda operator with "goes to" or "go to" or "arrow" or "become(s)." For example, you read `x=> x+5;` as "x goes to x+5." Similarly, you read `(x,y)=>x+y;` as "x and y go to x+y."

Author's Note: The C# compiler can convert a lambda expression to either a delegate instance or an expression tree. This book is not discussing LINQ in detail, but you have learned about delegates and saw several examples of them in Chapter 10. So, let us focus on delegate instances here.

Note When a lambda expression is converted to a delegate type, the result depends on the input parameters and return type. If a lambda expression doesn't have a return type, it can be converted to one of the `Action` delegates types; if it has a return type, it can be converted to one of the `Func` delegate types.

12.T2 Can you write a simple program to demonstrate the usage of a lambda expression?

Answer:

To make things simple, I'll show you a simple program (see Demonstration 1) that calculates the sum of two integers (10 and 5) using various approaches as follows:

- In the first approach, you'll notice the use of a normal method (which you are familiar with). You can use this method to calculate the sum of the ints.
- Then I show you how to use a delegate instance to do this.
- The last two segments of code show you the use of an anonymous method and a lambda expression, respectively.

Each program segment generates the same output, and these options give you a choice of which approach to choose for a program. For a better understanding, read the comments in the code.

Demonstration 1

```
Console.WriteLine(" Using a normal method call.");
int a = 10, b = 5;
Console.WriteLine(" Invoking the Sum() method without using a delegate.");
Console.WriteLine($"The sum of {a} and {b} is : {Sample.Sum(a, b)}");

// Using an in-built delegate
Func<int, int, int> del1 = Sample.Sum;
Console.WriteLine("\nUsing delegate now.");
Console.WriteLine("Invoking the Sum() method using a delegate.");
Console.WriteLine($"The sum of {a} and {b} is : {del1(a, b)}");

// Using Anonymous method (C# 2.0 onwards)
Console.WriteLine("\nUsing an anonymous method now.");
Sample.Mydel del2 = delegate (int x, int y) { return x + y; };
Console.WriteLine("Invoking the Sum() method using an
                   anonymous method.");
Console.WriteLine($"The sum of {a} and {b} is : {del2(a, b)}");
```

```
// Using a lambda expression(C# 3.0 onwards)
Console.WriteLine("\n Using lambda expression now.");
Func<int, int, int> del3 = (x, y) => x + y;
Console.WriteLine($"The sum of {a} and {b} is : {del3(a, b)}");

class Sample
{
    public delegate int Mydel(int x, int y);
    public static int Sum(int x, int y)
    {
        return x + y;
    }
}
```

Output

You'll receive the following output when you run this program:

```
Using a normal method call.
Invoking the Sum() method without using a delegate.
The sum of 10 and 5 is 15

Using delegate now.
Invoking the Sum() method using a delegate.
The sum of 10 and 5 is 15

Using an anonymous method now.
Invoking the Sum() method using an anonymous method.
The sum of 10 and 5 is 15

Using lambda expression now.
The sum of 10 and 5 is 15
```

Analysis:

Let's review the statements used for the anonymous method and lambda expression. In the case of the anonymous method, I have used the following:

```
delegate (int x, int y) { return x + y; };
```

In the case of the lambda expression, I have used the following:

```
(x, y) => x + y;
```

In most cases, compilers can identify the input parameters and return type when it deals with a lambda expression. In programming terms, this is called *type inference*. Still, in some special cases, you may need to keep this type of information to allow the compiler to evaluate the expression properly. But this is a simple case, and the compiler can understand it properly (in this context, notice the delegate declaration) even if you do not mention the type of the input parameters.

POINT TO REMEMBER

A lambda expression can accept one or multiple parameters. You can also use a lambda expression that does not accept any parameters.

- In the previous program, the lambda expression used multiple parameters. You have seen that you can list them in parentheses separated by commas as follows: `(x,y)=> x+y;`.
- If a lambda expression accepts only one parameter, you can omit the parentheses. For example, you can use either `(x)=> x*x;` or `x=>x*x;`. Both of them can serve the same purpose.
- Finally, `() => Console.WriteLine("No parameter.");` can be considered an example of a lambda expression that does not have any parameter.

12.T3 Suppose you have the following code:

```
class Sample2
{
    bool IsPositive1(int x) { return x > 0; }
}
```

Can you write an equivalent code using a lambda expression?

Answer:

The following code uses a lambda expression and replaces the plain method `IsPositive1` as follows:

```
class Sample2
{
    bool IsPositive2(int x) => x > 0;
}
```

12.T4 What is a Turing machine?

Answer:

In simple words: a Turing machine is an abstract machine that can manipulate symbols of a memory tape of infinite length following some rules. This tape is divided into cells where each cell can contain a symbol (including a blank). This machine has a 'head' that can read those symbols at a particular moment. It is the mathematical basis of different programming languages.

Types of Lambda Expressions

12.T5 What are the different types of lambda expressions?

Answer:

Lambda expressions are categorized into two types, called expression lambdas and statement lambdas. Expression lambdas appear with a single expression, whereas a statement lambda contains a block of statements. So, in the case of a statement lambda, you may notice the use of curly braces, semicolons, and return statements. A statement lambda can contain any number of statements, but in general, they contain two or three statements.

Also, at the time of this writing, you cannot use a statement lambda for expression-bodied methods, but you can use expression lambda in those contexts. The documentation at `https://docs.microsoft.com/en-us/dotnet/csharp/programming-guide/concepts/expression-trees/` also says the following:

> *The C# compiler can generate expression trees only from expression lambdas (or single-line lambdas). It cannot parse statement lambdas (or multi-line lambdas).*

Author's Note: If you use more than three lines in a lambda expression, it may complicate the understanding, and, in those cases, you can opt for a normal method instead of a lambda expression. Also, I've excluded the discussion of the expression tree because it is a LINQ-related feature, but a discussion of LINQ is beyond the scope of this book.

12.T6 What is an expression?
Answer:

As per Microsoft, an expression can be a combination of the operators and operands. It can be evaluated to a single value, method, object, or namespace. An expression can include a method call, an operator with the operands, a literal value (a literal is a constant value that does not have a name), or simply a name of a variable, type member, method parameter, namespace, or type. Here is a simple example of an expression statement:

```
int flag=1;
```

Here `flag` is a simple name, and `1` is the literal value. Literals and simple names are the two simplest types of expression.

Restrictions

12.T7 Can you mention some of the restrictions associated with lambda expressions?
Answer:

Here I mention two important restrictions from the online documentation at `https://docs.microsoft.com/en-us/dotnet/csharp/language-reference/operators/lambda-expressions`:

- A lambda expression can't contain a `goto, break`, or `continue` statement if the target of that jump statement is outside the lambda expression block. It's also an error to have a jump statement outside the lambda expression block if the target is inside the block.
- A lambda expression can't directly capture an `in`, `ref`, or `out` parameter from the enclosing method.

You'll see the code segments covering these concepts in 12.P12 and 12.P13.

The discussion of attributes is out of the scope of this book. But if you are familiar with it, Microsoft wants you to note that since the lambda expressions are invoked through the underlying delegate type but the delegate's `Invoke` method does not check attributes on these expressions, the attributes do not have any effect on these expressions.

12.T8 Can you overload a lambda operator?

Answer:

At the time of this writing, the answer is no.

Programming Skills

By using the following questions, you can test your programming skills in C#. Note that if I do not mention the namespace, you can assume that all parts of the program belong to the same namespace.

Basic Concepts

12.P1 Predict the output of the following code segment:

```
Console.WriteLine("***Experimenting lambda expressions with
                   different parameters.***");

Action del1 = () => Console.WriteLine("Hello");
del1();

Func<int,int> del2 = x => x * x;
Console.WriteLine($"Square of 9 is {del2(9)}");

Action<int,int> del3 = (int x, int y) =>
{
    int sum = x + y;
    Console.WriteLine($"The sum of {x} and {y} is {sum}");
};
del3(10, 20);
```

Answer:

This code can compile and run successfully. You'll get the following output:

```
***Experimenting lambda expressions with different parameters.***
Hello
Square of 9 is 81
The sum of 10 and 20 is 30
```

Additional Notes:

This program shows you that a lambda expression can use zero, one, or more parameters.

Expression-Bodied Members

12.P2 Can you compile the following code?

```
Test test = new();
Console.WriteLine($"The sum of 5 and 10 is
                  {test.CalculateSum1(5,10)}");
Console.WriteLine($"The sum of 25 and 100 is
               {test.CalculateSum2(25, 100)}");
class Test
{
    public int CalculateSum1(int a, int b)
    {
        int sum = a + b;
        return sum;
    }

    public int CalculateSum2(int a, int b) => a + b;
}
```

Answer:

This code can compile and run successfully. You'll get the following output:

```
The sum of 5 and 10 is 15
The sum of 25 and 100 is 125
```

Explanation:

Notice that `CalculateSum1` and `CalculateSum2` are doing the same thing. But the second one is more concise and readable. The general syntax for an expression body definition is as follows:

```
member => expression
```

Microsoft introduced expression body definitions for methods and read-only properties in C# 6, and this feature was expanded in C# 7.0. Expression body definitions can be used with the following type members: methods, properties, constructors, finalizers, and indexers.

12.P3 Predict the output of the following code segment:

```
Console.WriteLine("---12.P3---");
class Test
{
     int CalculateSum(int a, int b) =>
        {
         int sum = a + b;
         return sum;
        }
}
```

Answer:

You'll receive compile-time errors with many error messages. For your reference, I list a few of them here:

```
CS1525 Invalid expression term '{'
CS1519 Invalid token 'return' in class, record, struct, or
       interface member declaration
CS1519 Invalid token '{' in class, record, struct, or
       interface member declaration
```

Explanation:

Expression syntax to define nonlambda methods is not applicable for statement lambdas. You can use it only for the expression lambdas.

12.P4 Predict the output of the following code segment:

```
Employee emp = new(1);
emp.Name = "Kevin Turner ";
Console.WriteLine($"{emp.Name} works in the {emp.Company} as
                    an employee.");
Console.WriteLine($"His ID is {emp.Id}.");
Console.ReadKey();
```

```
class Employee
{
    readonly int empId=0;
    readonly string company = "XYZ company";
    string name = string.Empty;
    public Employee(int id) => empId = id;
    public string Company => company;
    public string Name
    {
        get => name;
        set => name = value;
    }
    public int Id
    {
        get => empId;
    }
}
```

Answer:

This code can compile and run successfully. You'll get the following output:

```
Kevin Turner works in the XYZ company as an employee.
His ID is 1.
```

Explanation:

You have seen the use of the expression-bodied members, but you can apply this concept to properties, constructors, and finalizers. In this program, you have seen this concept in a constructor, a read-only property, and a read-write property. For your immediate reference, go through the following code segment and read the comments to understand what is happening:

```
// Usual implementation of a constructor.
//public Employee(int id)
//{
//    empId = id;
//}
// Following code shows an expression-bodied constructor
public Employee(int id) => empId = id; // ok
```

```
// Common implementation of a read-only property
//public string Company
//{
//    get
//    {
//        return company;
//    }
//}

// Read-only property. C#6.0 onwards, it is supported.
public string Company => company;

// Common implementation of a read-write property
//public string Name
//{
//    get
//    {
//        return name;
//    }
//    set
//    {
//        name = value;
//    }
//}

// C#7.0 onwards, you can use the expression-body definition
// for the get and set accessors
public string Name
{
 get => name;
 set => name = value;
}
```

Local Variables in Lambda Expressions

12.P5 Predict the output of the following code segment:

```
List<int> numbers = new() { 12, 23, 37, 45, 52 };
Console.WriteLine("The list contains the following numbers:");
foreach (int number in numbers)
{
    Console.Write(number+"\t");
}
Console.WriteLine("\nFinding the numbers which are greater
                    than 30.");
#region Using method call syntax
Console.WriteLine("\nUsing the method call syntax:");
IEnumerable<int> numbersAbove30 = numbers.Where(x => x > 30);
foreach (int number in numbersAbove30)
{
    Console.WriteLine(number);
}
#endregion
```

Answer:

This code can compile and run successfully. You'll get the following output:

```
The list contains the following numbers:
12      23      37      45      52
Finding the numbers which are greater than 30.

Using the method call syntax:
37
45
52
```

Explanation:

You can use local variables in a lambda expression, but the variable must be in scope.

In a similar program, you can use either the query syntax or the method call syntax. Here, I have used the method call syntax with a lambda expression. If you are familiar with LINQ programming, you know about query syntax. By using it, you can write an equivalent code to find the numbers that are greater than 30 as follows:

```
#region Using the query syntax
var query = from num in numbers
            where num > 30
            select num;
Console.WriteLine("Using the query syntax now.");
foreach (int number in query)
{
    Console.WriteLine(number);
}
#endregion
```

Tuples in Lambda Expressions

12.P6 Can you predict the output of the following code segment?

```
var input = Tuple.Create(1, 2.3);
Console.WriteLine("The input tuple is as follows:");
Console.WriteLine("First Element: " + input.Item1);
Console.WriteLine("Second Element: " + input.Item2);

Sample.DoubleMaker del =
  (Tuple<int, double> input) => Tuple.Create(input.Item1 * 2,
                                             input.Item2 * 2);

var result = del(input);
Console.WriteLine("\nThe resultant tuple is as follows:");
Console.WriteLine("First Element: " + result.Item1);
Console.WriteLine("Second Element: " + result.Item2);

class Sample
{
 internal delegate Tuple<int, double> DoubleMaker(Tuple<int, double> input);
 static internal Tuple<int, double> MakeDouble(Tuple<int, double> input)
```

```
    {
        return Tuple.Create(input.Item1 * 2, input.Item2 * 2);
    }
}
```

Answer:

This code can compile and run successfully. You'll get the following output:

```
The input tuple is as follows:
First Element: 1
Second Element: 2.3

The resultant tuple is as follows:
First Element: 2
Second Element: 4.6
```

Explanation:

From C# 7.0 onward, you have built-in support for tuples. If you do not know about tuples, let me make things simple for you.

To get the same resultant tuple, you could use the normal method call as follows:

```
Console.WriteLine("\nUsing normal method call.");
result = Sample.MakeDouble(input);
Console.WriteLine("The resultant tuple is as follows:");
Console.WriteLine("First Element: " + result.Item1);
Console.WriteLine("Second Element: " + result.Item2);
```

How does this work? Notice that the tuple has only two components. You can pass this tuple to the MakeDouble method to get a tuple in which the tuple items are two times bigger than the original tuple items. This is the reason you see the following method (I have not used this method when I used the lambda expression):

```
static internal Tuple<int, double> MakeDouble(Tuple<int, double> input)
{
  return Tuple.Create(input.Item1 * 2, input.Item2 * 2);
}
```

You can see that inside the tuple, the first component is an `int`, and the second one is a `double`. I've multiplied the input arguments by 2 to get the double of each component and return the result with another tuple. Since I have invoked the method from a static context, I made the `MakeDouble` method static.

Now you know how to use tuples with a method. So, let's understand how to use it with a lambda expression. In many applications, you'll see the use of tuples with built-in delegates (for example, `Func`, `Action`, etc.) and lambda expressions. In 12.P7, you'll see the use of `Func` delegate in this context. In this example, you have seen the use of a user-defined delegate.

As a first step, I declared the following delegate inside the `Sample` class:

```
internal delegate Tuple<int, double> DoubleMaker(Tuple<int, double> input);
```

Now I have the delegate. So, I can use a lambda expression like the following:

```
Sample.DoubleMaker del =
  (Tuple<int, double> input) => Tuple.Create(input.Item1 * 2,
                                             input.Item2 * 2);
```

If you do not use a named component, by default, the fields of the tuple are named `Item1, Item2, Item3,` and so forth. So, to get the intended result, you can use the following lines of code:

```
var result = del(input);
Console.WriteLine("\nThe resultant tuple is as follows:");
Console.WriteLine("First Element: " + result.Item1);
Console.WriteLine("Second Element: " + result.Item2);
```

12.P7 Predict the output of the following code segment:

```
var input = Tuple.Create(1, 2.3);
Console.WriteLine("The input tuple is as follows:");
Console.WriteLine("First Element: " + input.Item1);
Console.WriteLine("Second Element: " + input.Item2);

Func<Tuple<int, double>, Tuple<int, double>> del =
  (Tuple<int, double> input) => Tuple.Create(input.Item1 * 2,
                                             input.Item2 * 2);
```

```
var result = del(input);
Console.WriteLine("\nThe resultant tuple is as follows:");
Console.WriteLine("First Element: " + result.Item1);
Console.WriteLine("Second Element: " + result.Item2);
```

Answer:

This code can compile and run successfully. You'll get the following output:

```
The input tuple is as follows:
First Element: 1
Second Element: 2.3

The resultant tuple is as follows:
First Element: 2
Second Element: 4.6
```

Explanation:

You saw equivalent code in 12.P6. The only difference is that this time you saw the use of the built-in Func delegate.

Event Subscription

12.P8 Predict the output of the following code segment:

```
Sender sender = new Sender();
EventHandler myEvent =
            (object sender, EventArgs e) =>
              Console.WriteLine("The flag is changed.");
Console.WriteLine("Registering the event.");
sender.MyIntChanged += myEvent;
Console.WriteLine("Setting the flag to 1.");
sender.Flag = 1;
Console.WriteLine("Setting the flag to 2.");
sender.Flag = 2;

Console.WriteLine("\nUnregistering the event.");
sender.MyIntChanged -= myEvent;
Console.WriteLine("Setting the flag to 3.");
```

```
sender.Flag = 3;
class Sender
    {
        private int _flag;
        public int Flag
        {
            get
            {
                return _flag;
            }
            set
            {
                _flag= value;
                OnMyIntChanged();
            }
        }

        public event EventHandler? MyIntChanged;
        public void OnMyIntChanged()
        {
            MyIntChanged?.Invoke(this, EventArgs.Empty);
        }
    }
```

Answer:

This code can compile and run successfully. You'll get the following output:

```
Registering the event.
Setting the flag to 1.
The flag is changed.
Setting the flag to 2.
The flag is changed.

Unregistering the event.
Setting the flag to 3.
```

Explanation:

This program shows that you can do an event subscription using a lambda expression.

12.P9 Predict the output of the following code segment:

```
Sender sender = new Sender();

Console.WriteLine("Registering the event.");
// Using lambda expression as an event handler
// Bad practise
sender.MyIntChanged += (object sender, System.EventArgs e) =>
                    Console.WriteLine("The flag is changed.");
Console.WriteLine("Setting the flag to 1.");
sender.Flag = 1;
Console.WriteLine("Setting the flag to 2.");
sender.Flag = 2;
Console.WriteLine("\nUnregistering the event.");
// Unregistering now (it is a bad practise)
sender.MyIntChanged -= (object sender, System.EventArgs e) =>
        Console.WriteLine("Unregistered event notification.");

Console.WriteLine("Setting the flag to 3.");
sender.Flag = 3;
class Sender
{
    private int _flag;
    public int Flag
    {
        get
        {
            return _flag;
        }
        set
        {
            _flag = value;
            OnMyIntChanged();
        }
    }
```

```
    public event EventHandler? MyIntChanged;
    public void OnMyIntChanged()
    {
        MyIntChanged?.Invoke(this, EventArgs.Empty);
    }
}
```

Answer:

This code shows you a bad practice. Here is a possible output:

```
Registering the event.
Setting the flag to 1.
The flag is changed.
Setting the flag to 2.
The flag is changed.

Unregistering the event.
Setting the flag to 3.
The flag is changed.
```

Explanation:

This is confusing output. Why? Notice the last line of the output. You may wonder why you see the message "The flag is changed" after you unsubscribe from the event. The reason is that if you use the following lines to subscribe to the event:

```
sender.MyIntChanged += (object sender, System.EventArgs e) =>
                    Console.WriteLine("The flag is changed.");
```

and, then later at some point of time, you unsubscribe it with the following line:

```
// Unregistering now (it is a bad practise)
sender.MyIntChanged -= (object sender, System.EventArgs e) =>
        Console.WriteLine("Unregistered event notification.");
```

there is no guarantee that the compiler will unsubscribe this event. This is why you should follow the approach shown in 12.P8.

POINTS TO NOTE

You probably know that to avoid memory leaks in real-world applications, once you subscribe to an event, you should unsubscribe once the intended job is done. You have seen the program segments in 12.P8 (good practice) and 12.P9 (bad practice). Experts recommend you store the anonymous method/lambda expression in a delegate variable and then add this delegate to the event. As a result, you can keep a track of it, and if you want, you can unsubscribe from the event properly. So, a common suggestion is that you should not use anonymous functions to subscribe to an event when you really want to unsubscribe from the event at a later point in time.

Static Lambda

12.P10 Can you compile the following code?

```
Sample sample = new();
sample.del(97, 3);
class Sample
{
    internal Action<int, int> del = static (x, y) =>
                                    Console.Write(x + y);
}
```

Answer:

This code can compile and run successfully in C# 9 and later versions. You'll get the following output:

```
100
```

So, if you run this code in .NET Core 3.1 (which supports C# 8.0), you'll see many errors, and one of them is as follows:

```
CS8400   Feature 'static anonymous function' is not available in C# 8.0.
Please use language version 9.0 or greater.
```

Natural Type

12.P11 Can you compile the following code?

```
// Code Segment-1
Func<string, double> del = (string s) => double.Parse(s);
double flag2 = del("23.4");
Console.WriteLine(flag2);

// Code Segment-2
var flag1 = (string s) => double.Parse(s);
Console.WriteLine(flag1("23.4"));
```

Answer:

This code can compile and run successfully. Both of these code segments will produce the same output.

```
23.4
23.4
```

Explanation:

Actually, a lambda expression in itself doesn't have a type. But the informal "type" of a lambda expression refers to the delegate type or `Expression` type to which the lambda expression is converted. Microsoft (`https://docs.microsoft.com/en-us/dotnet/csharp/language-reference/operators/lambda-expressions`) says the following:

> *Beginning with C# 10, a lambda expression may have a* ***natural type****.*
>
> *Instead of forcing you to declare a delegate type, such as* `Func<...>` *or* `Action<...>` *for a lambda expression, the compiler may infer the delegate type from the lambda expression.*

So, the compiler can infer the `Parse` method in this example as the `Func<string, double>` type in code segment 2.

Bonus Questions

12.P12 Predict the output of the following code segment (unsafe code is allowed in this program):

```
Action del = new Test().SampleMethod;
del();

class Test
{
    internal unsafe void SampleMethod()
    {
        int a = 10;
        int* p = &a;
        Console.WriteLine($"a={a}");
        Console.WriteLine($"*p={*p}");
    }
}
```

Answer:

This code will compile and produce the following output:

```
a=10
*p=10
```

12.P13 Predict the output of the following code segment:

```
Action del = () =>
{
    int _flag = 10;
    while (_flag < 15)
    {
        Console.WriteLine(_flag);
        _flag++;
       goto xx;

    }

};
del();
xx: Console.WriteLine("Level xx");
```

Answer:

This code cannot compile. You'll get the following error:

```
CS0159   No such label 'xx' within the scope of the goto statement
```

12.P14 Predict the output of the following code segment:

```
Func<int, int,string> del = (x, int y) => (x > y) ? "Yes." : "No.";
string result=del(10, 7);
Console.WriteLine(result);
```

Answer:

You'll receive the following compile-time error:

```
CS0748   Inconsistent lambda parameter usage; parameter types must be all
explicit or all implicit
```

Explanation:

You can see that the compiler could not infer the type. As per the error message, here are the possible remedies:

```
Func<int, int, string> del = (x, y) =>
                             (x > y) ? "Yes." : "No."; // OK
```

Or,

```
Func<int, int, str ing> del = (int x, int y) =>
                              (x > y) ? "Yes." : "No."; // OK
```

In the context of type inference, Microsoft (https://docs.microsoft.com/en-us/dotnet/csharp/language-reference/operators/lambda-expressions) provides the following guidelines:

- The lambda must contain the same number of parameters as the delegate type.
- Each input parameter in the lambda must be implicitly convertible to its corresponding delegate parameter.
- The return value of the lambda (if any) must be implicitly convertible to the delegate's return type.

12.P15 Predict the output of the following code segment:

```
int a = 99;
Sample.Increment(ref a);
class Sample
{
    public delegate int Mydel(int x);
    public static void Increment(ref int a)
    {
        // Using anonymous method
        Mydel del = delegate (int x)
        {
            x = a;
            return x + 1;

        };
        Console.WriteLine(del(a));
    }
}
```

Answer:

This code cannot compile. You'll get the following error:

```
CS1628   Cannot use ref, out, or in parameter 'a' inside an anonymous
method, lambda expression, query expression, or local function
```

If you comment out the line `x=a;` in the previous code, you can see the output 100.

CHAPTER 13

Generics

Generics are an integral part of advanced programming. They are one of the coolest features of C#. Let's see what Microsoft says about them (see `https://docs.microsoft.com/en-us/dotnet/csharp/fundamentals/types/generics`):

> *Generic classes and methods combine reusability, type safety, and efficiency in a way that their non-generic counterparts cannot. Generics are most frequently used with collections and the methods that operate on them. The System.Collections.Generic namespace contains several generic-based collection classes. The non-generic collections, such as ArrayList are not recommended and are maintained for compatibility purposes.*

This is one of the reasons you'll find few real-life applications that do not use generics at their core. This chapter focuses on generics and covers the following topics:

- The motivation behind generics
- The fundamentals of generic programs
- Use of generic interfaces
- Use of generic constraints
- Use of covariance and contravariance using generics
- Self-referencing generic type
- Experimenting with generic method's overloading and overriding
- Analyzing the static data in the context of generics

Let us review and test your understanding of these topics now.

V. Sarcar, *Test Your Skills in C# Programming*, https://doi.org/10.1007/978-1-4842-8655-5_13

Theoretical Concepts

This section includes the theoretical questions and answers on generics in C#.

Motivation and Uses

13.T1 What are the key motivations behind a generic program?

Answer:

When you use a generic type in your application, you do not commit to a specific type for its instances. For example, when you instantiate a generic class, one time your object can deal with an `int` type, and another time your object can deal with a different type such as a `double` type, `string` type, `object` type, and so on. In short, this kind of programming allows you to make a type-safe class without having to commit to any particular type.

Surely, this is not a new concept, and it is not limited to C#. You can see similar kinds of programming in other languages as well; for example, you can see them in Java or C++ (using templates) also. At the core, the following are some advantages of using a generic application in C#:

- Your program will be reusable.
- You ensure better type safety in your program.
- Your program can avoid typical runtime errors that may arise due to improper casting.
- Your program can perform better because you can avoid boxing for value types.

A discussion of assemblies is beyond the scope of this book. Still, it will be helpful if you remember one more point in this context. Microsoft (see `https://docs.microsoft.com/en-us/dotnet/standard/generics/`) says the following:

> *Generics streamline dynamically generated code. When you use generics with dynamically generated code you do not need to generate the type. This increases the number of scenarios in which you can use lightweight dynamic methods instead of generating entire assemblies.*

13.T2 I know that inheritance also promotes reusability. Then why do I use generics?

Answer:

Inheritance and generics work in different ways. Using inheritance, you inherit from a base type, and often you use casting and boxing. Generics scores high in this area: they provide better type safety and reduce casting and boxing. You also know that in the case of generics, you provide a template that contains placeholder types so that you do not commit to a specific type for its instances.

13.T3 You said, "Your program can avoid typical runtime errors that may arise due to improper casting." Can you explain?

Answer:

In 13.P2, you'll see the following code, which raises a compile-time error:

```
List<int> myList = new();
myList.Add(10);
myList.Add(20);
myList.Add("InvalidElement");
Console.WriteLine(" The list elements are:");
foreach (int myInt in myList)
{
    Console.WriteLine((int)myInt);
}
```

But if you use a nongeneric version of this program and write something like this:

```
using System.Collections;

ArrayList myList2 = new();
myList2.Add(10);
myList2.Add(20);
// No compile time error
myList2.Add("InvalidElement");
foreach (int myInt in myList2)
{
     // Will encounter runtime exception for the
     // final element  which is not an int
    Console.WriteLine((int)myInt);
}
```

then there is no compile-time error. However, the mistake is severe because now you'll face a runtime error saying the following:

```
System.InvalidCastException: 'Unable to cast object of type 'System.String'
to type 'System.Int32'.'
```

You also understand that catching a bug earlier is good practice. So, a compile-time error is always better than a runtime error.

Generic Methods

13.T4 Here is a program segment for you. Is SomeMethod a generic method?

```
class A
{
    T SomeMethod<T>(T arg)
    {
        // Some code
    }
}
```

Answer:

Yes.

13.T5 Here is a program segment for you. Is SomeMethod a generic method?

```
class Generic<T>
{
    T SomeMethod(T arg)
    {
        // Some code
    }
}
```

Answer:

As per Microsoft's description, the answer to this question is no. Why? Refer to Microsoft's documentation (`https://docs.microsoft.com/en-us/dotnet/standard/generics/`):

Generic methods can appear on generic or nongeneric types. It is important to note that a method is not generic just because it belongs to a generic type, or even because it has formal parameters whose types are the generic parameters of the enclosing type. A method is generic only if it has its own list of type parameters.

13.T5 Here is some sample code for you:

```
interface ISample<T>
{
    // Some code
}
class Implementor1<U, T1> : ISample<T1>
{
    // Remaining code
}

class Implementor2<T2, U> : ISample<T2>
{
    // Some code
}
```

Will this code compile?

Answer:

Yes. The key thing to remember is that the implementing class needs to supply the arguments required by the interface. For example, in this case, an implementor class must include the parameter, which is present in the interface.

Restrictions

13.T6 Can you mention some of the restrictions in generics?

Answer:

Here are some important restrictions:

- In 13.T7 (and 13.P22), you'll learn that static data is unique for each of the closed types but *not* for different constructed types.

- You cannot apply the DllImport attribute to a generic method. This attribute is often used with the extern modifier that is used to tell that the method is defined outside the C# code. Here you just mention the method name because the actual code is placed in a different location. In addition, these methods are static. So, the following segment of code:

  ```
  using System.Runtime.InteropServices;
  class GenericClassDemo2<T>
  {
      [DllImport("Somefile.dll")] // Error CS7046
      private static extern void SomeMethod();
  }
  ```

  will raise a compile-time error saying the following:

  Error CS7042 The DllImport attribute cannot be applied to a method that is generic or contained in a generic type.

- *You cannot use a pointer type as a type argument.* So, the last line in the following code segment:

  ```
  class Sample<T>
  {
      static unsafe void ShowMe()
      {
          int a = 10; // ok
          int* p; // ok
          p = &a; // ok

          T* _flag; // error
      }
  }
  ```

  will raise the compile-time error saying *the following*:

  ```
  CS0208 Cannot take the address of, get the size of, or declare a
  pointer to a managed type ('T')
  ```

- When you apply generic constraints, you have to follow certain rules. You'll see some of them in the "Programming Skills" section. For example, in 13.P10, you'll see that to remove the compile-time error CS0401, you need to place the `new()` constraint at the end of the constraint list.

Bonus Questions

13.T7 How does the static data work in the context of generic programming?

Answer:

Static data is unique for each of the closed types. So, you can see that the generic types do not share the same `static` member among them. You can refer to the program 13.P22 in this context.

13.T8 Is there any other way to share data among closed types?

Answer:

One probable solution is to make a nongeneric base class to hold the static fields (without type parameters). Then you make a generic type that can inherit from it.

13.T9 Can you give examples of built-in generic classes?

Answer:

I often use the `List` and `Dictionary` classes instead of `ArrayList` and `Hashtable` classes in my programs. You may know that `List` and `Dictionary` are generic classes, but the other two are non-generic classes.

You'll see the use of `List<int>` in 13.P2. So, let me show you the use of `Dictionary`. Consider the following code:

```
Dictionary<int, string> employees = new();
employees.Add(1, "Sam");
employees.Add(2, "Bob");
employees.Add(3, "Kate");
Console.WriteLine("The dictionary elements are:");
foreach( KeyValuePair<int,string> element in employees)
{
    Console.WriteLine($"ID: {element.Key} Name: {element.Value}");
}
```

Once you compile and run this program, you'll see the following output:

```
The dictionary elements are:
ID: 1 Name: Sam
ID: 2 Name: Bob
ID: 3 Name: Kate
```

Programming Skills

By using the following questions, you can test your programming skills in C#. Note that if I do not mention the namespace, you can assume that all parts of the program belong to the same namespace.

Basic Concepts

13.P1 Can you compile the following code?

```
Price<int> intOb = new();
Console.WriteLine($"The int version shows {intOb.Display(123)}");
Price<string> stringOb = new();
Console.WriteLine($"The string version shows {stringOb.Display("hello")}");
Price<double> doubleOb = new();
Console.WriteLine($"The double version shows {doubleOb.Display(456.78)}");
class Price<T>
{
    public T Display(T value) => value;
}
```

Answer:

Yes, this code can compile and run successfully. You'll get the following output:

```
The int version shows 123
The string version shows hello
The double version shows 456.78
```

Explanation:

You have seen a simple example of using generics in a program.

13.P2 Can you compile the following code?

```
List<int> myList = new();
myList.Add(10);
myList.Add(20);
myList.Add("InvalidElement");
Console.WriteLine(" The list elements are:");
foreach (int myInt in myList)
{
    Console.WriteLine((int)myInt);
}
```

Answer:

No. You'll receive the following compile-time error:

```
CS1503   Argument 1: cannot convert from 'string' to 'int'
```

Additional note:

This is the power of generics. You can catch an error early (at compile time).

Finding the Default Values

13.P3 Predict the output of the following code segment:

```
Sample.PrintDefault<int>();
Sample.PrintDefault<int?>();
Sample.PrintDefault<sbyte>();
Sample.PrintDefault<double>();
Sample.PrintDefault<bool>();
Sample.PrintDefault<string>();
Sample.PrintDefault<object>();
Sample.PrintDefault<System.Numerics.Complex>();
Sample.PrintDefault<List<int>>();
Sample.PrintDefault<List<string>>();
class Sample
```

```
{
    internal static void PrintDefault<T>()
    {
        T? defaultValue = default;
        string? printMe = (defaultValue == null) ? "null" :
                                         defaultValue.ToString();
        Console.WriteLine($"The default value of {typeof(T)}
                                                  is {printMe}.");
    }
}
```

Answer:

This code can compile and run successfully. You'll get the following output:

```
The default value of System.Int32 is 0.
The default value of System.Nullable`1[System.Int32] is null.
The default value of System.SByte is 0.
The default value of System.Double is 0.
The default value of System.Boolean is False.
The default value of System.String is null.
The default value of System.Object is null.
The default value of System.Numerics.Complex is (0, 0).
The default value of System.Collections.Generic.List`1[System.Int32]
  is null.
The default value of System.Collections.Generic.List`1[System.String]
  is null.
```

Explanation:

In an introductory course, you have probably seen the use of the `default` keyword in `switch` statements, where `default` is used to refer to a default case. But in generic programming, it has a special meaning. Here you can use `default` to initialize generic types with the default values. In this context, note the following points:

- The default value for a reference type is `null`.
- The default value of a value type (other than the struct and bool types) is 0.

- For the bool type, the default value is `false.`
- For the struct (which is a value type) type, the default value is an object of that struct with all the fields set with their default values. (In other words, the default value of a struct is a value produced by setting all value types fields to their default values and all reference type fields to null.)

Additional Note:

Starting in C# 7.1, you can use the `default` literal. It can produce the same value as `default(T)` produces. In this example, you have seen the simplified version of the default expression. So, instead of writing this:

```
T? defaultValue = default(T);
```

I have used the following:

```
T? defaultValue = default;
```

13.P4 Can you predict the output of the following code segment?

```
Sample.PrintDefault<MyClass>();
Sample.PrintDefault <MyStruct> ();
class MyClass
{
    int _flag;
    string _name;
    public override string ToString()
    {
        string temp = $"_flag: {_flag} and _name: {_name}";
        if (_name != null)
            return temp;
        else
            return $"_flag: {_flag} and _name: null";
    }
}
```

```
struct MyStruct
{
    int _flag;
    string _name;
    public override string ToString()
    {
        string temp= $"_flag: {_flag} and _name: {_name}";
        if (_name != null)
            return temp;
        else
            return $"_flag: {_flag} and _name: null";
    }
}

class Sample
{
    internal static void PrintDefault<T>()
    {
        T? defaultValue = default;
        string? printMe = (defaultValue == null) ? "null" :
                                         defaultValue.ToString();
        Console.WriteLine($"The default value of {typeof(T)}
                                               is {printMe}.");
    }
}
```

Answer:

This code can compile and run successfully. You'll get the following output:

```
The default value of MyClass is null.
The default value of MyStruct is _flag: 0 and _name: null.
```

Explanation:

You may note that `Console.WriteLine` simply invokes the `ToString()` method. This is why to show you the default values inside a class and struct, I have overridden the `ToString()` method.

Implementing a Generic Interface

13.P5 Can you compile the following code?

```
IVehicle<string> vehicle = new Car<string>();
string color = vehicle.GetColor("green");
vehicle.Describe();
Console.WriteLine($"Its color is {color}.");

interface IVehicle<T>
{

    T GetColor(T color);

    public void Describe();

}
class Car<T> : IVehicle<T>
{
    public T GetColor(T color) => color;
    public void Describe() => Console.WriteLine("This is a car.");

}
```

Answer:

Yes, this code can compile and run successfully. You'll get the following output:

```
This is a car.
Its color is green.
```

Explanation:

You can see that similar to a generic class, you can have a generic interface. In this program, you have two methods, called `GetColor(..)` and `Describe()`. It describes that a generic interface can contain nongeneric methods too.

When you implement a generic interface method, you can apply the same approach that you follow to implement a nongeneric interface method. This program demonstrates this fact. The Microsoft documentation (`https://docs.microsoft.com/en-us/dotnet/csharp/programming-guide/generics/generic-interfaces`) also says that the rules of inheritance that apply to classes also apply to interfaces.

13.P6 Suppose you've got the following two interfaces:

```
interface IColor<T> { }
interface IBrand<T, U> { }
```

Can you predict whether the following segments will compile?

```
// Segment 1:
class Car1<T> : IColor<T> { }
// Segment 2:
class Car2<T> : IBrand<T, U> { }
// Segment 3:
class Car3<T> : IBrand<T, string> { }
// Segment 4:
class Car4<U> : IBrand<T,int> { }
// Segment 5:
class Car5<T> : IBrand<string, int> { }
// Segment 6:
class Car6 : IColor<string> { }
// Segment 7:
class Car7 : IBrand<double,string> { }
```

Answer:

Only segments 2 and 4 will not compile.

For segment 2, you'll see the following error:

```
CS0246  The type or namespace name 'U' could not be found (are you missing
a using directive or an assembly reference?)
```

For segment 4, you'll see the following error:

```
CS0246  The type or namespace name 'T' could not be found (are you missing
a using directive or an assembly reference?)
```

Explanation:

The error messages are self-explanatory: for segment 2, Car2 doesn't include the parameter U, and for segment 4, Car4 doesn't include the parameter T.

For segment 1 and segment 3, Car1 and Car3 have the required parameters, respectively.

For segments 5, 6, and 7, there were no issues at all because in these cases, the respective classes worked on interfaces whose constructions are closed. If you have any confusion, review the following terms again: `Sample<T>` is an open constructed type, but when you write something like `Sample<int>` or `Sample<string>`, it is a closed constructed type. A generic class can inherit from concrete, closed constructed, or open constructed base classes.

Understanding Generic Constraints

13.P7 Predict the output of the following code segment:

```
// Employees
Employee e1 = new("Suresh", 1.5);
Employee e2 = new("Kate", 5.2);
Employee e3 = new("John", 7);

// Employee StoreHouse
EmployeeStoreHouse<Employee> empStore = new ();
empStore.AddToStore(e1);
empStore.AddToStore(e2);
empStore.AddToStore(e3);

// Display the Employee Positions in Store
empStore.DisplayStore();

interface IEmployee
{

}
class Employee : IEmployee
{
    string _name;
    double _yearOfExp;
    public Employee(string name, double exp)
    {
        _name = name;
        _yearOfExp = exp;
    }
```

```
    public override string ToString()
    {
        return $"Name: {_name} Exp:{_yearOfExp}";
    }
}
class EmployeeStoreHouse<T> where T : IEmployee
{
    readonly List<Employee> database = new();
    public void AddToStore(Employee element)
    {
        database.Add(element);
    }
    public void DisplayStore()
    {
        Console.WriteLine("The current database:");
        foreach (Employee emp in database)
        {
            Console.WriteLine(emp.ToString());
        }
    }
}
```

Answer:

This code can compile and run successfully. You'll get the following output:

```
The current database:
Name: Suresh Exp:1.5
Name: Kate Exp:5.2
Name: John Exp:7
```

13.P8 Let us modify the previous program (13.P7). This time remove the interface declaration as follows:

```
//interface IEmployee
//{
//
//}
```

Other parts of the program are unchanged. Can you compile the code now?

Answer:

No. You'll receive the following compile-time errors:

```
CS0246   The type or namespace name 'IEmployee' could not be found (are you
missing a using directive or an assembly reference?)

CS0311   The type 'Employee' cannot be used as type parameter 'T' in the
generic type or method 'EmployeeStoreHouse<T>'. There is no implicit
reference conversion from 'Employee' to 'IEmployee'.
```

Explanation:

You can see these issues due to the generic constraint, which is described as follows:

```
class EmployeeStoreHouse<T> where T : IEmployee
```

which means that T must implement the IEmployee interface.

POINTS TO REMEMBER

In general, you'll often notice the use of the following constraints:

`where T: struct` means that type T must be a value type. (Remember that struct is a value type.)

`where the T: class` means that type T must be a reference type. (Remember that class is a reference type.) In a nullable context in C# 8.0 or later, T must be a non-nullable reference type.

`where T: class?` means that type T must be a reference type (either nullable or non-nullable. (Remember that class is a reference type.)

`where T: ISample` means that type T must implement the `ISample` interface.

`where T: new()` means that type T must have a default (parameterless) constructor. (If you use it with other constraints, place it at the last position.)

`where T: S` means that type T must be derived from another generic type S. It is sometimes referred to as a *naked type constraint*.

There are other constraints also, such as `where T: default`, `where T: unmanaged`, `where T:<interface_name>?`, etc. If interested, you can learn about them from at `https://docs.microsoft.com/en-us/dotnet/csharp/programming-guide/generics/constraints-on-type-parameters`.

Starting with C# 7.3, you can also use enum constraints. So, you can use `where T: System.Enum` wherever applicable.

13.P9 Can you compile the following code?

```
// Employees
Employee e1 = new("Suresh", 1.5);
Employee e2 = new("Kate", 5.2);
Employee e3 = new("John", 7);

// Employee StoreHouse
EmployeeStoreHouse<Employee> empStore = new
                EmployeeStoreHouse<Employee>();
empStore.AddToStore(e1);
empStore.AddToStore(e2);
empStore.AddToStore(e3);

// Some other code

interface IEmployee
{

}
class Employee
{
    string _name;
    double _yearOfExp;
    //public Employee() { }
    public Employee(string name, double exp)
    {
        _name = name;
        _yearOfExp = exp;
    }
```

```
    public override string ToString()
    {
        return $"Name:{_name} Exp:{_yearOfExp}";
    }
}

class EmployeeStoreHouse<T> where T : new()
{
    readonly List<Employee> database = new();
    public void AddToStore(Employee element)
    {
        database.Add(element);
    }
    // Some other code
}
```

Answer:

No. You'll receive the following compile-time error:

```
CS0310  'Employee' must be a non-abstract type with a public parameterless
constructor in order to use it as parameter 'T' in the generic type or
method 'EmployeeStoreHouse<T>'
```

Explanation:

Notice that the public constructor was commented out. To remove this error, you have to uncomment it, because you have declared the generic constraint as follows:

```
class EmployeeStoreHouse<T> where T : new()
```

13.P10 Can you compile the following code?

```
// Employees
Employee e1 = new();
Employee e2 = new();

// Employee StoreHouse
EmployeeStoreHouse<Employee> empStore = new();
empStore.AddToStore(e1);
```

```
empStore.AddToStore(e2);
class Employee
{
    public Employee() { }
    // Some other code, if any

}
class EmployeeStoreHouse<T> where T : new(),Employee
{
    readonly List<Employee> database = new();
    public void AddToStore(Employee element)
    {
        database.Add(element);
    }
    // Some other code, if any
}
```

Answer:

No. You'll receive the following compile-time error:

```
CS0401   The new() constraint must be the last constraint specified
```

Additional Note:

The error message is self-explanatory. To remove this error, you need to place the `new()` constraint as follows:

```
class EmployeeStoreHouse<T> where T : Employee,new() // OK
```

It is also important to note that in this program, you could write the following constraint too:

```
class EmployeeStoreHouse<T> where T : class, new() // Also OK
```

But if you change the order of class and `new()` as follows:

```
class EmployeeStoreHouse<T> where T : new(),class // error
```

you'll see multiple compile-time errors, as shown here:

```
CS0401   The new() constraint must be the last constraint specified

CS0449   The 'class', 'struct', 'unmanaged', 'notnull', and 'default'
constraints cannot be combined or duplicated, and must be specified first
in the constraints list.
```

13.P11 Can you compile the following code?

```
// Some code
class Employee
{
    readonly int _id;
    public Employee(int id)
    {
        _id = id;
    }
    // Some other code, if any

}
class EmployeeStoreHouse<T> where T : class, new(int)
{
    readonly List<Employee> database = new();
    public void AddToStore(Employee element)
    {
        database.Add(element);
    }
    // Some other code, if any
}
```

Answer:

No. You'll see multiple compile-time errors; one of them is as follows:

```
CS0701   'int' is not a valid constraint. A type used as a constraint must
be an interface, a non-sealed class or a type parameter.
```

So, it is important to note that you cannot use a parameterized constructor constraint in a situation like this. The following code raises these errors:

```
class EmployeeStoreHouse<T> where T : class, new(int) // error
```

Additional Note:

In the context of the `T: class` constraint, you should remember Microsoft's guidelines whenever applicable. This guideline (see `https://docs.microsoft.com/en-us/dotnet/csharp/programming-guide/generics/constraints-on-type-parameters`) specifies the following:

> *When applying the where T: class constraint, avoid the == and != operators on the type parameter because these operators will test for reference identity only, not for value equality.*

It further states the following:

> *If you must test for value equality, the recommended way is to also apply the where T: IEquatable<T> or where T: IComparable<T> constraint and implement the interface in any class that will be used to construct the generic class.*

13.P12 Can you compile the following code?

```
// Some other code, if any
// Employee StoreHouse
EmployeeStoreHouse<Employee, Person> empStore = new();

interface IEmployee
{
    // Some code
}
class Employee: IEmployee
{

    // Some other code, if any

}
```

```
class Person
{
    public Person()
    {
        // some code
    }
    // Some other code, if any
}
class EmployeeStoreHouse<T,U> where T : Employee?, IEmployee?
                              where U: new()
{
    // Some other code, if any
}
```

Answer:

Yes, this code will compile successfully.

Additional note:

This program segment shows how to apply constraints to multiple parameters. It also describes how to apply multiple constraints on a single parameter.

Covariance

13.P13 Can you compile the following code?

```
Console.WriteLine("Normal usage:");
Func<Vehicle> vehicle = Vehicle.GetOneVehicle;
vehicle();
Func<Bus> bus=Bus.GetOneBus;
bus();
Console.WriteLine("Testing covariance:");
vehicle = bus;
vehicle();
```

```
class Vehicle
{
    public static Vehicle GetOneVehicle()
    {
        Console.WriteLine("Making a vehicle.");
        return new Vehicle();
    }
}
class Bus : Vehicle
{
    public static Bus GetOneBus()
    {
        Console.WriteLine("Making a bus.");
        return new Bus();
    }
}
```

Answer:

Yes, this code can compile and run successfully. You'll get the following output:

```
Normal usage:
Making a vehicle.
Making a bus.
Testing covariance:
Making a bus.
```

Explanation:

Because of the covariance support, the following line did not raise any compile-time errors:

```
vehicle = bus;
```

13.P14 Can you compile the following code?

```
Bus bus1 = new Bus();
Bus bus2 = new Bus();
// Creating a bus list
// Remember that List<T> implements IEnumerable<T>
```

```
List<Bus> busList = new();
busList.Add(bus1);
busList.Add(bus2);

IEnumerable<Vehicle> vehicleList = busList;
foreach (Vehicle vehicle in vehicleList)
{
    vehicle.Describe();
}
class Vehicle
{
    public virtual void Describe()
    {
        Console.WriteLine($"A vehicle is ready with hash code
                               {GetHashCode()}");
    }
}
class Bus : Vehicle
{
    public override void Describe()
    {
        Console.WriteLine($"A bus is ready with hash code
                                {GetHashCode()}");
    }
}
```

Answer:

Yes, this code can compile and run successfully. Here is a possible output:

```
A bus is ready with hash code 18643596
A bus is ready with hash code 33574638
```

Explanation:

In this example, you have seen the built-in construct `IEnumerable<T>`. This is a widely used interface in C# programming. Now you can use a `foreach` loop to do something meaningful on each item in a collection and process them one by one. Nearly every class in the .NET Framework that contains multiple elements implements this interface. For example, the commonly used `List` class also implements this interface.

Again, in this program, I've used Vehicle as the parent class and Bus as the derived class. Let me retrieve the definition of generic interface IEnumerable from Visual Studio, as shown here:

```
public interface IEnumerable<out T> : IEnumerable
    {
        //
        // Summary:
        //     Returns an enumerator that iterates through the
        //     collection.
        //
        // Returns:
        //     An enumerator that can be used to iterate
        //     through the collection.
        new IEnumerator<T> GetEnumerator();
    }
```

Have you noticed the out parameter? It means that T is covariant. Why? See the official documentation (https://docs.microsoft.com/en-us/dotnet/csharp/language-reference/keywords/out-generic-modifier) that says the following:

> *For generic type parameters, the out keyword specifies that the type parameter is covariant. You can use the out keyword in generic interfaces and delegates.*

This is why the following line works fine:

```
IEnumerable<Vehicle> vehicleList = busList;
```

where busList is a list of buses and described as follows:

```
List<Bus> busList = new();
busList.Add(bus1);
busList.Add(bus2);
```

The compiler allows you to convert from buses to vehicles because the type parameter is covariant. Let us think about this conversion. The out keyword on T ensures that T is used only in output positions, which means that you want to use it for the return type of a method. This conversion is also type-safe because instead of a Bus, you cannot use a different type such as a Train. Why? Notice that there's no way to feed a Train into an interface where T can appear only in output positions.

Note In many real-life applications, it's a common practice to use methods that return `IEnumerable<T>`. This is helpful when you do not want to disclose the actual concrete type to others and to have the ability to loop through the items (not to modify the collection, though, for example, to add or remove items).

Contravariance

13.P15 Can you compile the following code?

```
Vehicle vehicle = new();
Bus bus = new();
Console.WriteLine("Normal usage:");
ContraDelegate<Vehicle> vehicleDel = Sample.ShowVehicle;
vehicleDel(vehicle);
ContraDelegate<Bus> busDel = Sample.ShowBus;
busDel(bus);
Console.WriteLine("Testing contravariance now.");
busDel = vehicleDel;
busDel(bus);

// A generic contravariant delegate
delegate void ContraDelegate<in T>(T t);
// A generic non-contravariant delegate
// delegate void ContraDelegate<T>(T t);
class Vehicle
{
    public virtual void ShowMe()
    {
        Console.WriteLine(" The ShowMe() of the Vehicle is called.");
    }
}
```

```
class Bus: Vehicle
{
    public override void ShowMe()
    {
        Console.WriteLine(" The ShowMe() of the Bus is called.");
    }
}
class Sample
{
    internal static void ShowVehicle(Vehicle vehicle)
    {
        vehicle.ShowMe();
    }
    internal static void ShowBus(Bus bus)
    {
        bus.ShowMe();
    }
}
```

Answer:

Yes, this code can compile and run successfully. You'll get the following output:

```
Normal usage:
 The ShowMe() of the Vehicle is called.
 The ShowMe() of the Bus is called.
Testing contravariance now.
 The ShowMe() of the Bus is called.
```

Explanation:

The following segment of code is easy to understand because it matches the delegate signature. (See the output of the previous program if required.)

```
ContraDelegate<Vehicle> vehicleDel = Sample.ShowVehicle;
vehicleDel(vehicle);
ContraDelegate<Bus> busDel = Sample.ShowBus;
busDel(bus);
```

Now comes the interesting part, which is the opposite of covariance. Notice the following assignment:

```
busDel = vehicleDel; // OK now
```

This assignment doesn't raise any compilation error because this time, I'm using a contravariant delegate.

```
// A generic contravariant delegate
delegate void ContraDelegate<in T>(T t);
```

Why do I say that this is a contravariant delegate? Microsoft (`https://docs.microsoft.com/en-us/dotnet/csharp/language-reference/keywords/in-generic-modifier`) says the following:

> *For generic type parameters, the in keyword specifies that the type parameter is contravariant. You can use the in keyword in generic interfaces and delegates.*

But it is important to note that if you do not make the delegate contravariant using the `in` parameter, this assignment will cause the compile-time error saying the following:

```
CS0029   Cannot implicitly convert type 'ContraDelegate<Vehicle>' to
'ContraDelegate<Bus>'
```

13.P16 Can you compile the following code?

```
Vehicle vehicle = new();
Bus bus = new();
Console.WriteLine("Normal usage:");
Action<Vehicle> vehicleDel = Sample.ShowVehicle;
vehicleDel(vehicle);
Action<Bus> busDel = Sample.ShowBus;
busDel(bus);
Console.WriteLine("Using contravariance now.");
busDel = vehicleDel;
busDel(bus);
```

```
class Vehicle
{
    public virtual void ShowMe()
    {
        Console.WriteLine(" The ShowMe() of the Vehicle is called.");
    }
}
class Bus : Vehicle
{
    public override void ShowMe()
    {
        Console.WriteLine(" The ShowMe() of the Bus is called.");
    }
}
class Sample
{
    internal static void ShowVehicle(Vehicle vehicle)
    {
        vehicle.ShowMe();
    }
    internal static void ShowBus(Bus bus)
    {
        bus.ShowMe();
    }
}
```

Answer:

This code can compile and run successfully. You'll get the following output:

```
Normal usage:
 The ShowMe() of the Vehicle is called.
 The ShowMe() of the Bus is called.
Using contravariance now.
 The ShowMe() of the Bus is called.
```

Explanation:

13.15 and 13.P16 are equivalent programs. The only difference is that this time you see me using the built-in `Action` delegate, which is contravariant. For your reference, let me show you its definition:

```
public delegate void Action<in T>(T obj);
```

Notice the presence of the `in` keyword in this delegate declaration.

13.P17 Can you compile the following code?

```
Bus aBus=new Bus();
Vehicle aVehicle=new Vehicle();
IContraInterface<Vehicle> vehicle = new Implementor<Vehicle>();
Console.WriteLine(vehicle);
vehicle.Display(aVehicle);

IContraInterface<Bus> bus = new Implementor<Bus>();
Console.WriteLine(bus);
bus.Display(aBus);

bus = vehicle;
Console.WriteLine(bus);
bus.Display(aBus);

interface IContraInterface<in A>
{
   void Display(A obj);
}

class Implementor<A> : IContraInterface<A>
{
    public void Display(A obj)
    {
        Console.WriteLine(obj);
    }
```

```
    public override string ToString()
    {
        Type listType = typeof(A);
        return "Implementor[" + listType + "]";
    }
}

class Vehicle
{
    public override string ToString()
    {
        return "One vehicle";
    }
}
class Bus : Vehicle
{
    public override string ToString()
    {
        return "One bus";
    }
}
```

Answer:

Yes, this code can compile and run successfully. You'll get the following output:

```
Implementor[Vehicle]
One vehicle
Implementor[Bus]
One bus
Implementor[Vehicle]
One bus
```

Explanation:

The `bus = vehicle;` line of code worked due to the contravariance. If you do not make this interface contravariant and use something like `interface IContraInterface<A>`, you'll receive the following compile-time error for this assignment:

```
CS0266   Cannot implicitly convert type 'IContraInterface<Vehicle>' to
'IContraInterface<Bus>'.An explicit conversion exists (are you missing
a cast?)
```

Let us think about this conversion one more time. Notice the interface definition in this program closely:

```
interface IContraInterface<in A>
```

The in keyword on A ensures that A is used only in input positions, which means that you want to use it for the method parameters, but not for the return type. Since no member in IContraInterface outputs an A, you did not face any trouble by casting a vehicle to a bus, and this is why the C# compiler allows this conversion.

POINTS TO NOTE

Covariance and contravariance in generic type parameters are applicable for reference types, but not for value types. In addition, you may have a question: "When I see something like `Func<in T, out TResult>` or `Func<in T1, in T2, out TResult>`, how should I interpret these definitions?" The answer is that these definitions tell that the Func delegates have a covariant return type but the contravariant parameter types.

Self-Referencing Generic Type

13.P18 Can you compile the following code?

```
Console.WriteLine("Self-referencing generic type demo.");
Employee emp1 = new Employee("Physics", 1);
Employee emp2 = new Employee("Mathematics", 2);
Employee emp3 = new Employee("Computer Science", 1);
Employee emp4 = new Employee("Mathematics", 2);
Employee emp5=null;
Console.WriteLine($"Comparing emp1 and emp3:
                 {emp1.CompareWith(emp3)}");
Console.WriteLine($"Comparing emp2 and emp4:
                 {emp2.CompareWith(emp4)}");
```

```
Console.WriteLine($"Comparing emp2 and emp5:
              {emp2.CompareWith(emp5)}");

interface IIdenticalEmployee<T>
{
    string CompareWith(T obj);
}
class Employee : IIdenticalEmployee<Employee>
{
    string _name;
    int _id;
    public Employee(string name, int id)
    {
        _name = name;
        _id = id;
    }
    public string CompareWith(Employee obj)
    {
        if (obj == null)
        {
            return "Cannot compare with a null object.";
        }
        else
        {
            if (_name == obj._name && _id == obj._id)
            {
                return "Identical Employees.";
            }
            else
            {
                return "Different Employees.";
            }
        }
    }
}
```

Answer:

Yes, this code can compile and run successfully. You'll get the following output:

```
Self-referencing generic type demo.
Comparing emp1 and emp3: Different Employees.
Comparing emp2 and emp4: Identical Employees.
Comparing emp2 and emp5: Cannot compare with a null object.
```

Explanation:

When you compare two instances of a class, either you use the built-in constructs or you write a custom comparison method. When you are interested in using built-in constructs, you have multiple options. For example, you can use either the `CompareTo` method of `IComparable<T>` or the `Equals` method of `IEquitable<T>`. But in many cases, you may want to write a custom comparison method. I've done the same in this program.

This program simply checks whether the `_name` and `_id` are the same for two employees. If both match, it says that employees are the same. (Using the word *same*, I mean only the content of these objects are the same, but not the reference to the heap.)

This program also shows that a type can name itself as the concrete type when it closes the type argument. So, you see a self-referencing generic declaration in this program.

Testing Overloading and Overriding

13.P19 Can you compile the following code?

```
Console.WriteLine("---13.P19---");
Sample<int, double> sample1 = new();
sample1.Display(5, 10.5);

Sample<int, int> sample2 = new();
sample2.Display(5, 15);

class Sample<T, U>
{
    public void Display(T p1, U p2)
    {
        Console.WriteLine("Inside Display(T p1, U p2)");
    }
```

```
    public void Display(U p1, T p2)
    {
        Console.WriteLine("Inside Display(U p1, T p2)");
    }
}
```

Answer:

No. The following line:

```
sample2.Display(5, 15);// Error: Ambiguous call
```

will raise the compile-time error:

```
CS0121  The call is ambiguous between the following methods or properties:
'Sample<T, U>.Display(T, U)' and 'Sample<T, U>.Display(U, T)'
```

Explanation:

It may appear to you that you have two overloaded versions of the Display method because the order of the generic type parameters are different. But there is potential ambiguity, which you can see when you exercised the following code segments:

```
Sample<int, int> sample2 = new();
sample2.Display(5, 15);// Error: Ambiguous call
```

13.P20 Can you compile the following code?

```
Sample sample = new();
sample.Display(5);
sample.Display<int>(5);
sample.Display(5, 10.7);
sample.Display<int,double>(5, 10.7);
class Sample
{
    public void Display<T>(T p1)
    {
        Console.WriteLine("Inside Display(T t1)");
    }
```

```
    public void Display<T,U>(T t1, U u2)
    {
        Console.WriteLine("Inside Display(T t1, U u2)");
    }
}
```

Answer:

Yes, this code can compile and run successfully. You'll get the following output:

```
Inside Display(T t1)
Inside Display(T t1)
Inside Display(T t1, U u2)
Inside Display(T t1, U u2)
```

Explanation:

This program shows you two important characteristics of generics.

- You can overload a generic method.
- You can call a generic method without using the type argument because the compiler can infer it.

So, the following lines are equivalent:

```
sample.Display(5);// Ok
sample.Display<int>(5);// Also OK
```

The same comment applies for the following lines too:

```
sample.Display(5, 10.7);// OK
sample.Display<int,double>(5, 10.7);// Also OK
```

In this context, it'll be useful for you to note the following information from Microsoft's documentation (`https://docs.microsoft.com/en-us/dotnet/csharp/programming-guide/generics/generic-methods`):

> *The compiler can infer the type parameters based on the method arguments you pass in; it cannot infer the type parameters only from a constraint or return value. Therefore type inference does not work with methods that have no parameters. Type inference occurs at compile time before the compiler tries to resolve overloaded method signatures. The compiler applies*

type inference logic to all generic methods that share the same name. In the overload resolution step, the compiler includes only those generic methods on which type inference succeeded.

13.P21 Can you compile the following code?

```
Parent parent = new();
parent.Display(5);

parent = new Derived();
parent.Display("5");
parent.Display("abc");

class Parent
{
    public virtual void Display<T>(T p1)
    {
        Console.WriteLine("Parent's Display");
    }
}
class Derived : Parent
{
    public override void Display<T>(T p1)
    {
        Console.WriteLine("Derived's Display");
    }
}
```

Answer:

Yes, this code can compile and run successfully. You'll get the following output:

```
Parent's Display
Derived's Display
Derived's Display
```

Analyzing Static Data

13.P22 Can you predict the output from the following code?

```
Console.WriteLine("***Testing static in the context of generic
  programming.***");
Sample<int> intOb = new();
Console.WriteLine("\nUsing intOb now.");
intOb.Increment();
intOb.Increment();
intOb.Increment();

Console.WriteLine("\nUsing strOb now.");
Sample<string> strOb = new();
strOb.Increment();
strOb.Increment();

Sample<int> intOb2 = new ();
Console.WriteLine("\nUsing intOb2 now.");
intOb2.Increment();
intOb2.Increment();

Sample<string> strOb2 = new();
Console.WriteLine("\nUsing strOb2 now.");
strOb2.Increment();
strOb2.Increment();
class Sample<T>
{
    public static int count;
    public void Increment() => Console.WriteLine($"Incremented
                               value is {++count}");

}
```

Answer:

This code can compile and run successfully. You'll get the following output:

```
***Testing static in the context of generic programming.***

Using intOb now.
Incremented value is 1
Incremented value is 2
Incremented value is 3

Using strOb now.
Incremented value is 1
Incremented value is 2

Using intOb2 now.
Incremented value is 4
Incremented value is 5

Using strOb2 now.
Incremented value is 3
Incremented value is 4
```

Explanation:

Static data is unique for each of the closed types. So, you can see that the generic types do not share the same `static` members among them.

CHAPTER 14

Threading

In today's world, multitasking is a common activity. For example, while I am writing this chapter, I'm also listening to a calm piece of music in the background. To implement this concept in C# programming, you need to learn about threads; more precisely, you need to be familiar with multithreading.

In this chapter, we will review the fundamentals of multithreading. Upon completion of this chapter, you'll be able to answer the following questions:

- What are the threads, and how can you create them?
- What is a multithreaded program? How does it differ from a single-threaded application?
- Why are the `ThreadStart` and `ParameterizedThreadStart` delegates important in thread programming?
- How do you block a thread using `Sleep` or `Join` methods?
- How can you use lambda expressions in a multithreaded program?
- How do you use important `Thread` class members?
- How is a foreground thread different from a background thread?
- What is synchronization, and why is it needed?
- How can you implement thread safety in C# using `lock` statements?
- How can you implement an alternative approach to `lock` statements using `Monitor`'s `Entry` and `Exit` methods?
- What is a deadlock, and how can you detect a deadlock in your system?
- What is the purpose of using the `ThreadPool` class? What are the pros and cons of using it?
- How do you cancel a running thread in the managed environment?

V. Sarcar, *Test Your Skills in C# Programming*, https://doi.org/10.1007/978-1-4842-8655-5_14

Let us review and test your understanding of these topics now.

Note Once you understand multithreading, you should learn about asynchronous programming. These two concepts are closely related. Keeping in mind the target readers, I will not be discussing asynchronous programming in this book. But, if you're interested, you can learn about it from the book *Design Patterns in C#* (2nd edition), which is published by the same publisher. A big chapter is included in that book to help you understand asynchronous programming in depth.

Theoretical Concepts

This section includes the theoretical questions and answers on multithreading in C#.

Threading Fundamentals

14.T1 What is a thread?

Answer:

Most of the programs you have seen so far probably had a single sequential flow of control. In other words, once the program starts executing, it goes through all the statements sequentially until the end. As a result, at any particular moment, there is only one statement that is under execution. A thread is similar to a program. It has a single flow of control. It also has a body between the starting point and endpoint, and it executes the commands sequentially. So, in short, you can define a thread as an independent execution path of a program. You may note that each program has at least one thread.

14.T2 What is the key advantage of using a multithreaded program over a single-threaded program?

Answer:

Since you can execute the independent segments of code in separate threads, you can complete a task faster.

In a single-threaded environment, if the thread blocks, the entire program is halted, which is not the case in a multithreaded environment. In addition, you can reduce the overall idle time by making efficient use of the central processing unit (CPU).

For example, consider the case of sending a large amount of data over a network. In this case, when one part of your program is sending a large block of data over the network, another part of the program can accept the user inputs, and still another part of your program can validate those inputs and prepare the next block of data for sending.

In short, since the independent pieces of code do not affect each other, you can run them in parallel to complete a job much faster. This is the core aim of multithreading.

14.T3 What do you mean by multithreading in programming?

Answer:

It's a programming paradigm to have a program divided into multiple subprograms (or parts) that can be implemented in parallel. But the fact is that unless you structure your code to run on multiple processors, you are not using the machine's full computing potential. To visualize this, you can refer to Figure 14-1. This figure demonstrates a simple scenario in a multithreaded program, where a parent thread, called the *Main thread*, creates two more threads, `threadOne` and `threadTwo`, and all these threads are running concurrently.

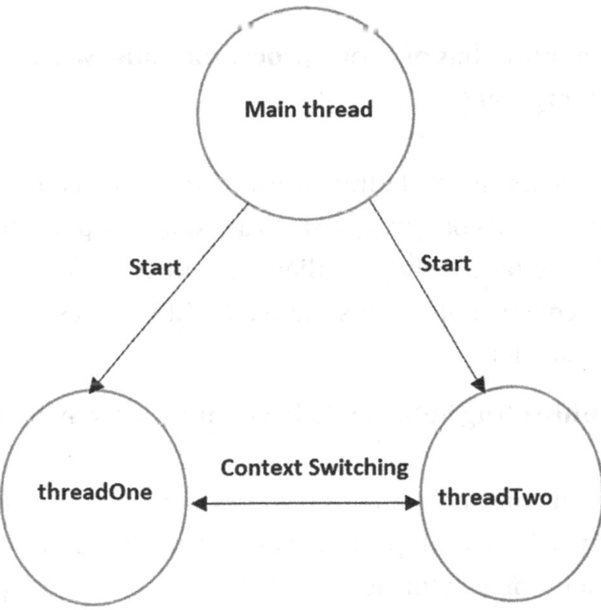

Figure 14-1. *In a multithreaded program, the main thread creates two more threads, threadOne and threadTwo. All of them are running concurrently*

14.T4 In Figure 14-1, I'm seeing the term *context switching*. What does it mean?

Answer:

In general, many threads can run in parallel on your computer. Actually, the computer allows one thread to run in one processor for some time, and then it can switch to a different one. This decision is made based on different factors. Normally, all threads have equal priority, and switching among them is done nicely. Switching between threads is termed *context switching*. It also enables you to store the state of the current thread (or process) so that you can resume the execution from this point later.

14.T5 Can you explain the difference between multithreading and multitasking?

Answer:

In simple words, multiprocessing involves more than one processor, and multithreading is used for a single process. When the OS divides the processor execution time among different applications, it is called multitasking, and when the OS divides the execution time among different threads within a single application, it is called multithreading. This is why multithreading can be considered a special case of multitasking.

14.T6 I have a computer that has only one processor. Can I write a multithreaded program using this computer?

Answer:

Theoretically, the answer is yes. In this case, the processor can switch among these subprograms (or, segments of code) very fast. As a result, it appears to human eyes that this code is executed simultaneously. In earlier days, most computers had a single core and, in those systems, concurrent threads shared the CPU cycles, but in actuality, they could not truly run in parallel.

14.T7 How can multithreading help me if I have a multicore system?

Answer:

Using the concept of multithreading, you can reduce the overall idle time by efficient use of the CPU. But if you have multiple processors, you can run multiple threads concurrently. As a result, you can further enhance the speed of your program.

Thread Safety

14.T8 I often hear about the term *thread safety*. What does it mean?

Answer:

When you have multiple threads that access a shared resource, you need to ensure thread safety. For example, consider a situation when one thread is trying to read the data from a file and another thread is still writing or updating in the same file. If you cannot manage the correct order, you may get surprising results. The concept of synchronization is useful in a similar situation.

14.T9 You said, "If you cannot manage the correct order, you may get surprising results." Can you give another example to illustrate this?

Answer:

In 14.P9, you can see a program that shows the problem of a nonsynchronized program. For now, let us consider a simple example to demonstrate the importance of thread safety.

Let's say you have an integer variable that is initialized with a value, say, 0. Further, assume that there are two threads; each of them will exercise some code to increment this value by 1 and save the result. Let's call these threads `Thread-1` and `Thread-2`. Since both these threads increment the value, you expect to see the final value as 2 inside this integer variable.

Now, consider the following situation, which can produce a different value:

- `Thread-1` reads the current value from the variable that is 0 now. So, it increments the value to 1 and is about to save this value.
- Before `Thread-1` saves this value, `Thread-2` starts reading the current value (which is the last saved value and still 0) from the variable. It also increments the value to 1 and is about to save this value.
- `Thread-1` saves the new value (1) back into the variable.
- Now, `Thread-2` also saves the new value back (1) into the variable.

As a result, the final value is 1.

POINTS TO REMEMBER

There are many ways through which you can coordinate multiple thread executions. Some common terms are frequently used in this context. For your easy understanding, let me explain them in simple words: the segment of code that you want to guard against simultaneous access from multiple threads is called the critical section. At any given moment, you allow only one thread to work in the critical section. This principle is termed mutual exclusion. You can enforce this principle through a synchronization object such as a mutex or semaphore. Often you will see the use of locks to ensure thread safety. Locks are a common mechanism to avoid accidental modification of shared resources due to simultaneous access of multiple threads in a shared location. You can say that a mutex enforces a lock-based mechanism to provide support for mutual exclusion.

14.T10 How can a locking mechanism ensure thread safety?

Answer:

Here is the idea: when a thread obtains a lock, it can enter the critical section. Once its job is done, it exits from this location and releases the lock. Now another thread can obtain the lock and proceed. In between, if any other thread wants to enter the critical section but sees that the lock is currently held by another thread, it cannot enter, and it'll suspend its activity until the lock is released.

14.T11 How can you create a lock?

Answer:

It is very simple and is often done with a private instance variable in the same object/ class, something like the following:

```
private object lockObject = new object();
```

You may also note that you can make a lock at your convenience. For example, if you deal with a static method, you could even write something like the following:

```
private static StringBuilder strLock = new StringBuilder();
```

Deadlock

14.T12 How multiple threads can cause a deadlock?

Answer:

When multiple threads are waiting for each other to complete a job but none of them can complete the job, you observe a hanging state. You can call it a deadlock. You can compare this situation with the following real-life examples:

- You can't get a job without experience, but you can't get experience without a job.
- After a fight between two close friends, each of them expects the other to initiate the friendship again.

Author's Note: In 14.P12, you'll see a program that can reach the deadlock state.

POINTS TO REMEMBER

In programming, without a proper synchronization technique, you may notice some surprising output (for example, you may notice some corrupted data), but with improper use of synchronization, the situation can become worse: you can encounter a deadlock.

ThreadPool Class

14.T13 What is the purpose of the `ThreadPool` class?

Answer:

Creating threads directly in a real-world application is normally discouraged. Some key reasons behind this are as follows:

- Maintaining too many threads incurs tough and costly operations.
- A big amount of time is wasted due to context switching, instead of doing the real work.
- When you start a thread, to work things properly at least some amount of time is invested. This time can be saved if you use a prebuilt thread.

To avoid directly creating threads, C# gives you the facility to use the built-in `ThreadPool` class. Using this class, you can use the already existing threads that can be reused to serve your purpose. The `ThreadPool` class is effective to maintain the optimal number of threads in your application. It can also help you write top-quality asynchronous programs. A discussion of asynchronous programming is beyond the scope of this book. Still, I suggest you note the following lines from Microsoft's online documentation (`https://docs.microsoft.com/en-us/dotnet/api/system.threading.threadpool?view=net-6.0`):

> *The thread pool enables you to use threads more efficiently by providing your application with a pool of worker threads that are managed by the system.*

This documentation also tells about the following examples:

- You create a `Task` or `Task<TResult>` object to perform some task asynchronously, by default the task is scheduled to run on a thread pool thread.
- Asynchronous timers use the thread pool.
- You use registered wait handles, a system thread monitors the status of the wait handles. When a wait operation completes, a worker thread from the thread pool executes the corresponding callback function.
- You call the `QueueUserWorkItem` method to queue a method for execution on a thread pool thread. (See 14.P13 in this context.)

14.T14 What is the size of a thread pool?

Answer:

Microsoft's online documentation says the following (see `https://docs.microsoft.com/en-us/dotnet/api/system.threading.threadpool?view=net-6.0`):

> *Beginning with the .NET Framework 4, the default size of the thread pool for a process depends on several factors, such as the size of the virtual address space. A process can call the GetMaxThreads method to determine the number of threads. The number of threads in the thread pool can be changed by using the SetMaxThreads method. Each thread uses the default stack size and runs at the default priority.*

This link also says the following:

> *The thread pool provides new worker threads or I/O completion threads on demand until it reaches the maximum for each category. When a maximum is reached, the thread pool can create additional threads in that category or wait until some tasks are complete. Beginning with the .NET Framework 4, the thread pool creates and destroys worker threads in order to optimize throughput, which is defined as the number of tasks that complete per unit of time. Too few threads might not make optimal use of available resources, whereas too many threads could increase resource contention.*

14.T15 How many thread pools can a process have?

Answer:

A process can have one thread pool only.

14.T16 What are the drawbacks associated with using a thread pool?

Answer:

Here are some challenges of using a thread pool:

- You cannot set a name for a pooled thread. So, if there is an issue, debugging can be tough.
- Inside the managed thread pool, threads are background threads. This means that they will die once all foreground threads complete their tasks. (In 14.P8, you will see a program to differentiate the foreground and background threads.)

Author's Note: You should not try to change the built-in working mechanisms of the thread pool. As per Microsoft, in most cases, the thread pool performs better with its own algorithm for allocating threads.

Bonus Q&A

14.T17 How is the `Yield()` method different from the `Sleep()` method?

Answer:

The `Yield()` method is useful for the current processor. It causes the current thread to allow other threads to complete their work. However, if there is no such candidate, your thread will soon be rescheduled and will continue the task. Microsoft (https://docs.microsoft.com/en-us/dotnet/api/system.threading.thread.yield?redirectedfrom=MSDN&view=net-6.0#System_Threading_Thread_Yield) ensures this by saying the following:

> *Yielding is limited to the processor that is executing the calling thread. The operating system will not switch execution to another processor, even if that processor is idle or is running a thread of lower priority. If there are no other threads that are ready to execute on the current processor, the operating system does not yield execution, and this method returns false.*

The `Sleep` method has the following overloaded versions:

```
public static void Sleep(int millisecondsTimeout);
public static void Sleep(TimeSpan timeout);
```

It suspends the current thread for a specified amount of time. So, compared to `Yield()`, it causes less CPU utilization. But you may note a special case that is mentioned as follows (https://docs.microsoft.com/en-us/dotnet/api/system.threading.thread.sleep?redirectedfrom=MSDN&view=net-6.0#overloads):

> *If the value of the millisecondsTimeout argument is zero, the thread relinquishes the remainder of its time slice to any thread of equal priority that is ready to run. If there are no other threads of equal priority that are ready to run, execution of the current thread is not suspended.*

14.T18 How does `Thread.Abort()` work?

Answer:

Earlier it was used to terminate a thread. The `Abort()` method has two different overloaded versions, which are as follows:

```
public void Abort();
public void Abort(object? stateInfo);
```

Starting with .NET 5, if you write something like this:

```
Thread.CurrentThread.Abort();
```

you'll see the following warning message:

```
SYSLIB0006   'Thread.Abort()' is obsolete: 'Thread.Abort is not supported
and throws PlatformNotSupportedException.'
```

So, what is the alternative? Microsoft recommends that you use `CancellationToken`. You'll see an example of this in 14.P15. If you want to learn more about this, I suggest you read the online documentation at `https://docs.microsoft.com/en-us/dotnet/standard/threading/cancellation-in-managed-threads`.

14.T19 What is thread signaling?

Answer:

Consider a scenario where one thread waits until receiving a notification from another thread. This is called *thread signaling*. You will often see the use of `Mutex`, `Semaphore` (on Windows), and `EventWaitHandle` (on Windows) in the context of thread interactions or thread signaling.

Author's Note: This chapter is already very big. Here I covered thread synchronization briefly. But the detailed discussions of `Semaphore` and `EventWaitHandle` are beyond the scope of this book.

Programming Skills

By using the following questions, you can test your programming skills in C#. Note that if I do not mention the namespace, you assume that all parts of the program belong to the same namespace.

Basic Concepts

14.P1 Predict the output of the following code segment:

```
Thread.CurrentThread.Name = "main";
Console.WriteLine($"The {Thread.CurrentThread.Name} thread has started.");

Thread threadOne = new(Sample.ExecuteMethod1);
threadOne.Name = "thread-one";

Thread threadTwo = new(Sample.ExecuteMethod2);
threadTwo.Name = "thread-two";
```

```
Console.WriteLine($"Starting {threadOne.Name} shortly.");
// threadOne starts
threadOne.Start();

Console.WriteLine($"Starting {threadTwo.Name} shortly.");
// threadTwo starts
threadTwo.Start();

Console.WriteLine("Control comes at the end of the Main method.");
class Sample
{
    public static void ExecuteMethod1()
    {
        for (int i = 0; i < 5; i++)
        {
            Console.WriteLine($"The
              {Thread.CurrentThread.Name} from ExecuteMethod1
               prints {i}");
        }
    }
    public static void ExecuteMethod2()
    {
        for (int i = -5; i < 0; i++)
        {
            Console.WriteLine($"The
            {Thread.CurrentThread.Name} from ExecuteMethod2
            prints {i}");
        }
    }
}
```

Answer:

This code can compile and run successfully, but you cannot predict the output. Here is some sample output when I execute this program for the first time:

```
The main thread has started.
Starting thread-one shortly.
Starting thread-two shortly.
Control comes at the end of the Main method.
The thread-one from ExecuteMethod1 prints 0
The thread-one from ExecuteMethod1 prints 1
The thread-one from ExecuteMethod1 prints 2
The thread-one from ExecuteMethod1 prints 3
The thread-one from ExecuteMethod1 prints 4
The thread-two from ExecuteMethod2 prints -5
The thread-two from ExecuteMethod2 prints -4
The thread-two from ExecuteMethod2 prints -3
The thread-two from ExecuteMethod2 prints -2
The thread-two from ExecuteMethod2 prints -1
```

Here is some other output after I executed the program a few more times:

```
The main thread has started.
Starting thread-one shortly.
Starting thread-two shortly.
The thread-one from ExecuteMethod1 prints 0
The thread-one from ExecuteMethod1 prints 1
The thread-one from ExecuteMethod1 prints 2
The thread-one from ExecuteMethod1 prints 3
The thread-one from ExecuteMethod1 prints 4
Control comes at the end of the Main method.
The thread-two from ExecuteMethod2 prints -5
The thread-two from ExecuteMethod2 prints -4
The thread-two from ExecuteMethod2 prints -3
The thread-two from ExecuteMethod2 prints -2
The thread-two from ExecuteMethod2 prints -1
```

Analysis:

I showed two possible outputs, but still, the output may vary in your case. It is common in thread programming because your operating system employs context switching as per the design. Later you'll see that you can employ some special mechanisms to control the execution order.

I also want you to note that the following lines are equivalent:

```
Thread threadOne = new(Sample.ExecuteMethod1);
// Same as
// Thread threadOne = new Thread(Sample.ExecuteMethod1);
// Also same as
// Thread threadOne = new Thread(new ThreadStart(Sample.ExecuteMethod1));
```

POINTS TO NOTE

In many contexts (particularly in UI applications), you'll see the term *worker thread*. It is used to describe another thread that is different from the current thread. Technically, it is a thread that runs in the background, though no one claims that this is the true definition. In the context of C#, Microsoft says this: by default, a .NET program is started with a single thread, often called the *primary thread*. However, the program can create additional threads to execute code in parallel or concurrently with the primary thread. These threads are often called *worker threads*. (See `https://docs.microsoft.com/en-us/dotnet/standard/threading/threads-and-threading`.)

Understanding the `Join()` Method

14.P2 Predict the output of the following code segment:

```
Thread.CurrentThread.Name = "main";
Console.WriteLine($"The {Thread.CurrentThread.Name} thread has started.");

Thread threadOne = new(Sample.ExecuteMethod1);
threadOne.Name = "thread-one";

Thread threadTwo = new(Sample.ExecuteMethod2);
threadTwo.Name = "thread-two";

Console.WriteLine($"Starting {threadOne.Name} shortly.");
// threadOne starts
```

```
threadOne.Start();
Console.WriteLine($"Starting {threadTwo.Name} shortly.");
// threadTwo starts
threadTwo.Start();

// Waiting for threadOne to finish
threadOne.Join();
// Waiting for threadtwo to finish
threadTwo.Join();

Console.WriteLine("Control comes at the end of the Main method.");
class Sample
{
    public static void ExecuteMethod1()
    {
        for (int i = 0; i < 5; i++)
        {
            Console.WriteLine($"The
              {Thread.CurrentThread.Name} from ExecuteMethod1
              prints {i}");
            Thread.Sleep(1);
        }
    }
    public static void ExecuteMethod2()
    {
        for (int i = -5; i < 0; i++)
        {
            Console.WriteLine($"The
               {Thread.CurrentThread.Name} from ExecuteMethod2
               prints {i}");
            Thread.Sleep(1);
        }
    }
}
```

Answer:

This code can compile and run successfully. Here is some possible output:

```
The main thread has started.
Starting thread-one shortly.
Starting thread-two shortly.
The thread-one from ExecuteMethod1 prints 0
The thread-one from ExecuteMethod1 prints 1
The thread-two from ExecuteMethod2 prints -5
The thread-one from ExecuteMethod1 prints 2
The thread-one from ExecuteMethod1 prints 3
The thread-two from ExecuteMethod2 prints -4
The thread-one from ExecuteMethod1 prints 4
The thread-two from ExecuteMethod2 prints -3
The thread-two from ExecuteMethod2 prints -2
The thread-two from ExecuteMethod2 prints -1
Control comes at the end of the Main method.
```

Here is some other possible output:

```
The main thread has started.
Starting thread-one shortly.
Starting thread-two shortly.
The thread-one from ExecuteMethod1 prints 0
The thread-one from ExecuteMethod1 prints 1
The thread-one from ExecuteMethod1 prints 2
The thread-two from ExecuteMethod2 prints -5
The thread-one from ExecuteMethod1 prints 3
The thread-two from ExecuteMethod2 prints -4
The thread-one from ExecuteMethod1 prints 4
The thread-two from ExecuteMethod2 prints -3
The thread-two from ExecuteMethod2 prints -2
The thread-two from ExecuteMethod2 prints -1
Control comes at the end of the Main method.
```

Explanation:

The most important change in this program is that you see the line `Control comes at the end of the Main method.` at the end of each possible output.

Let's investigate this and compare this program with the first demonstration. In that demonstration, you saw that the main thread finishes before the spawned threads. But in real-world applications, you may not want the parent thread to finish before the child threads.

In simple scenarios, you may use the Sleep(int millisecondsTimeout) method. It is a static method and is often used. It causes the currently executing thread to pause for a specified period. The int parameter gives you the clue that you need to pass milliseconds as the argument. So, if you want the current thread to pause for 1 second, you pass 1000 as an argument to the Sleep method. But the Sleep method is not as effective as Join(), which is also defined in the Thread class. This is because the Join() method can help you to block a thread until another thread finishes its execution. In the following demonstration, I used this method, and you saw the following lines of code with supporting comments:

```
// Waiting for threadOne to finish
threadOne.Join();
// Waiting for threadtwo to finish
threadTwo.Join();
```

I wrote these statements inside the Main() method. So, once the original thread passes through these statements, it waited for threadOne and threadTwo to finish their jobs and effectively join the execution of these child threads. I have used sleep statements inside the Sample class methods to pause them for a small amount of time. It helps you to visualize the effect of multithreading in this program easily.

Handling Parameterized Methods

14.P3 Can you compile the following code?

```
Thread.CurrentThread.Name = "main";
Console.WriteLine($"The {Thread.CurrentThread.Name} thread has started.");

Thread threadOne = new(Sample.ExecuteMethod1);
threadOne.Name = "thread-one";

Thread threadThree = new(Sample.ExecuteMethod3);
threadThree.Name = "thread-three";

Console.WriteLine($"Starting {threadOne.Name} shortly.");
// threadOne starts
```

```
threadOne.Start();
Console.WriteLine($"Starting {threadThree.Name} shortly.");
// threadThree starts
threadThree.Start(25);

// Waiting for threadOne to finish
threadOne.Join();
// Waiting for threadtwo to finish
threadThree.Join();

Console.WriteLine("End of the Main method.");
class Sample
{
    public static void ExecuteMethod1()
    {
        for (int i = 0; i < 5; i++)
        {
            Console.WriteLine($"The
             {Thread.CurrentThread.Name} from ExecuteMethod1
              prints {i}");
            Thread.Sleep(1);
        }
    }
    public static void ExecuteMethod3(object? number)
    {

        int upperLimit = Convert.ToInt32(number);
        for (int i = upperLimit-3; i < upperLimit; i++)
        {
            Console.WriteLine($"The
              {Thread.CurrentThread.Name} from ExecuteMethod3
               prints {i}");
            Thread.Sleep(1);
        }
    }
}
```

Answer:

Yes, this code can compile and run successfully. Here is some possible output:

```
The main thread has started.
Starting thread-one shortly.
Starting thread-three shortly.
The thread-one from ExecuteMethod1 prints 0
The thread-one from ExecuteMethod1 prints 1
The thread-one from ExecuteMethod1 prints 2
The thread-one from ExecuteMethod1 prints 3
The thread-three from ExecuteMethod3 prints 22
The thread-one from ExecuteMethod1 prints 4
The thread-three from ExecuteMethod3 prints 23
The thread-three from ExecuteMethod3 prints 24
End of the Main method.
```

Explanation:

In the previous cases, you've seen the usage of the ThreadStart delegate. As a result, you were not able to deal with methods that accept parameters. But methods with parameters are very common in programming. So, this time you will see the use of the ParameterizedThreadStart delegate.

Confused? OK, let me retrieve the definition of the ParameterizedThreadStart delegate from the Visual Studio IDE. It is as follows:

```
//
// Summary:
//     Represents the method that executes on a
//     System.Threading.Thread.
//
// Parameters:
//   obj:
//    An object that contains data for the thread
//    procedure.
 public delegate void ParameterizedThreadStart(object? obj);
```

You can see that this delegate accepts an object parameter, and its return type is void. Since the parameter is an object, you can use it for any type as long as you can apply the cast properly to the right type.

Now you understand that ExecuteMethod3 matches this delegate's signature. So, instead of writing the short version:

```
Thread threadThree = new(Sample.ExecuteMethod3);
```

you could also write the following:

```
Thread threadThree = new Thread(new
 ParameterizedThreadStart(Sample.ExecuteMethod3)); // OK
```

14.P4 Suppose, in the previous program (14.P3), that I replace the following line:

```
Thread threadThree = new(Sample.ExecuteMethod3);
```

with the following line:

```
Thread threadThree = new Thread(new
                       ThreadStart(Sample.ExecuteMethod3));
```

Can you compile the code now?

Answer:

No. You'll receive the following compile-time error:

```
CS0123   No overload for 'ExecuteMethod3' matches delegate 'ThreadStart'
```

Explanation:

The error is self-explanatory. ExecuteMethod1 matches the signature of the ThreadStart delegate, but not ExecuteMethod3. Since ExecuteMethod3 accepts a parameter, you need to use (or match) the ParameterizedThreadStart delegate.

14.P5 Can you compile the following code?

```
Thread.CurrentThread.Name = "main";
Console.WriteLine($"The {Thread.CurrentThread.Name} thread has started.");

Thread threadOne = new(Sample.ExecuteMethod1);
threadOne.Name = "thread-one";

Thread threadFour= new(Sample.ExecuteMethod4);
threadFour.Name = "thread-four";

Console.WriteLine($"Starting {threadOne.Name} shortly.");
```

```
// threadOne starts
threadOne.Start();
Console.WriteLine($"Starting {threadFour.Name} shortly.");
// threadFour starts
threadFour.Start(new Boundaries(7, 11));

// Waiting for threadOne to finish
threadOne.Join();
// Waiting for threadtwo to finish
threadFour.Join();

Console.WriteLine("End of the Main method.");
class Boundaries
{
    public int lowerLimit;
    public int upperLimit;
    public Boundaries(int lower, int upper)
    {
        lowerLimit = lower;
        upperLimit = upper;
    }
}

class Sample
{
    public static void ExecuteMethod1()
    {
        for (int i = 0; i < 5; i++)
        {
            Console.WriteLine($"The
              {Thread.CurrentThread.Name} from ExecuteMethod1
               prints {i}");
            Thread.Sleep(1);
        }
    }
```

```
    public static void ExecuteMethod4(object? limits)
    {
        Boundaries? boundaries = limits as Boundaries;
        if (boundaries != null)
        {
            int lowerLimit = boundaries.lowerLimit;
            int upperLimit = boundaries.upperLimit;
            if (lowerLimit <= upperLimit)
            {
                for (int i = lowerLimit; i < upperLimit; i++)
                {
                    Console.WriteLine($"The
                     {Thread.CurrentThread.Name} from
                      ExecuteMethod4 prints {i}");
                    Thread.Sleep(1);
                }
            }
            else
            {
                Console.WriteLine("The lower limit cannot be
                 greater than the upper limit.");
            }
        }
    }
}
```

Answer:

Yes, this code can compile and run successfully. Here is the possible output:

```
The main thread has started.
Starting thread-one shortly.
Starting thread-four shortly.
The thread-one from ExecuteMethod1 prints 0
The thread-four from ExecuteMethod4 prints 7
The thread-one from ExecuteMethod1 prints 1
The thread-four from ExecuteMethod4 prints 8
```

```
The thread-four from ExecuteMethod4 prints 9
The thread-one from ExecuteMethod1 prints 2
The thread-four from ExecuteMethod4 prints 10
The thread-one from ExecuteMethod1 prints 3
The thread-one from ExecuteMethod1 prints 4
End of the Main method.
```

Additional Note:

You can see that there is a class called Boundaries. I created an instance of it and passed 7 and 11 as arguments. Similarly, you can pass as many arguments as you want to construct an object and then pass it to a method that matches the ParameterizedThreadStart delegate.

ExecuteMethod4 is a little bit bigger compared to ExecuteMethod1. This is because I have put a guard to block some invalid data. So, if you write something like this in the output:

```
threadFour.Start(new Boundaries(17, 11)); // Invalid input
```

you'll see the following line:

```
The lower limit cannot be greater than the upper limit.
```

Using Lambdas

14.P6 Can you compile the following code?

```
Console.WriteLine("Handling a method(using lambda expression)
                   that accepts a parameter and returns an
                   int.");
Console.WriteLine("Running this method in a different thread.");
Thread.CurrentThread.Name = "main";
int input = 0; // A initial value
Console.WriteLine($"The initial value of the input is {input}");
Console.WriteLine($"Inside the {Thread.CurrentThread.Name}
                   thread, the ManagedThreadId is
                   {Environment.CurrentManagedThreadId}");
```

```
Thread threadOne = new(
    (a) =>
        {
            Console.WriteLine($"The
             {Thread.CurrentThread.Name} is executing now.");
            // Do some activity if required
            try
            {
                int temp = Convert.ToInt32(a);
                input = temp + 5;
            }
            catch (Exception e)
            {
                Console.WriteLine($"Exception:{e}");
            }
        }
    );
threadOne.Name = "thread-one";
Console.WriteLine($"Starting {threadOne.Name} shortly.");
// threadOne starts
threadOne.Start(10);

// Waiting for threadOne to finish
threadOne.Join();

Console.WriteLine($"The current value of the input is {input}");
Console.WriteLine($"End of the {Thread.CurrentThread.Name} thread.");
```

Answer:

Yes, this code can compile and run successfully. Here is the output:

```
Handling a method(using lambda expression) that accepts a
  parameter and returns an int.
Running this method in a different thread.
The initial value of the input is 0
Inside the main thread, the ManagedThreadId is 1
Starting thread-one shortly.
The thread-one is executing now.
```

```
The current value of the input is 15
End of the main thread.
```

Explanation:

In the previous examples, you saw how to run methods on different threads. But each of these methods had a `void` return type. This program shows you a way to deal with the methods that have non-`void` return types. You can see that I have used a lambda expression in this context.

Another point is that though the following line was purely optional, I wanted you to see the use of `ManagedThreadId`:

```
Console.WriteLine($"Inside the {Thread.CurrentThread.Name}
                   thread, the ManagedThreadId is
                   {Environment.CurrentManagedThreadId}");
```

Instead of using `Environment.CurrentManagedThreadId`, if you use `Thread.CurrentThread.ManagedThreadId` and write something like this:

```
Console.WriteLine($"Inside the {Thread.CurrentThread.Name}
  thread, the ManagedThreadId is
 {Thread.CurrentThread.ManagedThreadId}"); // Not recommended
```

you'll see a message in Visual Studio saying the following:

```
CA1840   Use 'Environment.CurrentManagedThreadId' instead of 'Thread.
CurrentThread.ManagedThreadId'
```

It is because Microsoft says that `System.Environment.CurrentManagedThreadId` is a compact and efficient replacement of the `Thread.CurrentThread.ManagedThreadId` pattern. You can refer to the online link: `https://docs.microsoft.com/en-us/dotnet/fundamentals/code-analysis/quality-rules/ca1840` in this context.

14.P7 Can you compile the following code?

```
Thread.CurrentThread.Name = "main";
Console.WriteLine($"The {Thread.CurrentThread.Name} thread
        with priority {Thread.CurrentThread.Priority} is
        executing now.");

Thread threadOne = new(
    () =>
    {
```

```
        Console.WriteLine($"The {Thread.CurrentThread.Name}
          with priority {Thread.CurrentThread.Priority} is
          executing now.");
        for (int i = 0; i < 5; i++)
        {
            // Some code
        }
        Console.WriteLine($"The {Thread.CurrentThread.Name} is
                                 about to finish.");
    }
    );
threadOne.Name = "thread-one";
threadOne.Priority = ThreadPriority.Highest;

Console.WriteLine($"Starting {threadOne.Name} shortly.");
// threadOne starts
threadOne.Start();
Thread.Sleep(1);
Console.WriteLine($"The end of the {Thread.CurrentThread.Name} thread.");
```

Answer:

Yes, this code can compile and run successfully. Here is some possible output where the `main` thread finishes before `thread-one`:

```
The main thread with priority Normal is executing now.
Starting thread-one shortly.
The end of the main thread.
The thread-one with priority Highest is executing now.
The thread-one is about to finish.
```

Here is another possible output where the `main` thread finishes after `thread-one`:

```
The main thread with priority Normal is executing now.
Starting thread-one shortly.
The thread-one with priority Highest is executing now.
The thread-one is about to finish.
The end of the main thread.
```

Explanation:

At the time of this writing, a thread in C# can have the following priorities: `Lowest, BelowNormal, Normal, AboveNormal, and Highest`. From one of these possible outputs, you can see that though I have set the child thread priority higher than the main thread, there is no guarantee that the child thread will finish before the main thread. Several other factors may determine this output.

Conceptually, the priority determines how frequently a thread can get the CPU's time. In theory, the higher-priority threads get more CPU time than the lower-priority threads, and in preemptive scheduling, they can preempt the lower-priority threads. Actually, you need to consider many other factors. Consider a case where a low-priority thread does a very short task and a high-priority thread does a long-running task. Though the high-priority thread gets more chances to complete its task, it is possible that the low-priority thread gets a single chance to execute and it finishes immediately. Lastly, how task scheduling is implemented in an operating system also matters because CPU allocation depends on this too. This is why you shouldn't depend entirely on priorities to predict the output.

Foreground vs. Background Threads

14.P8 Can you predict the output of the following code segment?

```
Thread.CurrentThread.Name = "main thread";
Console.WriteLine($"The {Thread.CurrentThread.Name} is
                    executing now.");
Thread childThread = new(
    () =>
    {
        for (int i = 0; i < 5; i++)
        {
            Console.WriteLine($"The
             {Thread.CurrentThread.Name} prints {i}");
            Thread.Sleep(500);
        }
        Console.WriteLine($"The {Thread.CurrentThread.Name} is
                            about to finish.");
    }
    );
```

```
childThread.Name = "child thread";
Console.WriteLine($"Starting a {childThread.Name} shortly.");
// threadOne starts
childThread.Start();
childThread.IsBackground = true;
Console.WriteLine($"The end of the {Thread.CurrentThread.Name}.");
```

Answer:

This code can compile and run successfully. Here is some possible output:

```
The main thread is executing now.
Starting a child thread shortly.
The end of the main thread.
```

Explanation:

By default, a thread is a foreground thread. But I converted the child thread to a background thread by setting the `IsBackground` property to `true`. But if you comment out the following line in this example as follows:

```
// childThread.IsBackground = true;
```

you may receive the following output:

```
The main thread is executing now.
Starting a child thread shortly.
The end of the main thread.
The child thread  prints 0
The child thread  prints 1
The child thread  prints 2
The child thread  prints 3
The child thread  prints 4
The child thread is about to finish.
```

This tells you that the child thread (aka worker thread) was able to complete its task when you do not make it a background thread. It is because this time it could continue the task even after the main thread finished its execution.

Obviously, if you add the line `childThread.Join();`, the main thread will wait for the child thread to complete.

Understanding Thread Synchronization

14.P9 Can you predict the output of the following code segment?

```
Console.WriteLine("Exploring a non-synchronized version.****");
Thread.CurrentThread.Name = "main thread";
Console.WriteLine($"The {Thread.CurrentThread.Name} is executing now.");

SharedResource sharedObject = new();
Thread threadOne = new(sharedObject.ExecuteSharedMethod);
threadOne.Name = "Child thread-1";

Thread threadTwo = new(sharedObject.ExecuteSharedMethod);
threadTwo.Name = "Child thread-2";
// Child Thread-1 starts.
threadOne.Start();
// Child Thread-2 starts.
threadTwo.Start();
// Waiting for Child thread-1 to finish.
threadOne.Join();
// Waiting for Child thread-2 to finish.
threadTwo.Join();
Console.WriteLine($"The {Thread.CurrentThread.Name} is about to finish.");
class SharedResource
{
    public void ExecuteSharedMethod()
    {
        Console.WriteLine(Thread.CurrentThread.Name + " has
                     entered the shared location.");
        Thread.Sleep(1000);
        Console.WriteLine(Thread.CurrentThread.Name + " exits.");
    }
}
```

Answer:

This code can compile and run successfully, but you cannot predict the sequence of the output messages. Here is some possible output:

```
Exploring a non-synchronized version.****
The main thread is executing now.
Child thread-1 has entered the shared location.
Child thread-2 has entered the shared location.
Child thread-1 exits.
Child thread-2 exits.
The main thread is about to finish.
```

Author's Note: This output may vary in each run in your system. To get the same output, you may need to execute the application multiple times.

POINT TO NOTE

From this output segment, you can see that `Child thread-2` entered the shared location before `Child thread-1` finishes its execution. When you deal with shared data, this kind of situation is dangerous. Why? For example, suppose one thread is writing some data while another thread is reading the data. As a result, you can get inconsistent results.

14.P10 Predict the output of the following code segment:

```
Console.WriteLine("Exploring a synchronized version.");
Thread.CurrentThread.Name = "main thread";
Console.WriteLine($"The {Thread.CurrentThread.Name} is executing now.");

SharedResource sharedObject = new();
Thread threadOne = new(sharedObject.ExecuteSharedMethod);
threadOne.Name = "Child thread-1";

Thread threadTwo = new(sharedObject.ExecuteSharedMethod);
threadTwo.Name = "Child thread-2";
Random random = new();
if (random.Next() % 2 == 0)
{
```

```
        // Child Thread-1 starts.
        threadOne.Start();
        // Child Thread-2 starts.
        threadTwo.Start();
    }
    else
    {
        // Child Thread-2 starts.
        threadTwo.Start();
        // Child Thread-1 starts.
        threadOne.Start();

    }
    // Waiting for Child Thread-1 to finish.
    threadOne.Join();
    // Waiting for Child Thread-2 to finish.
    threadTwo.Join();
    Console.WriteLine($"The {Thread.CurrentThread.Name} is about to finish.");
    class SharedResource
    {
        private readonly object myLock = new();
        public void ExecuteSharedMethod()
        {
            lock (myLock)
            {
                    Console.WriteLine($"{Thread.CurrentThread.Name} has
                                   entered the shared location.");
                Thread.Sleep(1000);
                Console.WriteLine($"{Thread.CurrentThread.Name} exits.");
            }
        }
    }
```

Answer:

This code can compile and run successfully. Here is some possible output:

```
Exploring a synchronized version.
The main thread is executing now.
Child thread-1 has entered the shared location.
Child thread-1 exits.
Child thread-2 has entered the shared location.
Child thread-2 exits.
The main thread is about to finish.
```

Here is some other possible output:

```
Exploring a synchronized version.
The main thread is executing now.
Child thread-2 has entered the shared location.
Child thread-2 exits.
Child thread-1 has entered the shared location.
Child thread-1 exits.
The main thread is about to finish.
```

Explanation:

Now you see a synchronized program. From this output segment, you can see that once a thread enters into the shared location and finishes its job, no other thread can enter into that location. I have introduced a random number generator to show you that either `Child thread-1` or `Child thread-2` can enter into the shared location first.

14.P11 In the previous program(14.P10), if you replace the following code block:

```
lock (myLock)
 {
  Console.WriteLine($"{Thread.CurrentThread.Name} has entered
                     the shared location.");
  Thread.Sleep(1000);
  Console.WriteLine($"{Thread.CurrentThread.Name} exits.");
 }
```

with the following code block:

```
try
{
  Monitor.Enter(myLock);
  Console.WriteLine($"{Thread.CurrentThread.Name} has entered
                    the shared location.");
  Thread.Sleep(1000);
  Console.WriteLine($"{Thread.CurrentThread.Name} exits.");
}
finally
{
  Monitor.Exit(myLock);
}
```

what will be the change in the output?

Answer:

You will see the equivalent code. The `Monitor` class members are also used to implement synchronization. You've seen the use of a `lock` in 14.P10. So, you understand that it is a shortcut for `Monitor`'s `Entry` and `Exit` methods with the `try` and `finally` blocks.

POINTS TO NOTE

The `Monitor` class has some useful methods. For example, in this class, you can see the presence of many other methods such as `Pulse, PulseAll, Wait, and TryEnter.` Some of these methods have different overloaded versions too. Here are the simple descriptions of some of these methods:

- `Wait()`: Using this method, a thread can wait for other threads to notify.
- `Pulse()`: Using this method, a thread can send notifications to another thread.
- `PulseAll()`: Using this method, a thread can notify all other threads within a process.
- `TryEnter(object obj)`: This method returns the Boolean value `true` if the calling thread can obtain an exclusive lock on the desired object; otherwise, it will return `false`. Using a different overloaded version of this method, you can specify a time limit, in which you attempt to get an exclusive lock on the desired object.

Exploring Deadlocks

14.P12 Can you compile the following code?

```
Console.WriteLine("Exploring a potential deadlocked situation.");
Thread.CurrentThread.Name = "Main thread";
Console.WriteLine("The main thread has started already.");
SharedResource sharedObject = new();
Thread threadOne = new (sharedObject.MethodOne);
threadOne.Name = "Child thread-1";

Thread threadTwo = new (sharedObject.MethodTwo);
threadTwo.Name = "Child thread-2";
// Child Thread-1 starts.
threadOne.Start();
// Child Thread-2 starts.
threadTwo.Start();
// Waiting for Child Thread-1 to finish.
threadOne.Join();
// Waiting for Child Thread-2 to finish.
threadTwo.Join();
Console.WriteLine($"The {Thread.CurrentThread.Name} exits now.");

class SharedResource
{
    private object firstLock = new();
    private object secondLock = new();
    public void MethodOne()
    {
        lock (firstLock)
        {
            Console.WriteLine($"{Thread.CurrentThread.Name}
              enters into MethodOne(Part-1).");
```

```
            Console.WriteLine($"{Thread.CurrentThread.Name}
              exits MethodOne(Part-1).");
            lock (secondLock)
            {
             Console.WriteLine($"{Thread.CurrentThread.Name}
               has entered MethodOne(Part-2).");
             Thread.Sleep(500);
             Console.WriteLine($"{Thread.CurrentThread.Name}
               exits MethodOne(Part-2).");
            }
        }

    }
    public void MethodTwo()
    {
        lock (secondLock)
        {
            Console.WriteLine($"{Thread.CurrentThread.Name}
              enters into MethodTwo(Part-I).");
            Console.WriteLine($"{Thread.CurrentThread.Name}
              exits MethodTwo(Part-1).");
            lock (firstLock)
            {
             Console.WriteLine($"{Thread.CurrentThread.Name}
               has entered MethodTwo(Part-II).");
             Thread.Sleep(500);
             Console.WriteLine($"{Thread.CurrentThread.Name}
             exits MethodTwo(Part-2).");
           }
        }
    }
}
```

Answer:

This code can compile. Here is some possible output:

```
Exploring a potential deadlocked situation.
The main thread has started already.
Child thread-1 enters into MethodOne(Part-1).
Child thread-1 exits MethodOne(Part-1).
Child thread-1 has entered MethodOne(Part-2).
Child thread-1 exits MethodOne(Part-2).
Child thread-2 enters into MethodTwo(Part-I).
Child thread-2 exits MethodTwo(Part-1).
Child thread-2 has entered MethodTwo(Part-II).
Child thread-2 exits MethodTwo(Part-2).
The Main thread exits now.
```

But this program may hang (or freeze) when you run it. When this program hangs, you'll see only these lines in your output:

```
Exploring a potential deadlocked situation.
The main thread has started already.
Child thread-1 enters into MethodOne(Part-1).
Child thread-1 exits MethodOne(Part-1).
Child thread-2 enters into MethodTwo(Part-I).
Child thread-2 exits MethodTwo(Part-1).
```

Author's Note: You may not encounter the deadlock in your first run. But keep executing the program, and there will be a case where you surely see the deadlock. On my computer, I can see it once or twice out of 10 runs on average. But I could see frequent deadlocks when I replaced `Thread.Sleep(500);` with `Thread.Yield();`.

Investigation:

Once you encounter the deadlock, go to the **Debug** menu and click **Break All**. Analyze the thread window now. (You can open the thread window in Visual Studio by selecting the Debug menu, pointing to Windows, and then selecting Threads.) See Figure 14-2 and notice the arrows in this diagram. Note that the threads IDs can vary on your computer. From this figure, you can see the following:

```
Child thread-1(ID 21796) is waiting on lock owned by Thread 15808, i.e. for
Child Thread-2
```

and the following:

```
Child thread-2(ID 15808) is waiting on lock owned by Thread 21796, i.e. for
Child Thread-1
```

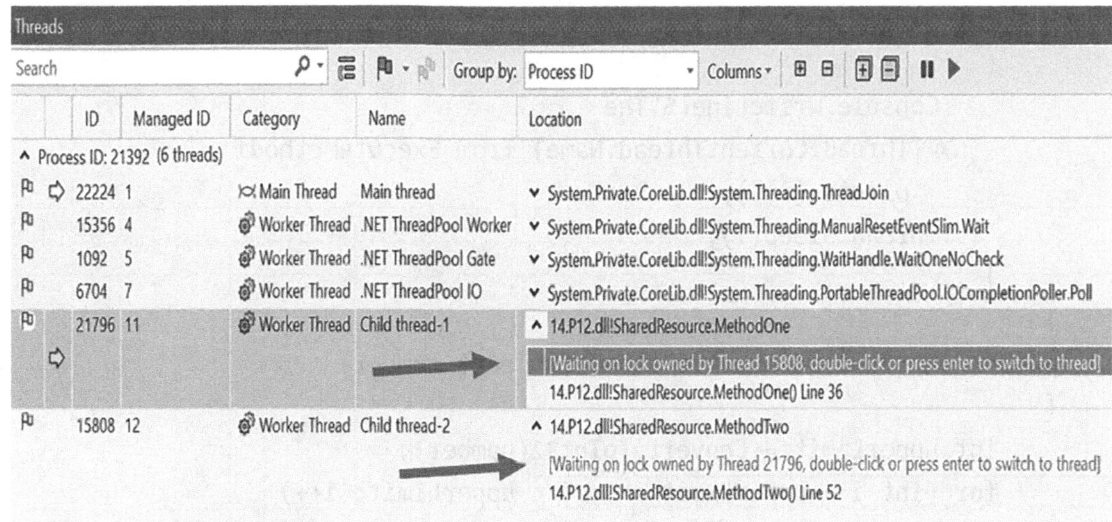

***Figure 14-2.** A deadlock situation: thread 15808 is waiting for thread 21796 to release the lock and vice versa*

Using ThreadPool

14.P13 Can you compile the following code?

```
Thread.CurrentThread.Name = "main";
Console.WriteLine($"The {Thread.CurrentThread.Name} thread has started.");

Thread threadOne = new(Sample.ExecuteMethod1);
threadOne.Name = "thread-one";
Console.WriteLine($"Starting {threadOne.Name} shortly.");
// threadOne starts
threadOne.Start();

ThreadPool.QueueUserWorkItem(Sample.ExecuteMethod3);
Console.WriteLine("Control comes at the end of the Main method.");
```

```
class Sample
{
    public static void ExecuteMethod1()
    {
        for (int i = 0; i < 5; i++)
        {
            Console.WriteLine($"The
             {Thread.CurrentThread.Name} from ExecuteMethod1
              prints {i}");
            Thread.Sleep(1);
        }
    }
    public static void ExecuteMethod3(object? number)
    {
        int upperLimit = Convert.ToInt32(number);
        for (int i = upperLimit - 3; i < upperLimit; i++)
        {
            Console.WriteLine($"The
             {Thread.CurrentThread.Name} from ExecuteMethod3
              prints {i}");
            Thread.Sleep(1);
        }
    }
}
```

Answer:

Yes, this code can compile and run successfully. Here is some possible output:

```
The main thread has started.
Starting thread-one shortly.
Control comes at the end of the Main method.
The thread-one from ExecuteMethod1 prints 0
The thread-one from ExecuteMethod1 prints 1
The thread-one from ExecuteMethod1 prints 2
The thread-one from ExecuteMethod1 prints 3
The .NET ThreadPool Worker from ExecuteMethod3 prints -3
```

```
The .NET ThreadPool Worker from ExecuteMethod3 prints -2
The thread-one from ExecuteMethod1 prints 4
The .NET ThreadPool Worker from ExecuteMethod3 prints -1
```

Explanation:

In 14.T13, you have learned about the purpose of the ThreadPool class. To avoid directly creating threads, you use this built-in class. This class is useful to maintain the optimal number of threads in your application.

On investigation, you'll see that ThreadPool is a static class that contains some static methods. Many of them have overloaded versions too. For your quick reference, I'm attaching a partial snapshot from the Visual Studio IDE, which shows the methods in the ThreadPool class at a glance (see Figure 14-3).

```
namespace System.Threading
{
    [...]public static class ThreadPool
    {
        [...]public static int ThreadCount { get; }
        [...]public static long CompletedWorkItemCount { get; }
        [...]public static long PendingWorkItemCount { get; }

        [...]public static bool BindHandle(IntPtr osHandle);
        [...]public static bool BindHandle(SafeHandle osHandle);
        [...]public static void GetAvailableThreads(out int workerThreads, out int completionPortThreads);
        [...]public static void GetMaxThreads(out int workerThreads, out int completionPortThreads);
        [...]public static void GetMinThreads(out int workerThreads, out int completionPortThreads);
        [...]public static bool QueueUserWorkItem(WaitCallback callBack);
        [...]public static bool QueueUserWorkItem(WaitCallback callBack, object? state);
        [...]public static bool QueueUserWorkItem<TState>(Action<TState> callBack, TState state, bool preferLocal);
        [...]public static RegisteredWaitHandle RegisterWaitForSingleObject(WaitHandle waitObject, WaitOrTimerCallback callBack, object? state, int millisecond
        [...]public static RegisteredWaitHandle RegisterWaitForSingleObject(WaitHandle waitObject, WaitOrTimerCallback callBack, object? state, long milliseco
        [...]public static RegisteredWaitHandle RegisterWaitForSingleObject(WaitHandle waitObject, WaitOrTimerCallback callBack, object? state, TimeSpan timeou
        [...]public static RegisteredWaitHandle RegisterWaitForSingleObject(WaitHandle waitObject, WaitOrTimerCallback callBack, object? state, uint milliseco
        [...]public static bool SetMaxThreads(int workerThreads, int completionPortThreads);
        [...]public static bool SetMinThreads(int workerThreads, int completionPortThreads);
        [...]public static bool UnsafeQueueNativeOverlapped(NativeOverlapped* overlapped);
        [...]public static bool UnsafeQueueUserWorkItem(WaitCallback callBack, object? state);
        [...]public static bool UnsafeQueueUserWorkItem<TState>(Action<TState> callBack, TState state, bool preferLocal);
        [...]public static bool UnsafeQueueUserWorkItem(IThreadPoolWorkItem callBack, bool preferLocal);
        [...]public static RegisteredWaitHandle UnsafeRegisterWaitForSingleObject(WaitHandle waitObject, WaitOrTimerCallback callBack, object? state, int milli
        [...]public static RegisteredWaitHandle UnsafeRegisterWaitForSingleObject(WaitHandle waitObject, WaitOrTimerCallback callBack, object? state, long mill
        [...]public static RegisteredWaitHandle UnsafeRegisterWaitForSingleObject(WaitHandle waitObject, WaitOrTimerCallback callBack, object? state, TimeSpan
        [...]public static RegisteredWaitHandle UnsafeRegisterWaitForSingleObject(WaitHandle waitObject, WaitOrTimerCallback callBack, object? state, uint mill
    }
}
```

***Figure 14-3.** A snapshot of the ThreadPool class from the Visual Studio 2022 IDE*

In this program, our focus is on the QueueUserWorkItem method. From the previous snapshot, notice that this method has three overloaded versions as follows:

```
public static bool QueueUserWorkItem(WaitCallback callBack);
public static bool QueueUserWorkItem(WaitCallback callBack,
                                     object? state);
public static bool QueueUserWorkItem<TState>(Action<Tstate>
                 callBack, Tstate state, bool preferLocal);
```

Now to see the details of this method, let's expand the first overloaded version of this method. Now you'll notice the following:

```
// Summary:
//     Queues a method for execution. The method executes when
//     a thread pool thread becomes available.
//
// Parameters:
//   callBack:
//     A System.Threading.WaitCallback that represents the
//     method to be executed.
//
// Returns:
//     true if the method is successfully queued;
//     System.NotSupportedException is thrown
//     if the work item could not be queued.
//
// Exceptions and other details are skipped here
 public static bool QueueUserWorkItem(WaitCallback callBack);
```

If you further investigate the method parameter, you'll find that WaitCallBack is a delegate with the following description:

```
//
// Summary:
//     Represents a callback method to be executed by a thread
//     pool thread.
//
// Parameters:
//   state:
//     An object containing information to be used by the
//     callback method.
public delegate void WaitCallback(object? state);
```

Now you understand that ExecuteMethod3() matches this delegate signature. So, you can use the following line in your program:

```
ThreadPool.QueueUserWorkItem(Sample.ExecuteMethod3);
```

or the following:

```
ThreadPool.QueueUserWorkItem(new WaitCallback( Sample.ExecuteMethod3));
```

The remaining code is easy to understand. *You can see that to run the* `ExecuteMethod1` *method, I created a thread, but for the* `ExecuteMethod3` *method, I used a pooled thread.*

Since you did not pass any argument for `ExecuteMethod3`, it took 0 as the argument. You can test this by using the following line:

```
Console.WriteLine(Convert.ToInt32(null)); //prints 0
```

But if you want to pass any other valid argument, you can use the overloaded version in this program:

```
public static bool QueueUserWorkItem(WaitCallback callBack, object? state);
```

and replace the following line:

```
ThreadPool.QueueUserWorkItem(Sample.ExecuteMethod3);
```

with something different as follows:

```
ThreadPool.QueueUserWorkItem(Sample.ExecuteMethod3,10);
```

Here is some sample output for this change (notice the changes in bold):

```
The main thread has started.
Starting thread-one shortly.
Control comes at the end of the Main method.
The thread-one from ExecuteMethod1 prints 0
The .NET ThreadPool Worker from ExecuteMethod3 prints 7
The .NET ThreadPool Worker from ExecuteMethod3 prints 8
The thread-one from ExecuteMethod1 prints 1
The .NET ThreadPool Worker from ExecuteMethod3 prints 9
The thread-one from ExecuteMethod1 prints 2
The thread-one from ExecuteMethod1 prints 3
The thread-one from ExecuteMethod1 prints 4
```

14.P14 Can you compile the following code?

```
Thread.CurrentThread.Name = "main";
Console.WriteLine($"The {Thread.CurrentThread.Name} thread has started.");
ThreadPool.QueueUserWorkItem(new WaitCallback(Sample.ExecuteMethod));
Console.WriteLine("Control comes at the end of the Main method.");
class Sample
{
    public static void ExecuteMethod()
    {
        // Some code
    }
}
```

Answer:

No. You'll receive the following compile-time error:

CS0123 No overload for 'ExecuteMethod' matches delegate 'WaitCallback'

Explanation:

If needed, see 14.P13's explanation again. Note that the delegate signature does not match the method signature in this program.

Managed Thread Cancellation

14.P15 Can you compile the following code? (You can get help from the comments if necessary.)

```
Thread.CurrentThread.Name = "main";
Console.WriteLine($"The {Thread.CurrentThread.Name} thread has started.");

CancellationTokenSource cts = new();
```

```
Thread threadThree = new(Sample.ExecuteMethod3);
threadThree.Name = "thread-three";
Console.WriteLine($"Starting {threadThree.Name} shortly.");
// threadThree starts
threadThree.Start(cts.Token);
// Let threadThree run for some time
Thread.Sleep(1000);

Console.WriteLine("About to set the cancellation request.");
cts.Cancel();
Thread.Sleep(1000);

// CancellationTokenSource implements IDisposable
// So, we can call the Dispose() method
cts.Dispose();

Console.WriteLine("Control comes at the end of the Main method.");
class Sample
{
    public static void ExecuteMethod3(object? token)
    {
        CancellationToken cToken = (CancellationToken)token;
        for (int i = 0; i < 100000; i++)
        {
           if (cToken.IsCancellationRequested)
            {
                Console.WriteLine($"\tThe
                  {Thread.CurrentThread.Name} was executing
                  ExecuteMethod3.");
                Console.WriteLine($"\tIn iteration {i+1},
                  the cancellation has been requested.");
                // Some cleanup operation
                break;
            }
```

```
            // The SpinWait causes a thread to wait for the
            // number of times defined by the iterations
            // parameter.
            Thread.SpinWait(500000);
        }
    }
}
```

Answer:

Yes, this code can compile and run successfully. Here is some possible output:

```
The main thread has started.
Starting thread-three shortly.
About to set the cancellation request.
        The thread-three was executing ExecuteMethod3.
        In iteration 33, the cancellation has been requested.
Control comes at the end of the Main method.
```

Additional Notes:

Note the following points:

- You have seen that you can cancel a running thread. Starting with .NET 4, this is the recommended approach for canceling a running thread. In 14.T18, you have seen that `Thread.Abort()` is obsolete now.
- You are now familiar with the `ThreadPool` class. So, you can replace the following code:

```
Thread threadThree = new(Sample.ExecuteMethod3);
threadThree.Name = "thread-three";
Console.WriteLine($"Starting {threadThree.Name}
                   shortly.");
// threadThree starts
threadThree.Start(cts.Token);
// Let threadThree run for some time
Thread.Sleep(1000);
```

- with the following code to get a similar result:

```
ThreadPool.QueueUserWorkItem(Sample.ExecuteMethod3,
                              cts.Token);
//ThreadPool.QueueUserWorkItem(new
//          WaitCallback(Sample.ExecuteMethod3),
//          cts.Token); // Also Ok
Thread.Sleep(1000);
```

- In this case, you'll see some output something like the following (notice the change in bold):

```
The main thread has started.
About to set the cancellation request.
        The .NET ThreadPool Worker was executing ExecuteMethod3.
        In iteration 25, the cancellation has been requested.
Control comes at the end of the Main method.
```

CHAPTER 15

Miscellaneous

Welcome to the final chapter of this book. You have seen many interesting features in C# 10 and its preceding versions. At the time of this writing, the C# 11 preview is newly available too. So, let's look at some of the newest features of C#. In addition, we'll cover some important topics that wouldn't fit into earlier chapters that can help you write better programs in the future. This chapter covers the following topics:

- Some of the latest changes in C# (I'll limit the discussion to those topics that are discussed in the first 14 chapters of this book)
- `switch` expressions with discard patterns
- Partial classes and methods
- Operator overloading
- Use of a record type in brief

Let us review and test your understanding of these topics now.

Theoretical Concepts

This section includes the theoretical questions and answers on miscellaneous topics.

Concept of Preview

15.T1 What do you mean by *preview* features?

Answer:

Preview features are not officially released for widespread use. They are made available for customers who want to get early access to them, do some experiments, and provide feedback about them. In general, you need to change some settings before you

V. Sarcar, *Test Your Skills in C# Programming*, https://doi.org/10.1007/978-1-4842-8655-5_15

test them. If the overall customer feedback of a preview feature is not satisfactory, the feature may remain in the preview phase for a longer period.

For example, I use the following settings in 15.P1, which you'll see in the "Programming Skills" section shortly:

```
<Project Sdk="Microsoft.NET.Sdk">
  <PropertyGroup>
    <OutputType>Exe</OutputType>
    <TargetFramework>net7.0</TargetFramework>
    <ImplicitUsings>enable</ImplicitUsings>
    <LangVersion>preview</LangVersion>
    <Nullable>enable</Nullable>
  </PropertyGroup>
</Project>
```

15.T2 What is meant by *preview channels*?

Answer:

At a particular time, you may work on any of the following channels:

- Preview channel
- Current channel
- Long-term support channel (LTSC)

The upcoming features that need to be tested before widespread use reside on the preview channel. When these features are stable, they are moved to the current channel. As per the name, LTSC enables a development team to get support from Microsoft for some specified time. Typically, this is for large organizations that cannot adopt the product updates for their customers as quickly as Microsoft recommends. Specifically, the documentation at `https://docs.microsoft.com/en-us/visualstudio/productinfo/vs-servicing` says the following:

- LTSC enables teams to remain supported on a minor version for up to 18 months after release.
- An LTSC release receives security and bug fixes but no additional new features.

Operator Overloading

15.T3 Can you overload operators in C#?

Answer:

Yes. But there are certain rules to follow. Note the following:

- You use the `operator` keyword to declare an operator. The keyword `operator` is followed by the operator symbol. Here is a sample:

```
Class Sample
 {
   public static Sample operator ++(Sample sample)
   {
      // Some code
   }
   // Some other code skipped
 }
```

- An operator declaration must satisfy the following rules:
    - You must include both a `public` modifier and a `static` modifier.
    - At least one input parameter of an operator (both unary and binary) must have type `T` or `T?` where `T` is the type that contains the operator declaration.
- In addition, all operators cannot be overloaded. Let me include some of them that you saw earlier. For example, you cannot overload the `default`, `delegate`, `new`, `switch`, `typeof`, and `with` operators.
- Certain operators need to be overloaded in pairs. For example:
    - == and != operators
    - < and > operators
    - <= and >= operators

Note You can learn more about operator overloading from `https://docs.microsoft.com/en-us/dotnet/csharp/language-reference/operators/operator-overloading`.

15.T4 It appears to me that anyone can misuse the concept when they overload contradictory operations using operator overloading; for example, I can use the ++ operator to decrement something. Is this correct?

Answer:

This is why you need to be careful. You should not implement any such operation to make a bad design. In addition, you must note that C# does not allow us to overload all the operators.

Partial Classes and Methods

15.T5 What is a partial class?

Answer:

When you split a class definition across multiple sections (or files), it is called a *partial class*. You can do the same for a method, struct, or interface too. Microsoft ensures that all parts are combined when you compile the application.

To split a class definition, you need to use the `partial` keyword modifier. The following code shows you a sample where I split the `Sample` class into two parts:

```
namespace Container
{
    public partial class Sample
    {
        public void Method1()
        {
            // Some code
        }
    }

    public partial class Sample
    {
        public int Method2()
        {
            // Some code
        }
    }
}
```

15.T6 Why do you need a partial class?

Answer:

Assume you are working on a large project and the class definitions are relatively big. So, if you split the class over separate files, multiple programmers can work together. In this context, Microsoft ensures that Visual Studio uses this approach when it uses Windows Forms. Let us review the complete comment at `https://docs.microsoft.com/en-us/dotnet/csharp/programming-guide/classes-and-structs/partial-classes-and-methods`:

> *When working with automatically generated source, code can be added to the class without having to recreate the source file. Visual Studio uses this approach when it creates Windows Forms, Web service wrapper code, and so on. You can create code that uses these classes without having to modify the file created by Visual Studio.*

In short, you can separate the "owner boundaries"; for example, the UI design code can be separated from the business logic code. As a result, developers can focus on any of these areas but work together.

15.T7 Why do you need a partial method?

Answer:

Truly, the usage is limited. Suppose you have a partial class and you split a method of this class into two parts (i.e., you have partial methods now). In this case, one part of the class can contain the signatures of the method, and the actual implementation can be provided in the other part. Obviously, you can provide the implementation in the same part too. In this context, note that providing a partial method implementation is optional for the following cases:

- The method returns `void`.
- The method does not have an `out` parameter.
- The method does not have an accessibility modifier.
- The method does not use any of the following modifiers: `virtual`, `new`, `override`, `sealed`, or `extern`.

Microsoft (refer to the link mentioned in 15.T6) says that partial methods are useful for the source generators (that can provide the implementations) and the templates that can generate boilerplate code.

Note There are many restrictions on using a partial class and methods. For example, you cannot apply the `partial` keyword to constructors, finalizers, overloaded operators, property declarations, or event declarations. In addition, at the time of this writing, the partial modifier is not available on delegate or enumeration declarations. In this chapter, you'll examine a few case studies for partial classes and partial methods. If you're interested, you can learn more about them from `https://docs.microsoft.com/en-us/dotnet/csharp/programming-guide/classes-and-structs/partial-classes-and-methods`.

15.T8 I am seeing people have started using the record type, but you have not discussed it in this book. Is there any specific reason for this? When should I use a record type?

Answer:

This book is reviewing most of the important features and concepts in C# that are used in everyday programming. To keep the book within a reasonable page limit, discussions on the record type as well as other concepts such as asynchronous programming and LINQ queries are absent from this book. If you like this book, you'll probably see many such discussions in an updated edition.

For a quick answer, let me remind you that class and objects are the foundation of object-oriented programming. You use classes to focus on the responsibilities and behavior of objects. You use the struct type to store small data that can be copied efficiently. C# 9 introduced the record type, which is a new reference type. You use it for value-based equality and comparison.

Starting with C# 10, you can also create the record struct type to define records as valuc types. This is useful when you want features of records for a type that is small enough to copy efficiently.

Programming Skills

By using the following questions, you can test your programming skills in C#. Here we focus on preview features, operator overloading, partial classes, and methods. Note that if I do not mention the namespace, you can assume that all parts of the program belong to the same namespace.

Preview Features

When you read this book, some or all these preview features will be included in the current channel. If you go through the discussions of these preview features, you'll have a better idea about how to test a preview feature in the future.

Raw String Literal

15.P1 Predict the output of the following code segment:

```
string language = "C#";
string version = "11";
string message = $"""
    Hello reader! How are you?
      {language} {version} is about to be released.
     Raw string literals are available in version: {version}.
    """;
Console.WriteLine(message);
```

Answer:

If you do not enable the preview feature option, you will see the following compile-time error:

```
CS8652  The feature 'raw string literals' is currently in Preview and
*unsupported*. To use Preview features, use the 'preview' language version.
```

Once you follow the Visual Studio IDE's suggestion, you'll receive the following output:

```
Hello reader! How are you?
  C# 11 is about to be released.
 Raw string literals are available in version: 11
```

Explanation:

You have seen an example of using a raw string literal. This literal starts with at least three double quotes (""") and ends with the same number of double quotes.

This kind of string literal can include arbitrary text, including whitespace, new lines, embedded quotes, and other special characters without requiring escape sequences. You can see that I have applied string interpolation with raw strings in this example.

Additional Note:

Following the online guidelines about C# language versioning, I added `<LangVersion>preview</LangVersion>` in my projects to test the preview features.

Note that `<EnablePreviewFeatures>True</EnablePreviewFeatures>` can also help you test the preview features in this context. It means that if you use the following segment, this project can compile and run too:

```
<Project Sdk="Microsoft.NET.Sdk">
  <PropertyGroup>
    <OutputType>Exe</OutputType>
    <TargetFramework>net7.0</TargetFramework>
    <ImplicitUsings>enable</ImplicitUsings>
    <EnablePreviewFeatures>True</EnablePreviewFeatures>
    <Nullable>enable</Nullable>
  </PropertyGroup>
</Project>
```

How does this setting work? Read the Microsoft guidelines at `https://docs.microsoft.com/en-us/dotnet/fundamentals/code-analysis/quality-rules/ca2252`.

> *You can also opt in to preview features at an assembly or module level. This indicates to the analyzer that preview type usage in the assembly is desired and, as a consequence, no errors will be produced by this rule. This is the preferred way to consume preview dependencies. To enable preview features inside the entire assembly, set the EnablePreviewFeatures property in a .csproj file.*

Newlines Support in String Interpolations

15.P2 Can you compile the following code?

```
//int? score = 75;
int? score = 40;
//int? score = null;
string message = $"Score: {score} Remarks:  {
score switch
{
    >= 60 => "First division",
```

```
    >= 40 => "Second division",
    _ => "Failed.",
}
}";
Console.WriteLine(message);
```

Answer:

This code can compile and run successfully. You'll get the following output:

```
Score: 40 Remarks:  Second division
```

Explanation:

Characters inside { and } can span multiple lines. Microsoft introduced this feature to read string interpolations with longer C# expressions easily. You often see them in `switch` expressions and LINQ queries.

Starting with C# 8.0, you can see the presence of `switch` expressions. If you are unfamiliar with it, let me show you an equivalent program that shows the `switch`-like semantics in a statement context.

```
//CheckNumber(75);
CheckNumber(40);
//CheckNumber(27);

void CheckNumber(double score)
{
    switch (score)
    {
        case >= 60:
            Console.WriteLine($"Score: {score} Remarks: First
                              division.");
            break;
        case >= 40:
            Console.WriteLine($"Score: {score} Remarks: Second
                              division.");
            break;
        default:
            Console.WriteLine($"Score: {score} Remarks:
                              Failed.");
```

```
            break;

    }
}
```

Author's Note: I have kept some commented lines to test the remaining cases. You can test them once you download the source code from the Apress website.

So, what is the difference between these two styles? You can see the following in the new style (i.e., the switch expression shown earlier):

- The variable name appears before the switch keyword. So, instead of the switch(score), I could use the score switch.
- Instead of using case >=40:, I have used >= only. This means that the case and : elements were replaced with =>.
- The default case is also replaced with the underscore (_) character. Basically, I have used a discard pattern here. So, if you use int? score = null; instead of int? score = 40;, you can see the following output: Score: Remarks: Failed.

In short, this new switch syntax is easier to read. With the newline support in string interpolations, your code is easier to read.

POINT TO REMEMBER

Discards are used for unassigned values, and they act as placeholders. In C# 7.0 onward, they are supported. But you must note that _ is also a valid identifier. Outside of the supported context, _ can be treated as a valid variable. If you have an identifier named _ already in scope, the use of _ as a stand-alone discard can result in unwanted outcomes.

Auto-default Struct

15.P3 Can you compile the following code?

```
struct Employee
{
    public string Name;
    public int Id;
```

```
    public Employee(string name, int id)
    {
        Name = name;
    }
    public override string ToString()
    {
        string emp = Name + " has ID " + Id;
        return emp;
    }
}
```

Answer:

This code produced a compile-time error in 3.P20 (Chapter 3). But the Visual Studio Preview Version 17.3.0 (Preview 1.1) allows you to compile this code. Notice that inside the Employee constructor, we did not initialize the ID; still, this code compiles. But now you'll see the following warning that is expected:

```
CS0649   Field 'Employee.Id' is never assigned to, and will always have its
default value 0
```

Explanation:

An auto-default struct is a new feature that was added in Visual Studio 2022 version 17.3. It ensures that all fields (or auto-properties) of a struct type are initialized to their default values if a constructor does not initialize them. It'll be helpful for you if you remember the discussions of 3.P16 and 3.P20 from Chapter 3 in this context.

Static Abstract Interface Members

15.P4 Can you compile the following code?

```
Test.Show();

interface ITest
{
    static abstract void Show();

}
```

```
class Test : ITest
{
    public static void Show()
    {
        Console.WriteLine("Implementing a static abstract
                                method in an interface.");
    }
}
```

Answer:

If you do not test this code in preview mode, you'll see the following error:

```
CS8703   The modifier 'abstract' is not valid for this item in C# 10.0.
Please use language version 'preview' or greater.
```

Once you enable your project file to test the preview features, the code will compile, and it can produce the following output:

```
Implementing a static abstract method in an interface.
```

Explanation:

Here is the Microsoft's recommendation (`https://docs.microsoft.com/en-us/dotnet/csharp/whats-new/csharp-11#static-abstract-members-in-interfaces`):

> *static abstract members in interfaces is a runtime preview feature. You must add the <EnablePreviewFeatures>True</EnablePreviewFeatures> in your project file.*

It continues as follows:

> *You can add static abstract members in interfaces to define interfaces that include overloadable operators, other static members, and static properties. The primary scenario for this feature is to use mathematical operators in generic types.*

Author's Note: In 6.P27, you saw a similar program. I added this program here to discuss these preview features together.

Testing Warning Wave 7

15.P5 Can you compile the following code?

```
Console.WriteLine("---15.P5---");
public class testingwarningwave
{
    // Some Code
}
```

Answer:

This code can compile, but you may see the following warning message:

```
CS8981   The type name 'testingwarningwave' only contains lower-cased ascii
characters
```

To see this warning, you have to enable the warning wave using the AnalysisLevel element in your project file such as the following:

```
<Project Sdk="Microsoft.NET.Sdk">

  <PropertyGroup>
    <OutputType>Exe</OutputType>
    <TargetFramework>net7.0</TargetFramework>
    <RootNamespace>_15.P5</RootNamespace>
    <ImplicitUsings>enable</ImplicitUsings>
    <Nullable>enable</Nullable>
    <AnalysisLevel>preview</AnalysisLevel>
  </PropertyGroup>
</Project>
```

Instead of seeing it as a warning, if you also include the element <TreatWarningsAsErrors>true</TreatWarningsAsErrors>, you will see a compile-time error, as shown in Figure 15-1.

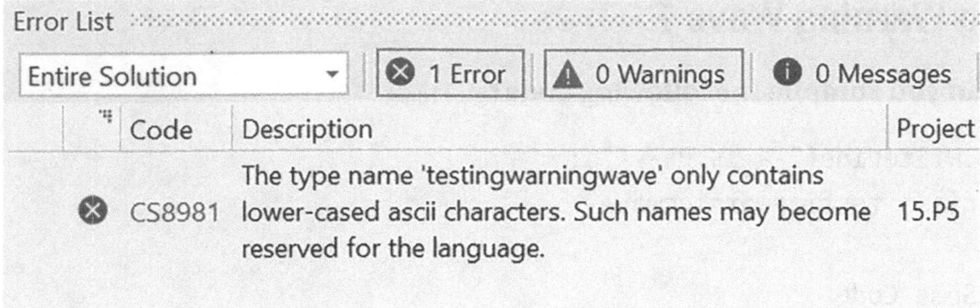

***Figure 15-1.** A compile-time error (CS8981) is generated*

Additional Note:

You can set a value for `AnalysisLevel` through the UI also; right-click the project, select *Properties*, select *Code Analysis*, and then select *.NET analyzers*, as shown in Figure 15-2.

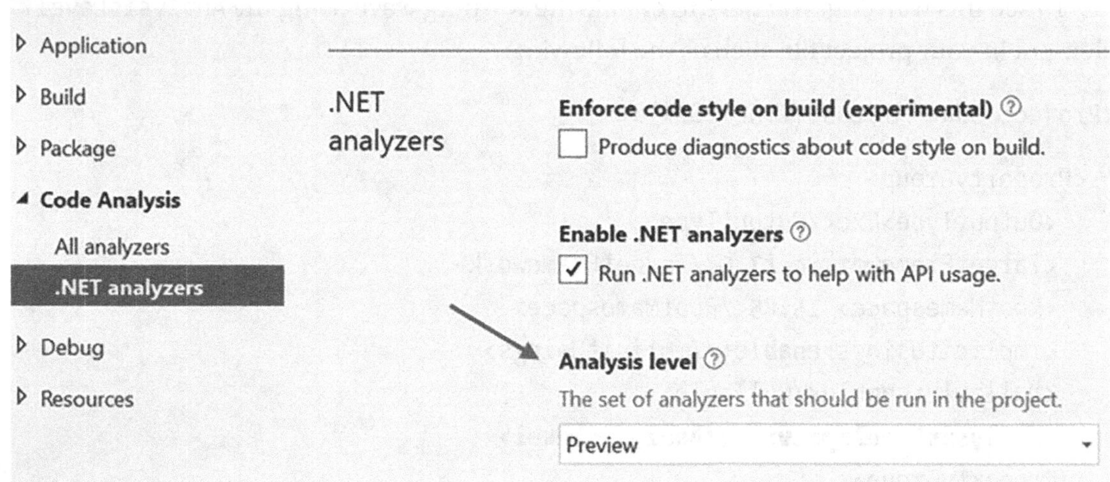

***Figure 15-2.** Setting the analysis level through the Visual Studio UI*

Operator Overloading

15.P6 Predict the output of the following code segment:

```
Sample sample1 = new(5);
Sample sample2 = new(7);
Console.WriteLine($"The sample1 contains {sample1}");
Console.WriteLine($"The sample2 contains {sample2}");
```

```
Console.WriteLine("\nTesting the unary operator ++ now.");
sample1++;
Console.WriteLine($"The sample1 contains {sample1}");
Console.WriteLine("\nTesting the binary operator + now.");
Sample sample3=sample1 + sample2;
Console.WriteLine($"The sample3 contains {sample3}");
class Sample
{
    int _flag;
    public Sample(int flag)
    {
        _flag = flag;
    }

    public static Sample operator ++(Sample sample)
    {
        sample._flag++;
        return sample;
    }
    public static Sample operator +(Sample sample1,
                                    Sample sample2)
    {
        return new Sample(sample1._flag + sample2._flag);
    }
    public override string ToString()
    {
        return $"the value: {_flag}";
    }
}
```

Answer:

This code can compile and run successfully. You'll get the following output:

```
The sample1 contains the value: 5
The sample2 contains the value: 7

Testing the unary operator ++ now.
```

```
The sample1 contains the value: 6

Testing the binary operator + now.
The sample3 contains the value: 13
```

Explanation:

This program shows that you can overload a unary operator (++) as well as a binary operator (+).

15.P7 Can you compile the following code?

```
Sample sample1 = new(5);
Console.WriteLine($"Inside sample1, {sample1}");

class Sample
{
    int _flag;
    public Sample(int flag)
    {
        _flag = flag;
    }

    public static void operator ++(Sample sample)
    {
        sample._flag++;
    }
    public override string ToString()
    {
        return $"current value is {_flag}";
    }
}
```

Answer:

No. You'll receive the following compile-time error:

```
CS0448    The return type for ++ or -- operator must match the parameter
type or be derived from the parameter type
```

Explanation:

Microsoft says the following (at https://docs.microsoft.com/en-us/dotnet/csharp/misc/cs0448?f1url=%3FappId%3Droslyn%26k%3Dk(CS0448)):

> *When you override the ++ or -- operators, they must return the same type as the containing type, or return a type that is derived from the containing type.*

15.P8 Can you compile the following code?

```
Console.WriteLine("---15.P8---");
// Some code

class Sample
{
    int _flag;
    public Sample(int flag)
    {
        _flag = flag;
    }

    public static void operator +(Sample sample1,
                                  Sample sample2)
    {
        // Some code
    }
    public override string ToString()
    {
        return $"current value is {_flag}";
    }
}
```

Answer:

No. You'll receive the following compile-time error:

```
CS0590   User-defined operators cannot return void
```

Partial Classes

15.P9 Can you compile the following code?

```
using Container1;

Sample sample = new();

sample.AboutMe();
Console.WriteLine($"12+7={sample.Add(12, 7)}");

namespace Container1
{
    public partial class Sample
    {
        public void AboutMe()
        {
            Console.WriteLine("Experimenting with the partial
                              class 'Sample'.");
        }
    }

    public partial class Sample
    {
        public int Add(int a, int b)
        {
            return a + b;
        }
    }
}
```

Answer:

Yes, this code can compile and run successfully. You'll get the following output:

```
Experimenting with the partial class 'Sample'.
12+7=19
```

Explanation:

You have seen an example of a partial class. You can see that though the `Sample` class has two parts, you can use them together.

15.P10 Predict the output of the following code segment:

```
using Container1;
using Container2;

Sample sample = new();

sample.AboutMe();
Console.WriteLine($"12+7={sample.Add(12, 7)}");

namespace Container1
{
    public partial class Sample
    {
        public void AboutMe()
        {
            Console.WriteLine("Experimenting with the partial
                                   class 'Sample'.");
        }
    }

}
namespace Container2
{
    public partial class Sample
    {
        public int Add(int a, int b)
        {
            return a + b;
        }
    }
}
```

Answer:

No. You'll receive the following compile-time error:

```
CS0104   'Sample' is an ambiguous reference between 'Container1.Sample' and
'Container2.Sample'
```

Explanation:

The error is self-explanatory. To avoid this error, you can put the partial class definitions in the same namespace. Microsoft (`https://docs.microsoft.com/en-us/dotnet/csharp/programming-guide/classes-and-structs/partial-classes-and-methods`) tells us the following in this context:

> *All partial-type definitions meant to be parts of the same type must be defined in the same assembly and the same module (.exe or .dll file). Partial definitions cannot span multiple modules.*

Partial Methods

15.P11 Predict the output of the following code segment:

```
using Container1;
Sample sample = new();
sample.SayHello();
namespace Container1
{
    public partial class Sample
    {
        internal partial void SayHello();
    }
    public partial class Sample
    {
        internal partial void SayHello()
        {
            Console.WriteLine("Hello, reader!");
        }
    }
}
```

Answer:

This code can compile and run successfully. You'll get the following output:

```
Hello, reader!
```

Explanation:

You have seen an example of using a partial class with a partial method.

15.P12 Can you compile the following code?

```
Console.WriteLine("---9.P12---");
namespace Container1
{
    public class Sample
    {
        internal partial void SayHello();
    }
}
```

Answer:

No. You'll receive the following compile-time errors:

```
CS8795   Partial method 'Sample.SayHello()' must have an implementation
part because it has accessibility modifiers.
CS0751   A partial method must be declared within a partial type
```

Explanation:

These error messages are self-explanatory. In 15.T7, you saw some restrictions on using a partial method. If required, you can read them again. So, if you remove the internal modifier, CS8795 will not appear. The following code is free from both these errors:

```
Console.WriteLine("---9.P12---");
namespace Container1
{
    public partial class Sample
    {
      // internal partial void SayHello();// Error:CS8795
      // partial void SayHello();// Error:CS0751, if class is
                                 // not partial
      partial void SayHello(); // No error

    }
}
```

Obviously, for this code, you'll see the warning saying `Message IDE0051 Private member 'Sample.SayHello' is unused`.

15.P13 Can you compile the following code?

```
Console.WriteLine("---9.P13---");
namespace Container1
{
    public partial class Sample
    {
       internal partial  void ShowNumber();

    }
    public partial class Sample
    {
        internal partial int ShowNumber()
        {
            return 5;
        }

    }
}
```

Answer:

No. You'll receive the following compile-time error:

```
CS8817   Both partial method declarations must have the same return type.
```

Additional note:

It should not be a surprise to you that partial methods are seen inside partial classes (or structs) and the method signatures should match.

15.P14 Can you compile the following code?

```
Console.WriteLine("---15.P14---");
namespace Container
{
    public partial class Sample
    {
        abstract partial int ShowNumber(); // ERROR CS0750
    }

}
```

Answer:

No. You'll receive the following compile-time error:

```
CS0750   A partial method cannot have the 'abstract' modifier
```

15.P15 Can you compile the following code?

```
Container.Parent parent = new Container.Sample();
Console.WriteLine($"The number is: {parent.ShowNumber()}");

namespace Container
{
    public abstract class Parent
    {
        public abstract int ShowNumber();

    }
    public partial class Sample:Parent
    {
         public override partial int ShowNumber();

    }
    public partial class Sample
    {
        public override partial int ShowNumber()
        {
            return 5;
        }
    }
}
```

Answer:

Yes. If you run this code, you will get the following output:

```
The number is: 5
```

This is the end of Part III of the book. This book helped you learn and review lots of C# constructs and features to help you continue your learning journey. Thank you and happy coding!

APPENDIX A

A Final Note

Congratulations! You have reached the end of the book and can now program confidently in C#. If you continue to study the program segments, examples, and Q&A discussions in the book, you will gain even more clarity about them and continue your success in the programming world.

As I've said before, C# is a vast topic, and this book is too small to cover all the features of C#. Still, in these 15 chapters, you learned, reviewed, and experimented with lots of C# constructs and features.

What is next? You should not forget the basic principle that learning is a continuous process. This book helped you learn the fundamental and commonly used constructs in C# so that you can understand a C# codebase better and enjoy future learning.

But learning by yourself will not be enough anymore. Feel free to participate in open forums and join discussion groups to get more clarity on C# programming. Researching topics on Google, Stack Overflow, Quora, and similar places can help you a lot.

A Personal Appeal

Over the years, I have seen a general trend in my books. When you like the book, you send me messages, write nice emails, and motivate me with your kind words and suggestions. But most of those messages do not reach the review sections of platforms like Amazon and others. Those pages are often filled with criticisms.

I understand that these criticisms help me to write better. But it is also helpful for me to know what you liked about a book. If I get a chance to update this book, those constructive suggestions can help me a lot with the new edition.

So, I have a request for you: you can always point out the areas to be improved, but at the same time, please let me know about the coverage that you liked. In general, it is always easy to criticize but an artistic view and open mind are required to discover the true efforts that are associated with hard work. Thank you and happy coding!

V. Sarcar, *Test Your Skills in C# Programming*, https://doi.org/10.1007/978-1-4842-8655-5

APPENDIX B

Recommended Reading

This appendix lists some useful resources. I suggest you read these books or the updated editions to know more about C# programming.

- *Design Patterns in C#: A Hands-on Guide with Real-world Examples by Vaskaran Sarcar (Apress, 2nd Edition, 2020).*
- *Simple and Efficient Programming with C#: Skills to Build Applications with Visual Studio and .NET by Vaskaran Sarcar (Apress, 2021).*
- *Interactive C#: Fundamentals, Core Concepts and Patterns by Vaskaran Sarcar (Apress, 2017).*
- *Getting Started with Advanced C#: Upgrade Your programming Skills by Vaskaran Sarcar (Apress, 2020)*
- *The C# Player's Guide by RB Whitaker (Starbound Software, 3rd edition, 2016)*
- *C# 10 in a Nutshell by Joseph Albahari (O'Reilly Media, 2022)*

The following are helpful online resources:

- `https://docs.microsoft.com/en-us/dotnet/csharp/`
- `https://docs.microsoft.com/en-us/dotnet/csharp/whats-new/csharp-11`
- `https://docs.microsoft.com/en-us/dotnet/core/introduction`

V. Sarcar, *Test Your Skills in C# Programming*, https://doi.org/10.1007/978-1-4842-8655-5

Index

V. Sarcar, *Test Your Skills in C# Programming*, https://doi.org/10.1007/978-1-4842-8655-5

E

F

G

H

I

J, K

L

U

V

W, X

Y, Z

Printed in the United States
by Baker & Taylor Publisher Services